Recreation Activities

FOR THE

Handicapped

by

FREDERICK M. CHAPMAN

Associate Professor of Recreation
University of Minnesota

THE RONALD PRESS COMPANY · NEW YORK

GV
183.5
C 46

Library of Congress Catalog Card Number: 59-14661

PRINTED IN THE UNITED STATES OF AMERICA

To

La Verne, Carol, Craig, Chico, and Copper

Foreword

Recreation in its general form came of age after World War I. The interest, concern, and investment of both money and energy are compelling testimony to this fact. The new status of recreation was the by-product of the metamorphosis of the average breadwinner as he progressed from a twelve-hour-a-day laborer, totally dependent upon his employer, to an individual with rights and the power to effect changes. The shorter working day and increased wages paved the way for greater recreational pursuits.

Hospital recreation is a veritable newcomer, receiving its impetus from World War II and emerging not only as a specific division within the broader field of recreation but also as a profession and as an acceptable form of treatment for the sick, disabled, or aged. It functions within the boundaries of special communities such as psychiatric hospitals, schools for the retarded or crippled, treatment centers for emotionally disturbed children, and special hospitals for geriatric patients. This rather young profession has all the vitality and energy which is typical of youth. It is filled with the desire and drive to accomplish despite occasional periods of restlessness.

While general recreation seeks to satisfy the needs of people in open communities, hospital recreation has as its clientele a highly select group of individuals—patients. Although they may suffer from widely divergent physical or mental illnesses, certain characteristics are discernible in all. All have regressed to a more dependent relationship. Many feel depressed, uncertain, and have little faith. The image of themselves has changed, leaving them confused and devoid of direction. Helping such persons to return to a more independent way of life becomes a major goal of those responsible for recreation for the handicapped.

To achieve this primary goal it becomes quite clear that good hospitals or special schools should have as their objectives, first, a clear-cut diagnosis of the problem and, second, a well-defined program for treating the specific illness. The procedure sounds elementary, but in reality, it has a wide variety of pitfalls starting with the diagnosis itself. The complex nature of each personality makes diagnosis extremely difficult under even the best circumstances. Careful, accurate evaluative studies are imperative before the planner can prescribe any form of treatment.

The present concept of treatment with its scope broadened to include total personality needs makes the treatment process considerably more involved. However, whether the patient suffers primarily from a physical, mental, or emotional disease, the concern must be first with the individual who has the disease and second with the disease itself. The constant goal must be to help patients to move out of the hospital as soon as possible. In the case of individuals with chronic illnesses, they must be provided the best help available within the confines of the hospital, with the emphasis on making them as independent as possible and affording them as many opportunities as they can profitably utilize to maintain self-esteem. These facts are not always given enough emphasis; and, as a result, some chronic patients achieve only a minor degree of hospital adjustment while others are actually allowed to deteriorate.

For a larger number of handicapped persons the task of the recreational worker is one of bridging the gap between illness and recovery, between hospital and home or community. The job entails more than just treating the individual during the acute phase of his illness. It encompasses a whole program of rehabilitation.

Although many patients benefit from the direct treatment of a particular illness within the hospital setting, they may be overwhelmed by countless fears when the time comes to leave. The apprehension about returning home, the doubts about their ability to readjust, the fears that the family may not accept them, the worry that their jobs may not be open to them, the uneasiness about finding acceptance in their social and religious groups—all of these can become overwhelming. Such fears tend to prolong the invalidism of the patient. The hospital must accept its responsibility in this area and move in with a practical program designed to reassure the individual that he can make a satisfactory adjustment by developing increased skills in living. This all-important hospital function is generally accepted, but too few institutions actually carry it to completion.

To those involved in recreation, the statements that "activity is necessary for life" and that "play is the basic language for all childhood" have become part of their professional orientation. Adults, too, never completely give up play. Many would be miserable without adequate recreational outlets. The types of activities chosen often reflect past experiences, the kind of leadership provided as well as the gratification obtained when certain activities were learned.

One of our basic psychiatric tenets is that illness represents a regression to an earlier period of adjustment. If we accept this as fact, we shall also have to recognize that a person who is physically or emotionally ill also shows regression in his recreational outlets. Some would benefit from reviving old ones that at one time had given gratification. Others may need some opportunities to improve their skills in certain types of activities. All of these can and should be provided for in hospitals. This book, *Recreation Activities for the Handicapped*, provides a great deal of usable information. Besides listing and describing various activities, it indicates the type of patient who might enjoy or benefit from a variety of activities. These are the guide lines and directives which will help bring hospital recreation into its proper perspective in the total treatment program.

EDWARD D. GREENWOOD, M.D.
The Menninger Foundation

Topeka, Kansas
January, 1960

Preface

This practical book contains a well-rounded program of activities for the handicapped. Because of its comprehensive nature, the book will serve the needs of a variety of groups. It will be of special aid to those studying in the fields of hospital recreation, medicine, nursing, occupational therapy, recreational therapy, social group work, and special education. Personnel responsible for the leadership of recreation activities in hospitals—city, county, military, private, state, Veterans Administration, and general—will find concise instructions for the conduct of activities useful in their day-to-day program planning for the handicapped. This book will also be of assistance to physicians in prescribing recreation activities for their patients, to teachers responsible for restricted groups in schools and colleges, and to families which desire to make a long convalescence less tedious and happier for their loved ones.

Part I of this book gives some insight into the nature of handicapped persons' behavior patterns and offers suggestions on how the handicapped can best be helped to cope with and overcome their problems. Leadership methods are discussed which emphasize the knack of establishing rapport vital in effecting rehabilitation.

Part II contains descriptions of over 250 activities divided among ten program areas—Arts and Crafts, Audio-Visual Activities, Dance Activities, Dramatic Activities, Hobbies and Special Interests, Musical Activities, Nature and Outing Activities, Social Recreation Activities, Special Events, and Sports and Games. The description of each activity gives information as to necessary equipment, procedures, variations, and the diagnostic group or groups to which the activity is best suited. Six diagnostic groups—the aged; children; general, medical, and surgical; neuropsychiatric; mentally retarded; and tubercular—are discussed in terms of their general needs, psychologies, and interests.

To help the reader locate materials for a recreation program, there are two indexes—one general and the other categorized by diagnostic groups. In addition, there are an interest finder, a device for detecting and classifying the interests of handicapped persons; a recreation calendar suggesting activities based on holidays and seasonal events; selected references to aid in procuring materials and pamphlets for a recreation program; and lists of agencies and organizations mentioned in the book.

The author is grateful for the wise counsel and suggestions of Gerald B. Fitzgerald, Director of Recreation Training, University of Minnesota. Appreciation is also extended to Richard J. Donnelly, Professor and Assistant Director, Department of Physical Education and Athletics, University of Minnesota, for his helpful advice in the development of the manuscript.

Several persons read Part I and rendered vital help in its presentation. The author is appreciative of the advice of Irving Kartus, M.D., Director, Menninger Memorial Hospital; James F. Pratt, Director of Adjunctive Therapy; and Jay Zimmerman, Adjunctive Therapist—all with The Menninger Foundation, Topeka, Kansas.

FREDERICK M. CHAPMAN

Minneapolis, Minnesota
January, 1960

Contents

I

PROGRAM
LEADERSHIP

Chapter 1

A Point of View

Everyone is handicapped in one way or another. The degree of misfortune depends upon the element of chance. The problem of leisure is a far more critical one for the handicapped than for so-called healthy people. Enforced time on one's hands can either lead to depression and boredom or be a source of creative activities. This book is dedicated to whoever is ill or handicapped and requires useful activity.

THE HANDICAPPED IN THE HOME AND COMMUNITY

Those who are handicapped and reside in a community require planned activity and resourceful leadership. Any person whose vocational or daily activities are restricted or limited may be considered to be handicapped. A physical or mental handicap presents a challenging hurdle for one who has to adjust in today's society.

Restlessness and anxiety characterize the plight of the bedridden, but with the helpful direction of a resourceful parent, relative, or friend, the confined person can at least use in part his faculties and interests. The creative use of leisure hours not only aids the handicapped person's morale but opens up new avocational interests. There are those who have vastly elevated their role in life through correspondence study and other self-improvement activities.

There is the possibility that a family may reject and overlook the less fortunate person. Perhaps the embarrassed sister and brother will not admit that their younger brother is retarded or crippled. They might even proclaim their superiority and lack of tie or relationship with such an invalid. However, emotional maturity is shown by the family who consider all members worthy and acceptable in the household. The "congenial abode" of today's modern family includes all as persons worthy of respect and love. As recounted in the *Prince and the Pauper*, it was formerly fitting to define a supposedly peculiar member of the family as mad or insane. Over the years, increasing attention has been given the atypical person so that he is now accepted as one of us. Through television, charitable drives, and special literature the public has become informed about epilepsy, mental illness, crippling disorders, mental deficiency, and other disabilities. Public schools are now preparing pupils to understand the afflicted, and community activities welcome any contribution the handicapped may make.

The role of handicapped persons in a community may be made more pleasant and enjoyable through recreation. Stimulating leadership is needed in order to provide a program of variety and balance. The State of California Recreation Commission has provided six guideposts for the recreation leader who works with handicapped persons *in a community*. They are summarized as follows:

1. Regard each participant as if he had no limitations and encourage the best of which the participant is capable.
2. Expect normal standards of behavior from the handicapped. Encourage fair play and follow the rules of the game.
3. Use imagination in the selection, adaptation, and invention of recreation activities especially suitable for the physically or mentally handicapped.
4. Present and encourage group activities that require cooperation and working together.
5. Be patient and allow the handicapped person to move at a slower pace.
6. Encourage the participant to improvise special ways of detouring around his own handicaps.[1]

[1] *Recreation for Handicapped People in California*, Publication 23, State of California Recreation Commission, Sacramento, California, 1955, p. 13.

THE HANDICAPPED IN HOSPITALS

From the medical viewpoint, recreation usually exists in a hospital as an adjunct to treatment and not just as a leisure time activity for enjoyment and relaxation. For at least twenty years at the Menninger Foundation in Topeka, Kansas,[2] specific types of recreational activities have been prescribed to alleviate specific symptoms of patients.

Recreation has been defined in various ways with frequent emphasis on the "fun of doing" aspect. Further characteristics include wholesomeness, enjoyment, and satisfaction, which in turn produce refreshment of strength and spirit in the individual. Another typical component is voluntary participation which should be encouraged as much as possible even though there are within the hospital obvious barriers and limitations to such freedom of choice.

Some physicians have specified that these varied activities should not be called "therapy," while others have stated that the only justifiable existence for recreation in a hospital is that of therapy. Dictionaries define therapy as being concerned with the treatment of diseases. Since the main object of hospitals is the care and treatment of the sick and injured, it must be assumed that recreation shall also contribute to this goal. Recreation in a hospital provides an opportunity for specifically prescribed therapeutic aims as well as necessary diversional outlets. The therapist or leader who utilizes the gamut of varied recreations with patients must also possess special ability and background.

Patients' previous leisure-time patterns before hospitalization do much to condition responsiveness to particular activities. The recreation program should be geared more to the needs of the patient than to his expressed interests. However, the desires and opinions of patients should be frequently reviewed in evaluating the program, although what the sick person did in his leisure time prior to hospitalization does not

[2] See William Menninger, M.D., "Recreation and Mental Health," *Recreation*, November, 1948.

necessarily provide the pattern to follow in the hospital. Through the direction of physicians, one who leads recreation activities in a hospital should be able to plan specific activities to meet stated objectives.

AN UNDERSTANDING OF THE AFFLICTED

The ill or handicapped person—whether in a community or hospital—has had traumatic and unpleasant experiences. Fear becomes real for the handicapped when it is known that life will be more difficult and less enjoyable. The one-time athlete crippled with poliomyelitis suddenly sees that he is no longer the proud possessor of a strong physique. Physical attractiveness is at a premium in modern society. The physically disabled believes himself to be less attractive than the ordinary citizen. In the active stages of treatment there are various tedious procedures that are necessary for proper care. Imagine the fear of being "stuck" daily with the hypodermic needle. The humdrum existence of being subject to pills, needles, and temperature-taking is not a pleasant one. The anticipation of a hobby, some entertainment, or just plain fun is unusually appealing to the restricted person. These are challenges to those who aid in the comfort of the disabled. The possibility of full-time work has been eliminated for the patient. He is left with increased leisure and the possibility of either boredom or cheerfulness. Whether he will learn to spend his time happily, either in creative or entertaining ways, will depend to a large extent on the guidance he is given.

Most people have a zest for life. Be it food, entertainment, travel, work, or play—there is something that intrigues the average person. However, depression and a feeling of worthlessness banish the incentive to be purposeful and productive. Worry, self-concern, and feelings of inferiority are dangerous elements which may halt useful activity. One of the major contributions of recreation can be that of cheering the empty hours and providing an outlet for untapped energy.

MEANINGFUL ACTIVITY

Life may not be profitable from the monetary standpoint for one who is crippled or atypical. His financial success is surely limited in this society of competition and survival of the fittest. However, he can escape a bare existence with the help of a planned program of leisure fulfillment. An economical activity which is not an excessive drain on the parent's or guardian's pocketbook is essential. Such pursuits as bird watching and rock collecting are only a few of the free recreational activities available.

Boredom breeds mischief, and misguided leisure results in behavior problems. The everyday life of children is characterized by play, and the lack of it may result in disintegration and lowered morale. An experience of institutionalized mentally retarded children in Illinois (prior to a state-wide expanded institutional recreation program) is worthy of note:

The buildings naturally showed the effects of children's idleness. The classrooms, drab, and unattractive to start with, were scarred from the pounding and picking of the unoccupied children. . . . With nothing constructive to do, and irritated by one another's restlessness, they frequently punched and bit those sitting beside them.[3]

A carefully planned activities program may mean the difference between feelings of boredom and of satisfaction. Improved discipline and better care of belongings result from busy hands and a relatively contented outlook. A sense of accomplishment is more probable when the parent, student, or therapist provides carefully selected activity daily. The future is indeed brighter when recreation fills the gaps of typically dreary hours.

[3] Bertha E. Schlotter and Margaret Svendsen, *An Experiment in Recreation with the Mentally Retarded* (rev. ed.; State of Illinois: Dept. of Public Welfare, 1951), p. 26.

Chapter 2

A Design for Programming

THE HANDICAPPED person needs a friend rather than an overseer. The worker should work *with* a person rather than being *in charge* of him. Therapeutic effectiveness is dependent upon the degree to which the handicapped person responds to suggestion and activity in a comfortable atmosphere.

ADJUSTING THE PHYSICAL ENVIRONMENT

The Menninger Foundation in Topeka, Kansas has done much with *milieu* as an important aspect in treatment. Milieu is the total environment and surroundings within which an activity takes place. It is believed that a patient will respond more favorably to a stimulus which is provided in an atmosphere conducive to the desired response. With the minimum of conflicts and distractions, a game, party, play, or show can take place more effectively for the patient's benefit.

It should be noted that all efforts are directed toward assuring the best atmosphere for the activity. The following are hints for the student of good programming in attaining the ideal milieu for activities:

1. *Temperature:* Be certain that the room or area is adequately ventilated and is neither hot nor stuffy. Whenever possible, conduct activities in fresh air and sunshine, but keep in mind that wind, strong breezes, and exposure to temperatures which are too cool could be detrimental to the patient.

2. *Space and setting:* Whenever possible, have the activity take place outdoors where there is a sense of freedom and a feeling of not being hemmed in (as is too often the case in a ward or sick room). Allow ample space for the type of activity planned.

3. *Clothing:* Physical comfort makes the participant more receptive to the game. Tight, binding, or itchy garments interfere with certain movements in sports. Appropriate attire for a party or dance helps the participant feel more a part of the occasion.

4. *Supplies and equipment:* Use equipment that is serviceable and of high quality. It is false economy to purchase cheap or inferior supplies or equipment. The safeness of the equipment is another consideration.

5. *Instruction and demonstration:* Explain briefly the rules of the game, have a trial run, and then do it! Do not waste time in lengthy explanations and perfectionistic approaches. Enter into the activity for the fun of it rather than for skill's sake. Demonstrate the relay or dance first, then do it as a group with the participants.

6. *Length and type of activity:* Select activities that are on the age and interest level of participants. Do not overwork special games or activities. Be original and plan a variety of things for the person who is to be reached. It is usually desirable to terminate the activity at its high point of interest.

7. *Avoidance of noise:* The undivided attention of the handicapped person is necessary in order for him to give complete cooperation. Distractions draw his mind elsewhere and lessen the effectiveness of the leader.

USING THE TEAM APPROACH

It takes more than love and empathy to ease the burdens of a sick person. Even though sympathetic understanding is of vital importance, skill on the part of trained persons is needed for best results. A combination of professional workers is more beneficial than one specialist working with the patient or handicapped individual. Combined efforts of members of a rehabilitation team can do much in raising morale and aiding recovery. Rehabilitation or at least improved adjustment to the environment can be an end result of planned activity.

The following twelve specialists should be available to give assistance. Their services may be provided in the home, school, hospital, or institution.

1. *Parent:* He or she is indeed a specialist in that there is special skill necessary in successfully bringing up a child. The son or daughter who is handicapped serves as a supreme test for parents.

2. *Physician:* The knowledge, wisdom, and experience of a medical doctor is essential in guiding the life of a handicapped person. Frequent consultation or occasional check-ups serve as bases for other specialists' contributions. Each rehabilitation member is responsible to, or works in cooperation with, the physician.

3. *Nurse:* Daily care and treatment of the sick and injured require a trained nurse's skill. The nurse's role is to carry out medical orders and help those in need of medical care.

4. *Recreation Worker:* This worker, leader, or therapist uses various recreation methods and is a morale-builder who brings cheerful activity into the leisure hours of the handicapped. Carefully planned and skillfully chosen activities assist in care and treatment.

5. *Occupational Therapist:* Individualized treatment and emphasis on work with hands constitutes a part of the therapist's duties. Her contribution helps in effective treatment of the sick and disabled. Therapeutically directed programs are planned to aid the patient in reaching recovery and rehabilitation goals.

6. *Teacher:* Special techniques are used by the teacher who aids the handicapped child. Concentrated lesson material on a tutorial basis helps in bringing this child up to par with pupils in the classroom.

7. *Volunteer:* One who gives freely in leading activities and providing personal services is a valuable addition to the over-all rehabilitation picture. The carefully chosen volunteer brings cheer and encouragement into restricted lives.

8. *Psychologist:* Mental testing and behavior observation assist other team members in learning more about the prognosis and which future course to follow. The psychologist is equipped to make evaluations and suggestions on mental ability.

9. *Librarian:* A librarian can help a crippled or handicapped child in the home to benefit from a well-selected series of reading materials. A librarian can also give advice about audio-visual aids, such as projected books, overhead projectors, slide projectors, and motion pictures.

10. *Dietitian:* When a special diet is necessary, the professionally trained dietitian is best able to plan meals of the right quantity and type of food.

11. *Physical Therapist:* The therapeutic use of light, heat, and water are necessary in special cases. Exercise, use of crippled limbs, and proper movement can be directed by the physical therapist.

12. *Social Worker:* A vital link between families, community, employers, and homes is provided by the social worker. This specialist can aid in vocational placement as well as in easing the transition to partial or complete participation in home and community activities.

There are more than twelve members on the medical team. Others are equally necessary for a vital treatment program. While the physician is responsible for treatment, he cannot always be available and must depend upon the competent and dedicated assistance of his team members. Many hours may be put in with the patient or handicapped person by the parent, student, or teacher. Since leisure hours of the disabled are unusually numerous, the wise use of activity is deemed to be of vital consequence.

A number of communities have established sheltered workshops wherein handicapped persons can contribute to their livelihoods. Under the guidance of a workshop director these persons engage in piecework and assembly line production. Individual assignments and work on sub-contracted jobs constitute a part of this paid work available in the workshop. Many employers have seen the high quality of materials turned out by the handicapped and are very willing to provide selected vocational opportunities. The disabled adult also finds this situation increases his income and is additionally rewarding for the fellowship and social contact. There is comfort in knowing that others also lead similar lives satisfactorily.

UTILIZING COMMUNITY RESOURCES

The handicapped person as a member of the community is entitled to the usual privileges of other taxpayers. City parks, schools, libraries, and public recreation programs are for the use of all community residents.

Local chambers of commerce, information centers, city newspapers, and public libraries are in a position to provide information to the public on current happenings and facilities. These sources can aid the parent and teacher in finding out where to take the handicapped child for worthwhile leisure activity. Some agencies have free loan services whereby books, games, and recreation supplies can be borrowed by responsible persons. Certain public recreation departments lend game kits to groups who want to sponsor a party or game night under private auspices. Group work agencies such as the Young Men's Christian Association, Young Women's Christian Association, Boy Scouts of America, and Girl Scouts of America sponsor selected activities exclusively for the handicapped. There are a number of scout troops operated successfully for mentally retarded boys or girls. Camps accept handicapped children under certain circumstances. Local health organizations sometimes know of camps featuring programs for crippled, diabetic, or mentally retarded children. The Salvation Army and similar agencies provide work opportunities for handicapped adults.

Some states have state-level recreation commissions. A number of universities have recreation consultative services or extension personnel who are ready to aid in recreation guidance. Information about state parks, literature, and speakers can be obtained from such sources. Several states have personnel in their state welfare, hospital, or mental hygiene departments who are able to furnish advice on recreation services for the handicapped. Use the services and facilities of the local community. The local town recognizes that handicapped persons are citizens and very worthy of being members of its society.

RECOGNIZING AGE-BEHAVIORAL CHARACTERISTICS

Most persons reach plateaus and stages in life which are typified by certain behavioral changes. The over-all interest at any given age range colors and influences the intensity and type of leisure activity. To illustrate, the small child likes to play "doctor" and imitate his elders, while the teen-ager wants rather desperately to dance, or at least fraternize with the opposite sex.

The age ranges in the following list are not hard and fast, but only suggestive of the general chronological period in question.

Preschoolers (Age up to 5): This child tends to be bossy, imitative, and generally without sex consciousness. He is gregarious, has varied short-term interests, and is susceptible to fights and clashes. His conflicts are varied and short in duration. He "makes up" easily and seeks play companionship. The child enjoys "messy" activity such as finger painting and splashing in mud or working with clay. The handicapped preschooler needs a wide range of activity involving action, work with hands, and colorful play.

Preadolescents (Ages 6–12): The younger boy or girl is approaching socialized behavior and desires to conform more than the preschooler. He likes to make-believe, listen to stories, and act out adventurous roles. His muscle movements tend to be more refined (compared to the preschooler), better directed, and meticulous in terms of selected games. Prior to puberty, girls tend to desire the company of girls, and boys want to associate with boys. The preadolescent is more cognizant of group responsibility and ready to join certain national organization programs such as scouting. Cooperation with others is more discernible. Boys in the range of eleven or twelve years indulge in a rougher type of conduct and even horseplay.

Adolescents (Ages 13–17): It is at this age that the handicapped teen-ager notices his inability to be accepted by other "normal" adolescents. He seeks attention of the opposite sex. The adolescent is very susceptible to fads and fancies of the time. He wants to conform and be like others of his age. The adolescent has a maturing body and senses his physiological potential. The adolescent wants recognition and enjoys competition.

Young Adults (Ages 18–30): The young adult sees a need for vocational self-support, if he is able to handle the same. A young person has refined certain skills and is at the peak of learning ability. He turns from exploratory co-ed interest to a more serious concern for one of the opposite sex. Puppy love is replaced by mature desires and thoughts of marriage. The young adult wants to produce something worthwhile and improve his role. He wants adventure, new experiences, and responsibility.

Adults (Ages 31–59): During this wide range of years the peak of one's productivity is reached. It is the time in which emotional maturity is most often attained. A handicapped adult has grown to accept, in some degree, his limited condition and status. He strives for a chance to prove his competence. The vigor of young adulthood is declining and being replaced by the desire and willingness to assume a contented spectator role. The adult is willing to share and help others who are in need. He is receptive to counsel and possibly to religious pursuits. The affairs of the world and political matters are a likely subject of interest to him. Discussion groups and similar passive group events tend to be received with favor by the handicapped adult.

Aged (Ages 60–up): The golden-ager is concerned with health, financial security, religion, and acceptance by others. Rehabilitation is not of as great concern to him as it is to younger persons and such goals as comfort, assurance, and worthwhile leisure activity are more realistic. The older person should be aided with consolation, kindness, and attention to his safety. He may be cranky, impatient, forgetful, and worried. The handicapped oldster needs proof that he is being cared for and not forgotten in the fast pace of life. *All* older persons are *not* handicapped and each should be maturely treated in accordance with his physical and mental ability. The twilight age provides an opportunity for service, hobbies, discussion, and spectator activity.

In general, the handicapped adult wants to be treated with as much dignity as possible. He does not want to be looked down upon. The provision of an attractive atmosphere, available supplies for leisure time use, and an active friendly attitude of a companion all help toward the best adjustment of one who is disabled.

Chapter 3

Leadership of Activities

PROVIDING recreation for the atypical becomes an important responsibility for the parent, physician, specialist, and nurse. Tangible activities may have educational carry-over into other pursuits. The activity and its equipment need to be laid out and even stressed for some who have lost their sense of adventure and imagination.

Since almost everyone has been, or will be, a past or prospective patient, the need for leisure time education appears necessary. Some persons are restricted and partially retarded in ability to communicate or discharge their everyday responsibilities. The handicapped person is physically or mentally altered in some manner so that his adjustment to an activity and his successful performance of it are limited. Unfortunately, the attitude of many persons makes the social and vocational adjustment of the handicapped even more difficult. The horizons of the handicapped need broadening by means of useful activity and goals which assist in sustaining at least the present level of performance.

The wise parent, leader, or therapist is not concerned with providing recreation just because of its possible amusement and entertainment value. The wide range of guided leisure pursuits can assist in personality, and sometimes physical, adjustment. The sick individual often has a particularly difficult time in adjusting to attitudes and prejudices of others.

Here again is the need to provide him with extra fortification and inspiration. The enjoyment of music or thrill of hobbies can carry a person, at least temporarily, beyond physical and mental barriers.

PROGRAM CONTENT

Recreation for the handicapped is any wholesome and beneficial activity pursued for pleasure and enjoyment that assists in treatment or adjustment of the person. The ten program areas of recreation are distinct and each of particular importance. They are as follows:

1. Arts and crafts
2. Audio-visual activities
3. Dance activities
4. Dramatic activities
5. Hobbies and special interests
6. Musical activities
7. Nature and outing activities
8. Social recreation activities
9. Special events
10. Sports and games

A balanced program would include activities within several or all of the ten program areas.

Diversional programs are also vital for the morale and adjustment of institutionalized persons. Motion pictures, television, and entertainment duplicate typical community life and surely are desirable if the disabled one is to return to this kind of living. Even for those chronically ill, the provision of entertainment and physical activity is humane and desirable. The use of volunteers or provision of equipment for recreation will serve as a nucleus for the program when leadership is not readily available.

Wise judgment is necessary in planning the type of activity most beneficial for the handicapped, because particular phases of a program may be of value to one person and not to another. For example, the aged individual may be more able and interested in arts and crafts than he is in sports and games participation; the typical patient afflicted with tuberculosis would indeed be harmed by playing tennis or blowing a trumpet. The danger points and possible excesses for any individual patient should be indicated by a physician. The wisdom and maturity of a leader or therapist are of further importance in ascertaining the types and numbers of activities.

Recreation is the re-creation of the mind and body in a purposeful release. This refreshment of spirit and strength can make the sick and injured more receptive to pills and injections. The hitting of a striking bag is an acceptable outlet for aggressions and tensions of the mentally disturbed.

Good planning characterizes the progressive program. Starting one thing at a time and being assured of its acceptance is more logical than a myriad of activities which have no predetermined goal. Scheduling of time so that there is no conflict with other treatments will result in an efficient program.

DIAGNOSTIC GROUPINGS FOR PROGRAMMING

The vast majority of handicapped persons will fall into one or more of the six diagnostic groupings for recreation programming purposes. The six groupings are intended only as a guide for the person who is responsible for recreation planning with the handicapped and not as a clinical or scientific chart of diagnostic arrangement. Some persons are afflicted with multiple or dual disorders and, of course, have a multiple or dual problem.

1. A—Aged
2. C—Children
3. GMS—General Medical and Surgical
4. MR—Mentally Retarded
5. NP—Neuropsychiatric
6. TB—Tubercular

The first two groupings, "Aged" and "Children," do not, in themselves, specify a general type of handicap. However, in planning recreation for older persons or children, one can be more conveniently guided by the distinctions in years than by the illness or handicap alone. The leader should be aware of his patient's age category and know whether or not he fits into the category of an aged person or child.

A guide to the conditions and handicaps that might fit under the six handicap groupings are indicated as follows:

A—Aged

As persons advance into their sixties, seventies, and eighties, more physical and mental problems appear to arise. It should not be assumed that all aged persons are sickly because of their age alone. However, bodily efficiency is slowed and curtailed. The condition of the older man or woman may be diagnosed in many different ways, but the common denominator of advanced age is still present. Most aged people move at a more relaxed pace and require a greater number of sedentary activities.

C—Children

The handicapped preschooler, preadolescent, and adolescent represent a group of persons who still have characteristics of children. Their interests and activities are still typical of the average boy or girl. Like the aged, they may be handicapped in any one of several areas. However, the approach to a handicapped child should be based more on the fact that he is a child than on his being a patient. Of course, the medical restrictions appropriate to the condition of the child still apply, but the child's attitudes and interest levels remain at the level of the child's age.

GMS—General Medical and Surgical

Anyone with an illness or injury of physical origin requires some restriction of activity. This person—in or out of the hospital—must not participate beyond the limits prescribed by medical authority.

MR—Mentally Retarded

Persons whose mentality is retarded present special problems unlike the physically or mentally ill. The problem is often considered to be more that of special education rather than of a medical nature. Limitation of intelligence may represent a congenital or acquired condition that requires appropriate social and educational methods. The impaired judgment of the mentally retarded may necessitate institutionalization in advanced cases. Retarded adults and children require activities that are colorful, simplified, and challenging to their particular age levels and mental capabilities.

NP—Neuropsychiatric

Persons who are marked by malfunction or injury of the brain and/or nervous system require specialized neurological or psychiatric help. Individuals with severe emotional disturbances behave differently from those in other diagnostic groupings. The mentally ill man or woman needs a variety of recreational activities for aid in social adjustment or treatment. The individual out of contact with reality may be physically well and hence able to participate in any number of medically approved activities.

TB—Tubercular

The pulmonary patient with tubercular infection requires selected activities that are not too strenuous for the individual and are in accordance with medical directive. Time and rest, as the basic treatment for the tubercular, allow opportunity for several recreational outlets.

INGREDIENTS OF LEADERSHIP

Leadership and followership are equally important abilities in working with the atypical. The exactness of medical treatment, the preciseness of medical and surgical procedures, and the necessary team dependency require that the leader stay in step as a competent follower. If one has the possibilities of leadership, with practice, intelligence, and empathy, he can develop effective human relationships.

Most successful leaders of the handicapped are emotionally mature. The term "emotionally mature" refers to the well-organized personality pattern of an experienced and socially integrated person. Maturity is not necessarily proportionate to chronological age, but means, rather, wise judgment which appears to have been seasoned by meaningful experience.

Some of the traits that characterize a well-qualified recreation specialist may be enumerated as follows:

Empathy	Humility
Fairness	Intelligence
Humor	Self-confidence
Honesty	Tact

Education and meaningful experience must accompany these personality traits for success. Intelligence is presumed as a prerequisite of formal education, and the latter is necessary to qualify technically the leader or therapist for work with the handicapped.

The successful recreation leader in a medical setting has a healthy self-concept and remains free of unusual self-concern about bodily health. The effective therapist is cheerful, well-adjusted, and respectful of other opinions. He is an energetic person who is able to channel and direct activities and projects to successful conclusions.

EVALUATION OF LEADERSHIP TRAITS

Evaluation implies careful appraisal of the traits or characteristics of an individual in the performance of given tasks. Careful judgment should be exercised before conclusions are formed regarding personality patterns, for the evaluator is often subject to bias and prejudice based upon his or her own past experiences in life. Whenever possible, written guides, scales, or schedules should be used in evaluating the performance of a person. This assures to a high degree a fair and consistent approach to all who are subjected to the evaluation. The qualities and attributes upon which the person is evaluated remain the same for each individual and thus guarantee some degree of consistency.

RELATIONSHIPS WITH THE HANDICAPPED

Rapport involves more than mere cooperation with participants and requires that the leader consistently look for ways in which he can make the handicapped person feel more at ease and comfortable. An out-going role must be played by the leader—because the handicapped person is not apt to take the lead in developing active participation in activities. This kind and persuasive manner should have no element of force in it. Unless prescribed to the contrary by the physician, the patient should be allowed to state whether or not he prefers to participate in the activity. Patience is a byword of the leader's technique. Time and again the handicapped person may not respond. Persistent efforts should be made by the leader in order to secure the proper reactions from specific individuals. The catatonic patient in the stuporous phase will rarely react very readily to any recreational activity. When the patient is in a stuporous state, the skilled therapist will actually take the patient's hands and place them on the ball. The therapist will then carefully explain to the patient that the ball is to be caught when it is thrown to him. The gradual establishment of a friendly understanding will help him on his long road to recovery. Unless in a phase of excitement, the catatonic patient does not usually express himself verbally, but he will often comprehend all that the leader is saying to him or about him in his presence.

Empathy is the ability to identify one's self with another and enter into the spirit or feeling of that person. This perception requires sympathy and experience. The understanding that leads to true empathy is vitally dependent upon the student, therapist, teacher, or parent learning reactions and characteristics of the handicapped. Seasoned and meaningful experience contributes to planning productive hours and to effective programming.

There have been monumental works written on the knack of winning confidence through thoughtful and considerate actions. Interpersonal relationships assume more than the casual acquaintance that one might strike up with another person. In many cases, in a hospital where there is a ratio of one recreation leader to one hundred or more patients, it is hard to conceive of developing therapeutic relationships with more than a few.

Attitude therapy plays a major role in dealing with emotional disturbances. It is particularly useful in working with neurospychiatric patients. Attitude therapy is a way in which the therapist responds to the patients' words and/or behavior. The medical doctor may prescribe an attitude that the team member is to assume at a certain time.

Prescribed attitudes are responses of staff persons to the patient's needs. Even though the therapist feels pity, he may still have to respond with kind firmness or other directed attitudes. Six commonly used attitudes that might accompany therapeutic activities are:

1. *Indulgence*—gracefully excusing things that the patient does as long as the divergence is not too great.
2. *Passive Friendliness*—The leader is available to the patient but does not force attention upon him.
3. *Active Friendliness*—Initiative is displayed by the leader in developing the patient's interest toward an activity, all in a friendly manner.
4. *Kind Firmness*—The leader displays a very positive yet kind attitude toward the patient which does not allow the patient's deviating from accepted rules or behavior.
5. *Matter-of-Factness*—The leader displays, in a friendly way, a passing and only casual recognition of the patient's conduct.
6. *Watchfulness*—The leader assumes a responsibility of consistent and careful watch over the patient's every action and removes the objects that might be of harm or danger to him.

An attitude of active friendliness should always characterize the leader's contact with the handicapped unless some other attitude or approach has been prescribed. It is in this kind of atmosphere that greatest progress can be realized in an activities program.

PITFALLS AND EMOTIONAL INVOLVEMENTS

A handicapped person in a confined world of his own has considerable time to think about those with whom he comes in contact during each day. The therapist should be aware of the patient's susceptibility to emotional involvement and avoid relationships of too personal a nature.

Pitfalls may beset the inexperienced leader who struggles to cope with the varied problems of the handicapped. Fear begets fear, and an appearance of anxiety and apprehension in the leader's approach to patients often upsets them in a similar manner. The seasoned hospital employee will utilize a technique that is reassuring as well as helpful to the patient.

The handicapped will sometimes see in the recreation leader or special teacher a substitute for a mother, father, husband, wife, or child. In institutions for the mentally retarded and epileptic where there are a number of children, the child's desire for parental love and response may be readily observed. Children may cling to and caress the play leader if there is no restraint. The discriminating leader will, from the beginning, tactfully resist such physical displays of affection. Naturally the leader will hold participants' hands in the normal course of activities, but overt displays of fondness and unnecessary physical contact are to be avoided. When working with children, it is wise to recognize that the activity leader could appear to serve as a parental substitute (as may the hospital aide or nurse). The leader must realize that this relationship is needed as much by the physically unattractive as by the attractive handicapped persons. A hardship for the handicapped person who had become overly fond of the recreation leader would certainly arise if his solicitous leader were transferred to another ward or left hospital employment.[1]

[1] For additional discussion on qualities of professional persons, see Paul Haun, M.D., "Qualities of the Professional in Hospital Recreation," *Journal of Health, Physical Education, and Recreation,* October, 1957.

IN-SERVICE TRAINING

Training or education on the job is an important and specified sequence in the supervisory growth of an employee. In-service training tends to commence and end at a specific point whereas supervision ideally continues throughout one's employment. In-service training is usually conducted by means of classes, lectures, or special methods which prepare the worker for a special skill.

"In-service" assumes that these lectures or courses are attended during working hours. A series of lectures by physicians, special teachers, or a schedule of weekly meetings may be geared to definite topics. Records might be kept on the time that workers participate in this training. Certificates of completion or attendance could be awarded to those who successfully complete the in-service training program. This type of training appears to be more formalized and academically directed than does the informal educational approach of supervision. In-service training is a part of supervision. Newly employed staff people might partake of an orientation training period wherein they attend a specified number of lectures and demonstrations.

THE VOLUNTEER LEADER

Volunteers supplement a staff's services to the handicapped and provide an invaluable and unique aid. Volunteers cannot take the place of paid professional leadership, but they do enrich and enlarge the recreation staff's services to patients. Volunteers may serve in nursing, occupational therapy, recreation, clerical, and other varied areas. However, the majority of volunteer contributions are of a recreational nature. It is wise to have a special volunteer coordinator in a large hospital. The coordinator works directly with representatives from the various volunteer groups and coordinates all voluntary services for the maximun benefit of the institution.

A system which results in a minimum of confusion to the volunteer and the maximum of service to the hospital is of major importance in working with volunteers. It is essential that a well-organized record system is maintained currently so that details of volunteer performance are available. If certificates of merit or recognition are to be awarded, there should be available an accurate record of hours spent or amount of money or objects given by volunteers. All volunteer service, whether it be articles or time given by people, must be recognized in some manner. One valuable form of recognition is the day-to-day "thank you" or appreciation extended verbally to volunteers who visit the sick and disabled. Letters and certificates of appreciation are proper for volunteers whose services have extended over a period of time or are of noteworthy consequence. Annual recognition dinners for volunteers have worked well in many hospitals.

A means of identification should also be considered so that other personnel within a hospital can identify these visitors on the wards. The initial clearance and orientation of volunteers is of signal importance. This should be done in conjunction with the medical or psychological staffs so that only approved individuals are allowed to enter this type of service.

Occasionally outside groups may want to present a play or stage performance for the handicapped. All content and script material should be cleared in advance so that objectional talent or lines may be excluded.

Institutions that welcome volunteers are increasing their effectiveness, and this free service needs only to be well organized and controlled. Some advantages in utilizing contributions of volunteers are:

1. Volunteers supplement particular skills that staff members may not possess.
2. Volunteers do not represent authority to the individual.
3. Contact with the outside community may be represented through the volunteer.
4. Volunteers present new faces and refreshing approaches in activities.

RECREATION SERVICES

The leadership of recreational activities in the home, school, hospital, or institution requires resourcefulness, skill, and good direction. It is important that activities of the handicapped be under the general direction or approval of a physician. The medical doctor is the best qualified in ascertaining the limits of patients' participation.

The administrative arrangement of recreation services for patients varies according to the type of hospital. Veterans Administration, private, military, state, and other hospitals all feature different plans for the supervision and administration of recreation. Regardless of the particular location of recreation services, or the titles of those who lead recreation activities, the effective direction of them requires a cooperative working liaison with other medical team specialists.

In order for recreational activities to be used successfully in a hospital, the leader must function under either medical prescription, clearance, or approval. All of these procedures assume medical direction and furnish the important tie-in of recreation with the coordinated treatment plan. Prescription includes the physician's written word on a special form. This direction gives basic information about the patient, his diagnosis, limitations, and desired goals. Clearance as a second procedure in activities leadership involves a medical "okay" for an individual or group to partake in some activity. This procedure could approve of patients' going to a spectator event or participating in some activity. Medical approval is a broader concept which involves approval of recreation activities by a physician. This method of sanction is less specific than prescription or clearance. Approval might feature only the signature of the ward physician or hospital medical director on a schedule of recreation activities for several patients, or possibly for the entire hospital patient population.

Prescription does not necessarily eliminate free choice in recreation. Most physicians are not professionally skilled in recreation leadership and prefer to leave decisions about specific activity up to the therapist. The prescription states limits and goals, but some freedom of choice for the patient is often allowed. Allowing the patient to choose is desirable, but the leader of recreation activity should remember that what the patient wants to do is not always of therapeutic value. The recreation specialist should know what activities to use in reaching the physician's goal within the limitations or restrictions of a prescription.

It is important that the person in charge of activities for the handicapped be skilled in leadership and that he reflect professional attitudes. The use of these recommended leadership methods along with the suggested activities in Part Two will provide a sound basis for success and satisfaction.

II

ACTIVITIES

Chapter 4

Arts and Crafts

ARTS AND CRAFTS are those activities that involve the creation of artistic and useful objects. A variety of media are combined in many ways to produce these tangible articles. Imagination, utility, aesthetic appreciation, skill, and patience characterize completed projects.

Considerable practice is needed in some cases for exquisite and attractive work. Those who lead the handicapped in arts and crafts programs are urged to secure complete directions and guidance in the construction and accomplishment of crafts. Such pursuits as basketry, ceramics, knitting, and rug weaving especially require qualified direction.

The productive use of hands and the sense of satisfaction gained from newly created objects are some of the psychological advantages inherent in hand crafts. Things made in activities programs should be useful and beneficial to the handicapped, whether he be in the home or hospital. Purposeful products may also be sold to the public. Profits from sales should be returned to those who made the objects or should go toward the purchase of supplies and equipment. Hospitals and institutions should never permit the production of crafts to turn into a thriving and profiteering business with increased pressures upon patients to turn out more and more work. This is not real rehabilitation.

Used Christmas cards, leather pieces, ribbon seconds, felt scraps, native clays, X-ray sheets, lumber pieces, and newspapers are a few scrap materials easily obtainable locally and often free of charge. Many worthwhile things can be made from these and other inexpensive supplies.

Creative expression is satisfied through a guided arts and crafts program, and the use of hands and limbs is enjoyably achieved in many craft activities. Coloring, cutting, weaving, and modeling are realized in many of these selected activities, yet only limited space and inexpensive supplies are needed for many crafts.

The thirty-eight recommended activities are representative of a balanced program for the several diagnostic groups of patients. The crafts are located in eight major categories:

1. Modeling
2. Painting and Drawing
3. Papercraft
4. Puppet making

5. Sewing
6. Weaving
7. Woodwork
8. Other Crafts

See *Dennison Paper Arts and Crafts for Teachers and Group Leaders*. This colorfully illustrated paper crafts guide contains ideas on classroom decorations, posters and bulletin boards, dramatics, and selected hints. Purchase it from a local stationery or department store or through the Dennison Manufacturing Company.

MODELING

Ceramics   • A • GMS • NP •

Equipment for Making Clay Bowls: Potters clay, kick wheel, kiln, glaze, and electric current.

Mold the clay so it is easy to work with and pliable. Place the clay on the kick wheel and set it in motion. With dampened fingers, mold the clay into a cylindrical shape. Form the clay into a bowl or dish. Make objects that can be used or sold.

Carefully study directions accompanying the kiln and place the completed clay product into it for firing. Bake the bowl, dish, or other clay creation in the kiln for three to nine hours, depending upon attainable temperature and size of kiln. For safety's sake, be certain that the kiln has the approval of the Underwriter's Laboratory, Incorporated. Skill and experience are necessary for firing of clay. Check with a nearby library for books on ceramics and pottery.

Front and top loading electric kilns are costly and should be carefully studied before purchase. Prices range from about $60 to $1400. Some kilns are obtainable in kit form for about $25 and may be assembled in an hour or less. Purchase such kits from your local arts and crafts dealer or the American Art Clay Company. These kits usually include a partially assembled kiln and instructions for putting it together, plus directions on the use of it for firing.

Clay Modeling   • C • GMS • MR • NP • TB •

Equipment: Plastic nonfiring modeling clay, a two by two foot piece of oilcloth, several toothpicks, nails, hairpins, and string.

Place the oilcloth on a table or board. Mold the clay in strips and various shaped sizes. Make a ball about four inches in diameter. With a tightly held string clutched between the two hands, cut the ball in half. Gouge out the center of each half sphere. Smooth off the rough edges and notice that this leaves two bowls. Use the toothpicks, nails, and hairpins as tools for decorating clay objects. Remold the clay into other shapes and forms. Secure plastic nonhardening clay for the best results. When working with mentally retarded children, be sure that the clay is nontoxic. Most craft dealers and some department stores sell this type of modeling clay.

Purchase for the advanced clay modeler several colors of modeling clay together with modeling tools. Consider making these tools out of boxwood or try ice cream bar sticks as temporary tools. Large paper clips that are partially straightened out sometimes can be used as a wire-end tool.

Papier Mâché   • A • C • GMS • NP • TB •

Equipment: Papier mâché paste (1 cup water, 1 tablespoon powdered alum, 1 pint cold water, 1 pint flour, 1 teaspoon oil of clove); fifteen or twenty pages of newspaper; nonrusting container; various colors of paint; small paint brush; shellac and small shellac brush.

Tear newspaper pages into fine strips and soak for twenty-four hours in the container. Make paste with above ingredients of water, powdered alum, cold water, flour, and oil of clove. Boil the cup of water and add powdered alum. Mix the flour into the cold water until there is a smooth mixture. Pour this mixture gradually into the boiling alum water. Stir constantly and cook until it shows a blue cast. Remove from the heat, add the oil of clove and stir well. Thin if necessary with water.

Squeeze water out of the soaked newspaper strips. Add paste to the pulp. Model forms, shapes, and objects out of the papier mâché mixture. Mold the mixture over solid objects to make masks, bowls, and so on. Thoroughly dry the completed products. Paint in decorative colors. After paint has dried, apply shellac for a glossy appearance.

For variety, try making papier mâché with colored crepe paper.

Equipment: One package of crepe paper, one large bowl, scissors, one tablespoon of salt, one cup of flour and one quart of water.

Cut the crepe paper (while still folded in the package) crosswise in small quarter-inch sections. Recut this in confettilike squares until the whole package is cut up and placed in bowl. Add the salt and cover mixture with water. Allow this to soak for an hour or until it is soft. Drain off the surplus water. Leave just enough water so that the paper is moist and pulpy. Add sufficient flour to make into a stiff dough (like cookie dough). Knead the doughy mixture until the cut-up crepe paper is blended in with the flour and water. Notice that it is soft and pliable like modeling clay.

Select several small trays, typewriter ribbon cans, cellophane tape cans, small cannisters, and old jewelry. Model the claylike mixture over the articles and allow to dry. Make ash trays around a circular piece of tin (end of a used tin can) or try making small objects which have no foundation at all.

PAINTING AND DRAWING

Crayoning   • C • *GMS* • *MR* • *NP* •

Equipment: Eight or more varied color crayons, paper, and/or coloring books.

Distribute crayons in a flat box along with paper or coloring books to any number of participants. If there are many persons, tear pages from a large coloring book and pass these out to them. Plain paper may allow more originality of expression. Be sure that crayons are of a nontoxic variety, especially when using with mentally retarded children. Large hexagonal crayons are easy to hold and do not break as readily as regular sized ones. Also, the color and quality of the more expensive crayons are much better than the cheapest brands. Purchase these in local department or stationery stores.

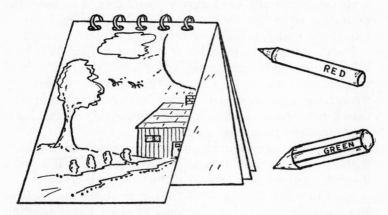

Many variations of crayon work are possible on wood or cloth in addition to paper. Save crayon shavings left over from crayon sharpening. Sprinkle a variety of color shavings onto a piece of white paper. Place another plain sheet of paper over it. Run a warm electric iron over this several times. Lift the top sheet and note that the shavings have melted into a very colorful design on both sheets. Secure varied effects by using certain colors and arranging the shavings in different formations (hearts, trees, cross, or squares).

Finger Painting   • C • GMS • NP • TB •

Equipment: Assorted finger paints, water, finger-paint paper, and newspaper. If finger-paint paper is not obtainable, use newspaper as a finger painting surface. If commercial finger paints are not available at local craft stores make your own finger paint. Use the following recipe:

1½ cups laundry starch	½ cup talcum (optional)
1 quart boiling water	½ tablespoon paint
1½ cups soap flakes	

Mix the starch with cold water to form a creamy paste. Add the boiling water and cook until mixture becomes glossy. Stir constantly. Add the talcum. Let mixture cool a bit, add soap flakes and stir until evenly distributed. Let cool and pour into eight jars with screw tops. Stir into each jar ½ tablespoon poster, powder, or easel paint of desired color.

Locate a large area for a finger-painting surface. Wet both sides of the finger-paint paper and flatten it out on a level surface. Place a lump of paint on the paper. With sweeping strokes, smear the paint over the wet surface. Use the fingers, fists, hands, or even elbows to create interesting effects. Place the completed picture on a newspaper to dry.

After the finger-paint picture is dry, press it on the back with a warm household iron. This will flatten it and make it suitable for use as a framed picture or book cover.

See *Craft Adventures for Children* by Gretchen Grimm and Catherine Skeels for additional ideas on finger painting and other children's crafts.

Lettering   • A • C • GMS • NP •

Equipment: Several crowquill and various sized speedball pen points, pen holder for crowquill pen points, pen holder for speedball pen points, metal edged foot ruler, ink and pencil erasers, hard lead pencil, eleven- by fourteen-inch masonite writing board, small T square to fit writing board, black drawing ink, white and colored sheets of drawing or construction paper, single-edged razor blade, roll of transparent tape, and small box to hold ink, pen points, and other writing equipment.

Select a sturdy table or stand upon which to put the various pieces of writing equipment. Tape the corners of the drawing paper to the writing board. Have the letterer practice different widths and types of letter styles with the pens. Draw penciled guide lines along the horizontal edge of the T square within which to do the hand lettering. Make posters for display that will advertise and interpret worthwhile recreation activities.

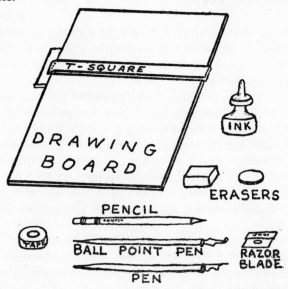

Purchase several relatively inexpensive celluloid lettering stencils that may be used with a T square as a guide. These allow for more perfect lettering and less chance of spoiled posters for the amateur. For the individual intrigued with lettering, purchase a mechanical lettering set (such as the LeRoy set from Keuffel and Esser Company).

Study the various types and styles of letters. The following describe the three major groups of letters:

1. Roman letters: All letters made up of wide and narrow lines (in same letter).
2. Gothic letters: All letters made up of uniformly wide lines (same width in each letter).
3. Text letters: Other letter types such as church text, Old English text, old fashioned script, and so on.

The following describe the two types of letter sizes:

1. Upper case: Capital letters.
2. Lower case: Small (noncapitalized) letters.

Paint-by-Number Kits · A · C · GMS · MR · TB ·

Equipment for Painting a Predrawn Picture: A predrawn canvas, capsules of paints arranged numerically to fit the predrawn canvas, paint brush, and board (all usually obtainable in stores in kit form).

Affix the canvas to a board and place the paint capsules in a readily available location. Have participants brush oil paint from each numbered capsule onto the same numbered areas in the picture. Let them paint the entire area enclosed in any numbered section, and if necessary, overlap lines rather than leave blank spaces where the predrawn lines are printed. After all numbers are covered, a beautiful and seemingly professionally painted picture is the reward for patient and detailed work.

Suggestions: Use the principle of paint-by-number kits in making mimeographed sheets with similar predrawn arrangements. Insert names of colors instead of numbers. Try this inexpensive method with crayons.

Trays, letter holders, waste baskets, dishes, and other articles with predrawn pictures on them are also available on the market. Predrawn canvases with premixed colors in sets may be purchased from local arts and crafts dealers. If these are unobtainable locally, try the Palmer-Pann Corporation for additional information.

A great sense of achievement is felt by some higher-grade mentally retarded persons who complete a paint-by-number scene. In contrast, certain neuropsychiatric patients become frustrated and distressed with such detailed work.

The opportunity for free artistic expression and creativity is limited when the painter has to follow specific numbers and lines.

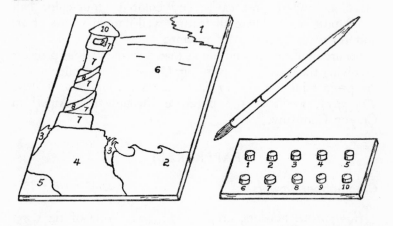

Painting   • A • C • GMS • NP • TB •

Equipment: Assorted colors of tempera powdered paint, small containers for the paints, water, paper, easel or board, and several long-handled paint brushes.

Place the paper on a board or flat surface. Mix water with several colors of tempera powder in the individual containers. Procure any object in the room or another picture for the patient to reproduce on paper. After some practice in painting, select fruit, bowls, and cylindrical articles for the patient to use as models.

Encourage the beginner to use free expression and free action in painting. Suggest for the advanced student of painting the use of oil paints, charcoal, pencil, water colors, and other media on paper and canvas.

Some painters are interested in art correspondence courses —systematic approaches to painting in a series of lessons. The tuition fees for some art correspondence courses are high. One well-known course for art students is the Famous Artists Course. Encourage the study of famous artists such as Vincent van Gogh, who created many admirable pictures while mentally ill. Go to a nearby library or art gallery for added information on the study of the famous painters. Write to the National Gallery of Art for information on copies of prints, black and white post cards, and colored (four-color half tone) post cards. These all feature well-known works of art and are available for small amounts.

Secure publications and books that describe various projects involving the medium of painting. One excellent collection of art project ideas is the *Project and Idea Folio No. 3 (Art Therapy)*, available for purchase through the American Crayon Company.

PAPERCRAFT

Crepe-paper Flowers   • A • GMS • NP • TB •

Equipment: Scissors, crepe paper, paste, role of tie wire, and instruction book on crepe-paper flower making.

Carefully read the detailed instructions on crepe-paper flower making in any specially written guide book. In brief, cut the flower's petals from a thickness of several sheets of crepe paper. Cup and shape petals with the fingers. Fasten the base of all petals, now shaped like a flower, with tie wire. Wrap additional tie wire to give the appearance of stems. Stretch the paper to complete flower shape.

When one has adequate practice and skill, he may teach crepe-paper flower making fundamentals to others. Guide booklets on crepe-paper craft are obtainable from the Dennison Manufacturing Company or some local stationery or department stores. The one entitled *How to Make Flowers* contains considerable detail and step-by-step directions on crepe-paper flower making.

For variety try gummed crepe paper (crepe paper with adhesive on one side) for making bright and gay paper crafts.

Gummed crepe paper is available for sale through local stationery stores. The typical bright crepe-paper colors are attractive when cut in flower designs. Use contrasting colors together on construction paper backgrounds for authentic looking flowers. See *Fun with Crafts* for more information on the uses of gummed crepe paper.

Paper-bag Mask   • C • GMS • MR •

Equipment: Paper bag large enough to slip over head, scissors, and assorted crayons.

Select one or more paper bags large enough to fit over the head. Have the child cut out holes for the eyes, nose, and mouth. Color the hair, eyebrows, cheeks, and other facial features. Trim off bottom of bag so it fits comfortably around neck.

Paper-bag masks may be made for holidays such as Halloween. Have several children make masks and compare them. Lead group singing and other activities at a party at which children don their masks.

Avoid too carefree use of masks, which may frighten or disturb some persons.

Go to a nearby grocer and ask for or purchase several Kraft paper bags for this purpose. Have volunteers donate clean and untorn bags.

See *Fun with Crafts* for easy-to-make paper craft projects.

Paper Hat   • A • C • GMS • MR • NP • TB •

Equipment: One double page of newspaper.

Double page of newspaper should be closed like a book. Fold newspaper in half so fold is parallel with the newsprint. Fold two lower corners in about four inches from upper

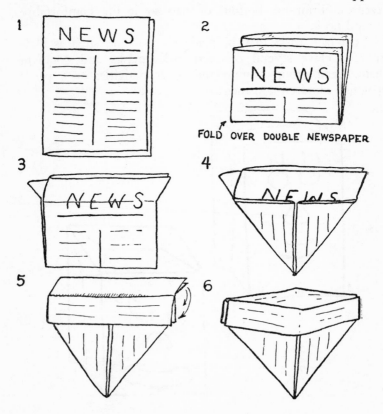

FOLD OVER DOUBLE NEWSPAPER

end. Fold one upper end over the two folded corners. Fold four inches of the other end over opposite side of hat. Pull hat open, crease edges, and place on head.

Tape bottom of hat so that it will stay intact longer without opening up. Have children place hats on their heads and march rhythmically to music. See *Papercraft* by Joseph Leeming for more ideas on paper folding, cutting, and games.

Paper Nut Cup   • A • C • GMS • NP • TB •

Equipment: Square piece of paper approximately six to nine inches square.

Fold the square sheet evenly so that a triangle is made. Open it up and fold in other direction so another triangle is made. Open up the square and fold in the four corners to the center point of square. Keep the four corners folded in. Turn the sheet over and bend the four corners over and back so that points touch center of folded square. Turn folded sheet over. Bend neatly and evenly into a rectangle. Open up and bend in opposite direction so that a rectangle results. Open up the four corners and push in the four pockets so that nut cup sits on four corners. Shape so that paper is stiff and stays in position.

For variety, before opening up the four corners in last step, color the nut cup with crayons. Serve nuts and candies in cup at the next meal.

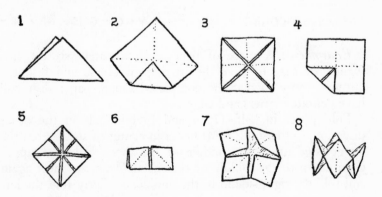

Paper-plate Letter Holder   • A • C • GMS • NP • TB •

Equipment: Two paper plates, six feet of yarn, paper punch, scissors, and crayons.

Cut one of the paper plates in half. Punch holes one-half inch apart all around the rim of the whole paper plate and the half paper plate. Place the half paper plate inverted over the whole plate with edges together. This forms a pocket. Color the back of the half plate and inside of the whole plate. Join the two halves together by sewing or looping yarn through holes all around the whole plate. Insert a separate loop through one of the top holes for hanging the completed letter holder. Hang on end of bed and use as a receptacle for letters, notes, and other personal belongings of the patient. If possible, paint the letter holder rather than using crayons. Use a brush and shellac to preserve the completed product.

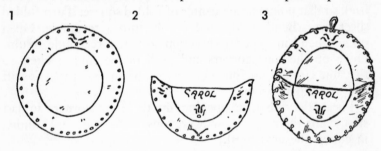

Paper Square Dish   • A • C • GMS • NP • TB •

Equipment: A piece of paper approximately six by nine inches. Be sure to have the participant crease and fold the corners firmly so that the completed square paper dish will have definite corners and edges.

Fold paper in half. Open and fold in half in the other direction, so that both folds bisect in center of sheet. Fold the lower edge up to the middle of the sheet. Fold the upper edge down to the middle of the sheet. Open the sheet again and fold the right side in to the middle. Similarly fold the left side in to the middle. Flatten sheet out and tear evenly on the top and bottom folds (on folded line) to the first vertical lines. Bend over the top and bottom folds and crease sharply. Bend the two end flaps in toward the center and crease them in the shape of a box. Lift up the two flattened sides and bend them over tops of the two crossed flaps. Crease the ends so they interlock over each set of crossed flaps on the ends.

Use the dish for small articles. For permanence, staple or

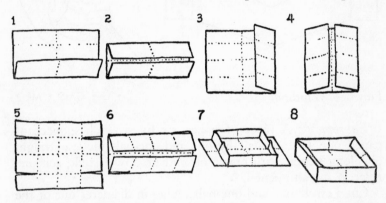

glue the two ends so they are affixed to the underneath crossed flaps, thereby keeping dish from slipping apart. Use heavy paper or colored construction paper.

Before folding the container, color with crayons or paint both sides of it, if plain paper is being used. This makes it, when folded, a very attractive paper dish.

To make a basket for Easter, Valentine, or other parties, glue handles on the paper dish.

Paper Whistle   • C • MR •

Equipment: Piece of paper, eight inches by three inches; pair of scissors.

Cut out whistle similar to the outline in the drawing. Bend the two flaps back and hold loosely between the first and second fingers of either hand. Blow into the opening between the two turned up end flaps. The exterior part of the whistle (not flaps held against the mouth) may be colored with crayons.

Use the paper whistle only where there is no restriction on the shrill noise that it makes.

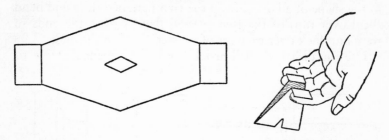

Pinwheel Windmill   • C • GMS • MR •

Equipment: A piece of paper, six by six inches; piece of paper, one and one-half by one and one-half inches; straight pin; long pencil with eraser on end or dowel stick; scissors; ruler; paste; and pencil.

Cut a circle one and one-half inches in diameter out of the smaller piece of paper. Paste this circle to the center of the six-inch square. As shown in the diagram, cut from each corner of square to the outside of circle. Gently bend (do not crease) every other corner, one at a time, just over the center.

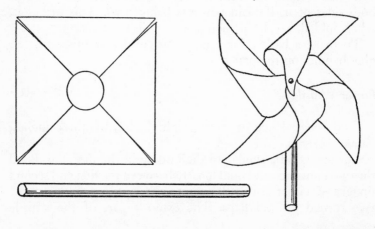

After the four corners are bent over and held on the circle of the square, push a straight pin through corners and center of the square. Stick pin point into the eraser of a pencil or dowel stick. Hold the pinwheel in a breeze or wave the windmill in the air so that it will spin. For durability and beauty, use heavy colored paper.

PUPPET MAKING

Finger Puppets • A • C • GMS • TB •

Equipment: Several peanuts, pen with ink, bits of cloth, yarn scraps, glue, pencil, and scissors.

Break or cut open the peanut shells so as to fashion a cap to fit over finger tips. Draw plan of puppet face on the peanut

shell. Create a puppet face with bits of yarn and cloth glued to the shell. Draw other facial outlines with pen and ink. Add a small cap and hair to the finger puppet.

After several are made, experiment with acting out scenes. Provide narration and move selected finger puppets as each "talks." One such "talk" adaptable to finger puppets is *Thumkins*. Do it with one finger puppet on the thumb and another on the first (pointer) finger. Say the following verse using the finger puppets in appropriate gestures and movements:

Thumkins

Where is Thumkins? (move first finger forward to words)
Where is Thumkins? (move first finger forward to words)
Here I am! (move thumb three times)
Here I am! (move thumb three times)
How are you this evening (or morning)? (move first finger)
How are you this evening (or morning)? (move first finger)
Hide-a-way! (thumb puppet tucks into palm of hand)
Hide-a-way! (thumb puppet tucks into palm of hand)

Do *Thumkins* to a tune and act it out at same time! Sing it to the tune of "Are You Sleeping?".

Hand Puppets   • A • C • GMS • MR • TB •

Equipment: Two pieces of terry cloth or other heavy cloth nine inches square, needle, thread, scissors, small paint brush, and paint of assorted colors.

Cut out of both cloth pieces a section that has two extended ends for thumb and small finger and a circular top part for index finger. The basic shape of a head and two arms is obtained. For more sturdy wear, sew over edges of pieces on open part. Stitch around edges of the "arms" and "head" as in a glove. Paint on a face and other decorations to give appear-

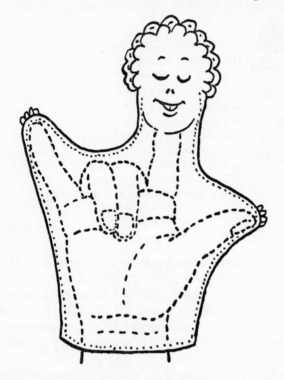

ance of arms, hands, and clothing, or sew on buttons and other objects for eyes, nose and mouth.

Place index finger in the head area of glove. Place thumb in one arm area and little finger in the other. Rest other fingers between arm and head inside of hand puppet. Hold puppet behind a cardboard box used as stage so that elbow and arm are not visible to audience. Act out a scene with someone behind the box stage narrating the action.

If only limited time is available, make hand puppets out of small paper bags. Color the faces, arms, hands, and clothing on the bag with crayons.

Try acting out *Three Little Lads* with hand puppets. If there are two puppets, assign every other line to be narrated by the person working the second puppet. Also try having all persons saying the piece in unison and acting out the various lines.

Three Little Lads

We're three little tykes!
Three little chums!
Three little lads at school!
We mean to be so good,
We mean to be true!
But sometimes get into mischief
Now, honest, didn't you?
When you were little chaps!
When you were little chums!
When you were little lads at school.

Marionettes   • A • GMS • TB •

Equipment: Instruction book on making marionettes, pine pieces, clamp, knife, sandpaper, pencil, marionette plans, soft leather strips, glue, hand drill and bits, paint, small paint brush, wood file, scissors, black thread, and cloth materials. The materials used in marionettes must be reasonably light so that the completed product is not too heavy to manipulate with the hands.

Carefully study the book on marionette construction. Follow instructions and make several marionettes. Note that most hands and heads for properly made marionettes are slightly out of proportion and large. Pencil in the features on head. Paint faces and dress the marionette according to its particular character or role.

Find or write a play in which the marionettes are to perform. Put on a performance for others in a theater built for marionette shows. For instructions on how to make an inexpensive theater for marionettes, see E. O. Harbin's *The Fun Encyclopedia.*

Study nursery rhymes, fables, fairy tales, and children's stories for ideas that can be adapted into plays. Assign parts for the available puppets and present a marionette show on the stage. See "Handy Stunts" (Kit I) from *Handy* for more ideas on plays to use with marionettes.

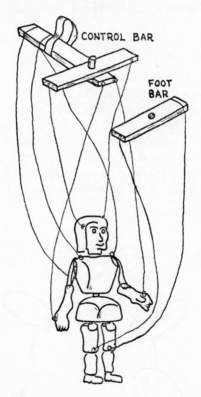

Remember that the making of marionettes is a time-consuming task that cannot be completed in a short period. Some participants become impatient with the meticulous and painstaking work required in making marionettes. Children often tire because of the time needed in making marionettes, but will enjoy marionette shows put on for their entertainment.

The use of marionettes with neuropsychiatric patients is questioned by some authorities. They object to the out-of-proportion facial and body characteristics of puppets. Certain manipulated actions of marionettes do not always duplicate typical normal adult behavior. This could tend to implement and support certain patients' hallucinatory behavior. Medical guidance is particularly suggested in any consideration of marionettes for neuropsychiatric patients.

Stick Puppets   • A • C • GMS • MR • TB •

Equipment: Tongue depressor or other flat stick about six to eight inches long, small picture of a face, cardboard, four paper fasteners, glue, scissors, and crayons.

Cut out and trim the small face from a magazine or elsewhere. Cut out piece of cardboard and glue to back of face. Cut pieces of cardboard to serve as the body, legs, and arms. Push paper fasteners through arms and legs and attach to body section. Glue back of body piece to stick. Glue face over

top part of body piece (neck) and to the stick. Color the body, arms, and legs.

Hold stick puppet up and watch arms and legs move freely as a story is acted out. Gaily recite a simple rhyme to the actions of a stick puppet.

SEWING

Knitting   • A • GMS • NP • TB •

Equipment: One pair of knitting needles (4¼ millimeter size), two one-ounce balls of dark-colored yarn, and two one-ounce balls of light-colored yarn.

Secure an instruction book on knitting and study the detailed directions and illustrations. Practice the essential knitting steps. Fit the stitches closely, but not tightly around the needles. Practice the two basic stitches of knitting, the knit stitch and purl stitch. Make a hat or other small object out of the amount of provided yarn. Collect from volunteers old neckties for use in making afghans.

One book that contains illustrated directions for knitting, crocheting, tatting, and embroidery is the *Learn-How Book*. Two other complete books on the subject of knitting are *The Good Housekeeping Needlecraft Encyclopedia* edited by Alice Carroll and *The Big Book of Knitting* edited by Isabella Stevenson.

Stuffed Toys   • A • C • GMS • MR • NP • TB •

Equipment: Several square feet of oilcloth or other heavy cloth, cotton, kapok or foam rubber, large needle, heavy yarn, and scissors.

Have the participant cut a pattern of an animal out of the oilcloth or heavy cloth and blanket stitch it with the heavy yarn a small part of the way around the animal outline. The participant then stuffs cotton or other material into the partially sewn animal. Stitch more of the outline and again have the participant stuff as much padding as possible into the inside. Complete stitching of the stuffed toy. For more substantial use, stitch the stuffed toy on a sewing machine. For variety, add yarn tails and sew a name onto the toy.

COTTON FOR STUFFING→

WEAVING

Basketry   • A • C • GMS • NP •

Equipment for Rectangular Basket: Wood strips from a sassafras or similar wood log, ¾ inches wide and ¹⁄₁₆ inch thick—eight that are 19 inches long, six that are 22 inches long, and four weaving strips that are approximately 5 feet long; wood board 10 inches by 6 inches by ¾ inches thick; five small nails (each about ¾ inches long); hammer; sharp knife; and large pan of water. If wood strips are not obtainable from nearby wooded areas, check with local arts and crafts dealer, or secure a straight sassafras log 5 to 6 feet long and 6 inches thick. Soak it in water for a day or more. Pound it all around evenly with a lead pipe for an hour or so. Starting at one end, carefully pull off strips from the log.

Soak the strips in water for at least a half hour so they will be pliable and bendable. Cross a 19-inch and 22-inch strip so they bisect each other at right angles. Slit one-half (9½ inches) of the middle 19-inch strip so that on one end it is ¾ inches wide and the other in two sections, each ⅜ inches in width. Start from this middle point and criss-cross the strips so that one is alternately over and under the other. Push the strips close to one another so there are only small spaces between the right-angle crossed strips. The bottom of the woven basket is completed after six of the long 22-inch strips have been crossed alternately over and under eight of the 19-inch strips.

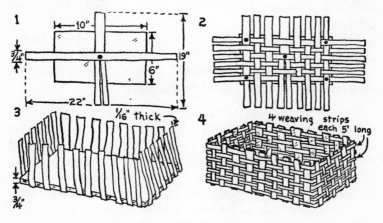

Place the bottom part of the basket on the wood board. Pound a nail through the strips on each corner and in the middle of the board area. Soak the basket for another half hour and whenever it is not being worked upon.

Bend the strips or "ribs" up and around the edges of the board. Crease the strips as much as possible so that they are at right angles around the board edges. Insert one of the 5-foot weaving strips through the one split strip and weave it alternately between strips around the edge of the board. Pull the strips tightly and form the sides of the basket. Carefully pull the nails out of the strips and remove the form board from the inside bottom of the basket. As one weaving strip ends, overlap it with another and keep going around the sides of the partially completed basket. Press the strips as close together as possible and form the corners so they too are at right angles.

At a height equal to about six or seven strips, the sides are completed. Bend over the ribs (that have gone around the bottom of the basket and formed uprights for sides) and tuck them in between the woven side strips. This interlocks and finishes off the strips on the top horizontal tier of the basket. If the basket has become dry, soak it again in water and crease again into a rectangular shape. Make a handle out of two long strips. Insert them through the woven strips on each side of basket. For added strength, staple the handles to the basket.

Use other materials for the strips such as heavy paper, cardboard or cattail stalks. See the *Handbook for Patrol Leaders* by William Hillcourt for more information and illustrations on simple basketry and weaving.

Place Mats: Weave place mats out of green cattail stalks. Go to a nearby swamp area and collect fourteen stalks for each place mat. Weave these together, tuck in the ends, and use as a place mat or decorative piece on a dresser or table. Children enjoy this type of nature weaving craft, and more ideas can be found in *Hand Weaving with Reeds and Fibers* by Osma Gallinger and Oscar Benson.

Braiding   • C • GMS • TB •

Equipment for Bracelets and Lanyards: Two strips of different colored round or flat lacing material, each about six feet long, and lanyard snap.

Locate the middle point of the long strips and cross them at that spot. Four working ends are now left. Place a lanyard snap at this middle point. Bend end A all the way over end B. Bend B back over the top of A. Bend C back and over B. Bend D over C and tuck it under and through A, thereby interlocking the beginning of a square braid. Follow this braiding pattern and pull the four strips tightly after each completed braid. When desired length for a bracelet or lanyard is reached, tuck the remaining short ends in and around lanyard snap.

Lacing material may be purchased in craft stores under a variety of trade names. Sometimes it is called "gimp" or craftstrip. The more expensive strips are made out of plastic and another type is an oilcloth-covered material.

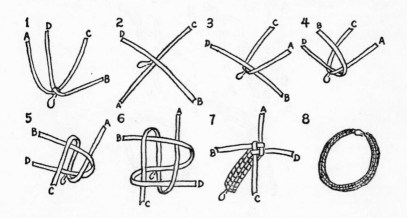

Three Strand Braiding: Make craftstrip necklaces or bracelets with three strands of craftstrip or cloth material. Tie a slip knot at the beginning and start by bending C over B so it is between A and B. Keep pieces pulled tightly after each overlapping braid. Bend A over C so it is between B and C. Repeat by bending B over A and then C over B. Continue doing this until the overlapping braid strands are braided all the way to their ends.

Use shoe laces or heavy string in place of the commercially purchased lacing material. Try plaid shoe laces of the longest obtainable lengths for attractive color variations. Check with your local arts and crafts dealer for sheets and leaflets on other uses for craftstrip projects. Inquire about braided lacing around metal strips for bracelets and other intricate patterns. Study literature that gives detailed diagrams on braiding craft. One such publication is *101 Uses for Craftstrip* by Cy Vaughn.

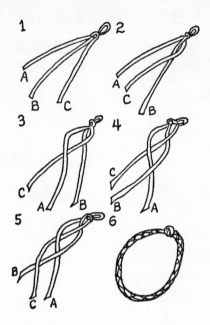

Looper Clip Weaving   • A • C • GMS • MR • NP • TB •

Equipment for Pot Holders: One package of assorted color jersey cloth looper clips (sometimes called loopers), one metal weaving frame, and one weaving needle.

Place the looper clips parallel on the frame with a looper clip stretched over each opposite set of prongs from top to bottom. This set of stretched looper clips is called the warp. Hook a looper clip with the weaving needle to a prong on the other opposite side and weave it over and under each alternate looper. This new set of looper clips now started is called the woof. Do this similarly until all the looper clips are crossed in an alternating manner. Starting at one corner with the hooked end of the weaving needle, gently lift each loop up from a prong and insert it through the looper clip on the adjoining prong. Go all the way around until the last loop is left and the pot holder is woven and lifted from the frame.

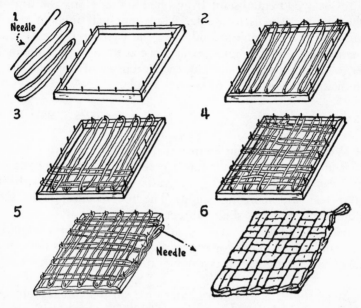

As a variation, make several pot holders and sew or loop them together for a table mat or small rug. Use yarn or string instead of looper clips. Have the advanced weaver make such projects as purses and scarves.

Suggestion: Make a square frame out of four pieces of wood, all of which are one inch thick. Make two of the pieces four inches long and two of them six inches long. Place each piece of the same length opposite one another and nail together. Place the completed frame flat on a table so that all four pieces are in contact with the table top. Secure 76 headless nails three-quarter inches long. Pound the nails half-way

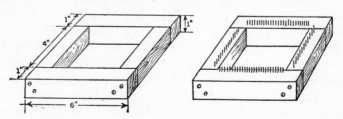

into the wood equidistant from one another along the top of the frame, 19 nails to a side. Allow one-half inch of space between the end of each side (on the two long pieces) and the nearest nail. The raised nails serve as prongs on the homemade loom. Slip a looper clip over each set of opposite nails in making a pot holder or woven article.

Rug Weaving   • A • GMS • MR • NP •

Working with a rug loom is a useful and creative activity that involves use of the hands. Looms are of varying sizes all the way from the six inch table variety up to floor models of four feet and more in height. The use of most table and floor looms requires skilled direction.

Seek the advice of an occupational therapist in the acquisition and use of looms for rug weaving. Study books that give detailed directions on weaving rugs on wood or metal looms.

Suggestions: Start the beginner on a small six-inch loom. A durable six-inch wood loom is available for purchase through The Handicrafters and other large craft suppliers. This type of fine and detailed work is very useful for certain types of neuropsychiatric patients. Exercise to limbs is also provided for selected general medical and surgical patients.

WOODWORK

Carving   • A • GMS • TB •

Equipment: Whittler's knife and five extra blades, sharp pen knife, coping saw, chisel, pencil, and various sized whittling blocks of pine, basswood, or balsa wood.

Draw an outline of the object or animal desired on the block of wood. Study how it will be carved. If there is a good amount of wood to be carved away, use coping saw to cut away unnecessary wood from the outline. Carve out some of the larger areas with a chisel. Do all fine carving with pen knife and whittler's knife. Use latter with specially made razor-sharp blades.

Umbrella handles, bottle stoppers, jewelry boxes, walking sticks, and lamp bases can be made by those with advanced skill. The skilled carver may also do chip carving of boxes, boards, and plaques with whittler's razor-sharp knives. Consider such woods as beech, holly, mahogany, oak, and box-wood for advanced wood carving.

Soap Carving: Use a large bar of white soap for soap sculpturing. Follow the procedure that is described for wood carving. Less hand strength is needed in soap carving.

Purchase razor-sharp knives such as the "X-acto" assortment of several knives and blades in a small wooden chest (about six dollars per assortment). Inquire at any arts and crafts dealer for this type of a whittling set. Use meticulous care in selecting persons for chip carving. Do not allow depressed patients (without consent of physician) or those with young and unsteady hands to participate in this activity.

Wood Burning   • A • C • GMS • NP • TB •

Equipment: Electric wood burning pencil, several wooden blocks, pencil, and electric current. Exercise care in handling of connected wood burning pencil and disconnect it from electricity after use.

Draw in pencil the general design that is wanted on wooden block or purchase predrawn plaques and wooden postcards upon which may be burned attractive scenes and pictures. Use wood burning pencil to burn in outline of object on wood.

When buying a wood burner, also get one or two extra replacement elements (points).

Workbench   • A • C • GMS • MR • NP •

Equipment: Heavy wood table or workbench, hammer, saw, hand drill, other woodworking hand equipment, assorted nails, various sizes of wood blocks and boards.

Suggest various simple articles that the participant might create out of wood. Allow him ample opportunity to experiment with the wood and nails. After practice, encourage the construction of such useful items as book ends, trays, boxes, book covers, and bread boards. Purchase precut wood kits at craft stores. Bird houses and bird feeder kits which include instructions and supplies are available. Use shellac, varnish, or paint for the finishing of well-made things.

Give careful supervision to the use of tools, especially when working with neuropsychiatric patients with depressed conditions. The mentally retarded enjoy woodworking, but require very close supervision.

For a complete illustrated description of the correct use and care of hand tools, secure a copy of the booklet entitled *A B C's of Hand Tools*.

OTHER CRAFTS

Leather Tooling   • *A* • *GMS* • *NP* • *TB* •

Equipment for Belts, Pocketbooks, and Wallets: Tooling leather or scrap leather pieces, small sponge, tracing paper, pencil, modeling tools, and water. Scrap leather may sometimes be obtained free or very reasonably from shoe repair shops or leather goods manufacturers.

Trace a chosen design onto tracing paper. Wet the leather from the back with sponge. Attach tracing paper to the leather on a hard surface. Trace the lines of design with pencil onto leather. Remove tracing paper.

Using the modeler (most common modeling tool), go over the lines of the design with hook end of tool. Press background of design down with spoon end of tool. Keep leather moist throughout the tooling process. Allow leather to dry when tooling process is complete. Small distinctive designs can be pounded into the leather with a mallet and stamping tools.

Study more advanced books on leather carving, lacing, and tooling. Refer these to the individual who wants to pursue this craft in more detail. Study *Handicrafts and Hobbies* by Marguerite Ickis for more ideas.

Buy Indian moccasin kits that are easy to assemble and practical for children or adults. Most arts and crafts dealers sell prepunched leather project kits. These have the necessary leather, lacing, and snaps needed to complete the wallet, keycase, coin purse, or whatever the item may be. Certain projects may be tooled when so specified. Plan to spend between $.15 and $1.50 for each kit. If there is no arts and crafts dealer in your locality that sells leather goods, try a mail inquiry to one of the larger dealers such as the J. C. Larson Company, or Tandy Leather Company.

Metal Enameling   • A • GMS • NP •

Equipment: Copper pieces approximately ¹⁄₁₆ inch thick by 1 inch square (round pieces are also useful), metal enamels, enameling fork, metal enameling kiln, enameling rack, spatula, brush, and vial of oil.

In accordance with instructions on most metal enameling kits, clean perfectly the metal that is to be enameled. Apply enamels to the metal with spatula or other method as desired. Preheat the kiln to 1500 degrees Fahrenheit. If the piece is enameled on both sides, place it on the enameling rack. With the enameling fork, push the rack and metal piece into the hot kiln. When the door is opened, the kiln temperature will drop to about 1325 degrees Fahrenheit and then rise again after door is closed. Fire for between two and three minutes, depending on the size of the metal piece. Remove the piece and rack from the kiln. Place it on a heat resistant surface to cool.

Consult your local arts and crafts dealer or The American Art Clay Company about metal enamel supplies that may be purchased. "Trinkit" and "Craftint" are the names of two copper enameling kits that contain the necessary supplies for this craft. They sell for approximately seven to fifteen dollars each retail.

Plaster Jewelry   • A • C • GMS • MR • NP • TB •

Equipment: Rubber molds, plaster of Paris powder, cold water, safety pins, tempera paint, small paint brush, shellac, and small shellac brush.

Mix the plaster of Paris powder with cold water until there is a smooth pouring consistency. Pour this smooth mixture into the molds and thump out any air bubbles. Place the filled molds on a level surface to set. Just as plaster is about to harden, place the back side of safety pin into the mixture. Let it dry. After three hours, carefully remove the plaster object from the mold and paint with tempera. Shellac the dried tempera paint surface for a glossy finish.

Suggestion: Make rubber molds with liquid rubber and a cast. About five molds can be made from a quart of liquid rubber. The price averages $3.50 per quart. Purchase this from a local arts and crafts store or the Cleveland Crafts Company.

Plastic Jewelry   • A • C • GMS • NP •

Equipment for Buttons and Jewelry: A sheet of plastic, approximately 9 inches by 12 inches by ⅛ inch or ³⁄₁₆ inch thick, coping saw, hand drill, file, four sheets sandpaper (heavy and fine grades), gloves, and electric household iron.

Cut the sheet into squares, circles, or other small shapes for buttons. Drill holes in the centers with hand drill. File the saw marks from edges of buttons. Then use coarse and fine grade sandpaper to smooth edges of the buttons.

Make lapel pins or other cut-outs if desired. Use the electric household iron (at a low heat) to warm the plastic for bending or twisting. Use gloves to handle and bend plastic into desired shape.

Sometimes plastic sheets are sold under a trade name such as Plexiglass. These sheets when sawed into appropriate sizes may be glued into small boxes and other shapes. Use plastic cement or acetone for the best bond. Purchase Plexiglass or plastic discs from a local arts and crafts store.

Sheet Cork   • A • GMS • NP • TB •

Equipment for Household Articles: Several square feet of sheet cork, scissors, pencil, water colors, water-color brush, shellac, and small shellac brush.

Consider luncheon sets, coasters, mats, and book covers as objects to make. Trace or draw a pencil design of the object desired on the sheet cork. Cut design out with scissors. Paint the drawn picture with water colors. After the paint has dried, use shellac finishing as a preservative. Glue sheet cork to cardboard, wood, or cloth. A recommended adhesive to use is a mixture of glue and paste in equal parts.

Variation: Do spatter printing on sheet cork. (See directions on page 171 for spatter printing.) It may be purchased from local arts and crafts dealers. Inquire of the Cleveland Crafts Company for information and prices.

Shell Craft   • A • GMS • NP • TB •

Equipment: Assortment of several types of small shells; assorted sizes of several plastic discs, two inches by two inches in area or smaller; several brooches or safety pins and strong transparent cement.

Arrange shells in several ways so that they are attractive and interesting. Place and glue shells individually in a definite color pattern close together. Let the finished shell-flower or shell-design dry. Attach with cement the safety pin back or brooch back to back of the plastic disc. After drying, the piece of shell jewelry is ready to wear.

For variety, purchase a package of assorted color sequins. Glue them in same manner as shells to plastic discs. Purchase these in packages of about 400 for about fifteen cents in department stores or craft stores. Assorted colors allow many more variations in colorful pins. Purchase shells or shell craft kits in local craft stores.

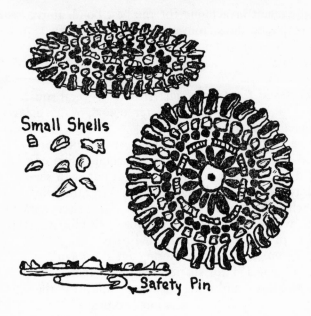

Small Shells

Safety Pin

Tie Dyeing   • C • GMS • NP • TB •

Equipment: Square piece of light-colored or white cloth about eighteen inches by eighteen inches, several feet of cord, dye, household electric iron, electric current, and scissors.

Locate the very center point of the cloth. Take hold of this point and let remainder of material hang freely. Tightly wrap cord several times around any areas not to be dyed, and tie it securely. Place the cloth into the liquid dye in accordance with directions on box of dye. Remove tied cloth from dye and let it dry. Untie the cord and press the cloth with electric household iron.

For variety, use two or three colors of dye and dip parts of tied cloth into each. Dye in a light dye solution. Let cloth dry, then retie over new parts of cloth and dye in darker solution.

Consult with local department or craft stores regarding available dyes and prices. One popular dye that can be satisfactorily used for tie dyeing is "Rit." Contact the Rit Products Corporation for more information on the use of dyes in craft projects. See the *Hobby Dyeing Book* for more ideas.

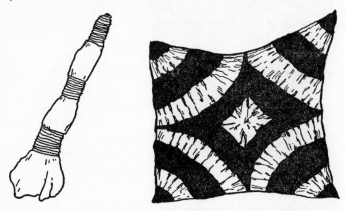

Wall Plaques   • A • C • GMS •

Equipment: Several jar lids with jar rubbers (both used under jar caps in home canning), several hairpins, adhesive tape, scissors, enamel, paint brush, small colored pictures from magazines, and paste.

Attach the hairpin to the underside of the lid with a piece of adhesive tape, allowing the loop end of pin to extend about

¼ inch. Enamel the front and back of lid. Let lid dry. Cut out a suitable small picture and paste it in the inner circle of the lid. Use several plaques in groupings to hang on wall near the bedside. Contact the Ball Jar Company for unusual uses for the product and for other craft projects that may be made from lids and jars.

Wire Twisting   • GMS • NP • TB •

Equipment for Making Wire Jewelry: Several feet of soft metal wire (copper, brass, or aluminum), one pair of ordinary pliers, and one pair of long-nose pliers.

Assist the participant in working out various kinds of twist patterns; for example:

1. Twist two wires together
2. Twist wire with right hand and then double and twist in reverse direction
3. Twist additional wires into the grooves of twisted wires
4. Twist into coils

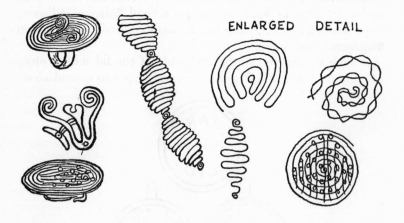

ENLARGED   DETAIL

Chapter 5

Audio-visual Activities

Audio-visual activities include all media that assist in clearly portraying things through sound and sight. These activities depend upon devices and equipment to interpret scenes, adventure, tones, and music interestingly. Life is made more meaningful when envisioned easily through audio-visual techniques. In this area of activities, the handicapped person can be taken temporarily into other settings, countries, and situations. The variety of leadership aids should not be overlooked for those who are confined to restricted geographic locations. In effect, these are devices that assist in making more interesting and entertaining the enforced leisure hours of those who are handicapped.

It is important that the recreation leader secure only necessary and needed audio-visual equipment. Certain opaque projectors, tape recorders, and 35-millimeter motion picture projectors can be very costly. Yet in some large hospitals, the purchase of these items is justified, since they are useful in providing a varied program. Audio-visual gear requires maintenance and should only be purchased new or in excellent used condition.

Too often, if the leader does not plan his program carefully, the majority of the activities may permit the handicapped to become observers or viewers, rather than active physical participants. A therapeutic climate can be more readily obtained through a series of activities that involve persons in actual physical participation in selected pursuits with their hands and body. The audio-visual emphasis should supplement an activities program. These sound and sight aids to leadership are especially beneficial for the individual who is physically restricted or immobile.

Audio-visual activities provide enjoyment for the participant as well as furnishing assistance to the leader. Some of these activities (motion picture projection and tape recording for example) may be used as aids in various phases of the evening entertainment or afternoon listening program. These are helps to the program planner in varied activity offerings as well as a medium of activity for the handicapped.

LISTENING, ANNOUNCING, AND SCRIPT WRITING

Radio Listening   • A • C • GMS • NP • TB •

Equipment: Table or floor radio and electric current.

A small table-model radio is a real companion to the convalescent. Some rooms in hospitals and institutions have "intercom" systems instead of individual bedside radios.

Some of the areas of content in radio programs are:

1. Disc jockey programs (popular music)
2. Dramatic serial programs (soap operas and family dramas)
3. Educational (travel stories, book reviews, studies)
4. Farm and rural news
5. Inspirational and philosophical chats
6. Morning wake-up music
7. Music (symphonic, classical, and opera)
8. News
9. Religious programs
10. Sports
11. Variety programs

Study the daily radio schedules that appear in newspapers. Suggest to the handicapped person some of the program types that fit his needs and interests.

Generally avoid the morning dramatic serial programs as their emotional involvements are many and varied. Watch for notice in newspapers of special events (speeches, ball games, and sporting events) to recommend for listening. Listen for regularly scheduled radio chats or discussions (some with music) that are often inspiring and encouraging.

In some larger cities there are educational stations (often associated with colleges or universities) that do not have commercial advertising. Look for this type of station as a source of symphonic music and educational programs.

Most stations commence daily programming at 6 A.M. and terminate daily broadcasting at midnight. Some broadcast on a twenty-four hour schedule. Urge the listener to be considerate of others in respect to the volume and length of time that the radio is on.

Variation: Tune in to police calls at extreme ends of the radio kilocycle band. If the radio has a short wave band, tune in to amateur stations and foreign broadcasts. On a Frequency Modulation (FM) band, tune in to the sound portions of television broadcasts. Short wave reception is usually best in the evening (and particularly when the weather is clear). Tune in to "Voice of America" broadcasts that are sometimes announced in English and directed toward persons in other lands. Try to receive other interesting broadcasts in English or foreign languages that originate from Ecuador, England, Australia, Canada, and Russia.

Radio Station Announcing   • GMS • NP •

Equipment: Microphone, speakers, electric current, wiring for microphone and sound equipment.

Obtain a microphone and sufficient wiring to string between rooms where the radio announcing activity is to take place. Connect the speaker and microphone to electric outlet for volume and power.

Use this small "public address" or announcement system for the transmittal of messages as well as recorded music. Practice enunciation of words and clarity of speaking. Present a half-hour "variety" program. Invite a nurse, teacher, or other guest for an interview over the air.

Suggestions: If the announcing activity increases in popularity and favor in the hospital, consider expansion into a regular radio station with outlets to all wards. Consult the hospital electrician, radio authorities, and personnel in other hospitals who have such stations in operation. Include other

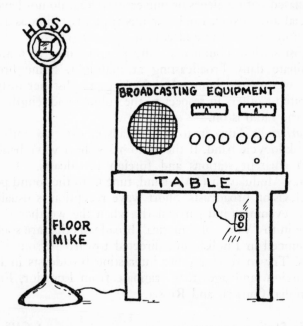

persons, such as script writers, radio actors, disk jockeys, and radio engineers. Consult medical staff as to the type of broadcast programs that are most desirable for those who are on the listening end.

Secure free assistance on hospital-operated radio stations through selected local commercial broadcasting stations. Write to the National Association of Broadcasters, National Broadcasting Company, Columbia Broadcasting System, Mutual Broadcasting System, or other networks for additional information on radio work.

Radio Programming   • GMS • NP •

In radio programming, type out a script for each actor. Use paper that does not rustle so that silence and proper sound sequences are made effective. Select deep voices for villains, high ones for heroines, slow and hesitant voices for the aged, and quick bright voices for the young. Remember that actors must come in on cues quickly and reflect character by their voice alone. Slow dull voices are monotonous and not suited for radio work. Use these radio starters in planning a variety of interesting programs:

1. "Push button program." A series of musical acts inter-mixed with conversation and humor.
2. "Cross-country travels." Question a group of persons from various parts of the country. Provide each partici-pant with background music that represents his section of the land.
3. "Information Please." Assemble a group of patients and nurses. Have the patients quiz the nurses on subjects of popular interest.
4. "Get acquainted program." Interview a physician, psy-chologist, or nurse on interesting phases of his or her life.
5. "Country music fest." Invite any who play the guitar or other instrument to play favorite western songs. Inter-sperse recordings of hill-billy music.
6. "Hobby-lobby." Interview or chat with one or more persons about interesting hobbies or avocations. Make suggestions on how others could also become hobbyists.

Record Listening   • A • C • GMS • MR • NP • TB •

Equipment: One four-speed phonograph, phonograph rec-ords, and electric current.

Select records prior to the listening period that present variety (in composers, instruments, and style) and are of probable interest to the listeners. After the people have as-sembled, describe the records to be played. Point out special effects and passages for which to listen in the recording. Place the record on the phonograph set at the proper speed (16, 33⅓, 45, or 78 revolutions per minute). Consider the advantages of prepared sheets describing records for the use of listeners.

Plan record listening hours for those who are interested in a certain type of music (symphonic, semiclassical, or jazz). Select a specific composer, orchestra, or singer and discuss interesting characteristics of the artist or artists. Have a number of portable phonographs for loan service to bedside record listeners.

Purchase "story records" for children. These have illustrated color guides with them and assist in portraying a specific story while the record is being played. Examples of several titles are: *Hansel and Gretel*, *Johnny Appleseed*, and *Peter and the Wolf*.

Accumulate an indexed library of records that is easily accessible. Let volunteers or students assist in the classification of record titles, musicians, and types of music. Some categories are:

1. Ballet music
2. Children's records
3. Choral techniques
4. Descriptive music
5. Folk dance music
6. Historical development of form
7. Holidays and seasons
8. Instrumental techniques
9. Jazz
10. Literature and drama correlation
11. Music of different nations
12. Myths and legends in music
13. Nature study in music
14. Opera
15. Portraiture and characterization
16. Popular adaptations of the classics
17. Popular music
18. Religious music
19. Rhythm patterns

If any number of records are to be purchased, ask for an educational record catalog at a music dealer's or music store. This guide lists record titles, descriptions, suggested age ranges, costs, and other helpful information. One such catalog is *The RCA Victor Educational Record Catalog*.

Consider the advantage in purchasing 45 and 33⅓ r.p.m. records rather than the 78 r.p.m. records. The 45's and 33⅓'s require a turntable speed of 45 and 33⅓ revolutions per minute, respectively. These records are nonbreakable, long lasting, convenient to handle, generally inexpensive, and high in quality.

Plan a record library that meets a variety of listening interests. One such selected library of titles that can be purchased for about $40.00 is the following:*

> *Album for the Young* (Tchaikovsky)
> *All Tempos* ("Perfect for Dancing" Series)
> *America's Favorite Marches*
> *Beloved Hymns*
> *The Blue Danube Waltz; Tales from the Vienna Woods*
>   (J. Strauss, Jr.)
> *Christmas Hymns and Carols*, Vol. 1
> *Heart of the Symphony*
> *Music for Special Occasions*
> *Music for Reading*
> *My Reverie*
> *Play that Barbershop Chord*
> *Square Dances* (with calls)
> *Strauss Waltzes*, Vol. 1
> *Toy Symphony* (Haydn); *Finale* from "Serenade in C"
>   (Tchaikovsky)

Script Writing   • A • GMS • NP • TB •

Find those persons who are at all interested in writing and dramatics. Encourage them to select characters and write parts for a play. Stress brevity (and short sentences) in creation of scripts. A first step is to sketch out the characters and

---

* RCA Victor 45 r.p.m. record albums listed by record titles.

action before writing out detailed script. Remember that the script-writer must describe what an audience does not see. Sound effects and well planned dialogue help in providing appropriate background.

Test the script and dialogue first by having its writer speak it to himself to see if it can be easily handled by an actor.

Have patients act out scripts that have been written by those on their own ward. Use those scripts that are especially well done for tape recording purposes. Play these back for the entertainment of the actors and script-writer. If there is a hospital-operated radio station, let selected patients put on the play over the radio hookup to wards.

Tape Recording   • GMS • NP •

Equipment: Tape recorder, plastic tape, and electric current.

Suggest to the participant that he rather carefully plan out in advance what he anticipates recording. If this is a reading, poetry or a speech, urge him to collect any needed material and rehearse the same before presentation on the tape. Tell the person about the importance of notes, enunciation, even speech or varied speech for appropriate parts, and clear voice, while in the process of recording.

In accordance with directions on the recorder, place the plastic tape on the machine in recording position. Instruct the participant to speak into the microphone. Set it at a speed of three and three-fourths ips (inches per second) for speech work. Use the speed of 7½ ips for all recordings of music. If the recording is for broadcast over a radio station, use the 7½ ips setting for music or speech. Play the tape back so it can be slightly amplified and heard by those in the room.

Some of the more expensive tape recorders have built-in radios for recording selections from the radio on the tape. Do not place the microphone directly in front of the radio speaker, as a poor recording would usually result.

Use the tape recorder in assisting in speech training and evaluating speech for those having physical or mental disabilities involving speech. Purchase plastic tape as it is stronger, more versatile, and reproduces sounds better than cheaper paper-backed tape.

Contact the state department of education or nearby university audio-visual service for information on possible free library use of tape recordings on such subjects as agriculture, art, conservation, history, music, or social studies.

Try some of these uses for recorded tapes:

1. Check in speech such items as voice improvement, grammar, spelling, speech analysis, and public speaking.
2. Use in listening to choral reading, story telling, and pre-recorded music for pantomiming.
3. Play to music appreciation groups. Record piano solos, bands, and vocal performances.
4. Use as music background for timing exercise groups in wards.
5. Listen to athletic events (World Series, football games, and so on) that were previously broadcast on the radio.
6. Record radio short-wave broadcasts and play back to those of foreign descent.
7. Make a "script" or coordinated sound for a film-strip (see page 83).

VISUAL ACTIVITIES

Flannelgraphs   • C • GMS • MR • TB •

Equipment: One flat piece of wood board, ½ inch thick by 8½ inches by 11 inches; piece of flannel, 9½ inches by 12 inches; 12 thumbtacks; felt or flannel scraps; paste; and colored pictures.

Stretch the flannel tightly over the board and tack it on the reverse side. Cut out a variety of colored pictures that will be useful in telling a story. Paste or glue the felt or flannel scraps to reverse sides of the pictures, or stick the smooth side of sandpaper to the backs of the pictures. A greater adhesion results and there is less chance of pictures falling off the flannelboard. Tell a story and illustrate it by firmly pressing the pictures to the board (so that reverse felt-covered side of picture contacts flannel-covered board). With a variety of pictures, "chalk talks" and stories are visualized and told to a group. Flannelgraphs may also be used to illustrate dance steps and game formations.

See Story Telling on pages 123-25 for more ideas to use with flannelgraphs.

Use flannelgraphs to portray Bible stories. Try these flannelgraph stories with children:

Noah and the Ark

Felt-backed pictures: Noah, partially built ark, completed ark, Noah's sons, several animals and birds, dove, land, and water on ground.

Noah was a good man who lived many, many years ago. One day God asked him to build a very large boat called an ark. Noah and his sons, named Shem, Ham, and Japheth, worked for many days cutting down trees. They sawed them and very carefully hammered them in place. The ark grew bigger and higher. Finally the huge boat was finished. It was made out of gopher wood so it would be able to sail for many days.

Then God asked Noah to gather all the birds and animals together to live on the ark with Noah and his family. Noah and his three sons guided the animals, two by two, into the ark. Many strange sounds could be heard. After the animals and birds were safely aboard, Noah and his family went into the ark. They closed the doors and windows as the rain began to fall.

Noah and his family could hear the water falling on the roof and splashing against the sides of the ark. It rained for forty days and forty nights. Suddenly the rain stopped and the sun began to shine. All was quiet as Noah peered out of the ark. There was water everywhere. He sent a dove to find dry land. When it returned with a small branch in its mouth, Noah knew that it had found the dry land. And the flood was over at last!

Johnny Appleseed

Felt-backed pictures: Johnny Appleseed, clouds, sun, birds, house, deer, apples, and apple trees.

When clouds turn pink at sunset, old timers say "Johnny Appleseed's orchard is in bloom."

He was a small quiet man. He never argued or fought with anyone. He lived in Pennsylvania years ago on a farm with fruit trees, flowers, and birds.

Big wagons, pulled by oxen and full of new settlers, headed for the West, stopped by his door. Johnny fed the settlers.

He, too, left for the West, on foot, and took a saucepan to cook in, a spoon to eat with, a Bible to read—and a bag of appleseeds. "They'll need orchards out there," thought Johnny.

After crossing the Ohio River by canoe, he set out on wilderness tracks that animals had made. Even though the forest was full of savage bears and wolves, Johnny carried no gun, because he didn't believe in killing anything. Into the woods, barefooted, he walked, and no rattlesnake ever struck him. Somehow the animals knew that he loved them, because they say that birds flew to him, and sat on his shoulder. Squirrels and rabbits fed out of his hand, and deer just looked at him and didn't run away.

Even the Indians loved him. He'd walk into their camp, no gun in his hand, and he'd cure their sick by using herbs and roots. Johnny's

heart was so full of love that it never had any room for fear, so he
came and went as he pleased.

Whenever he ate with settlers, he never had any money, but he'd
always leave appleseeds behind to pay for his food. He'd always leave
early in the morning, saying, "I've got work to do."

In the winter he went around to cidermills, collecting appleseeds.
During the rest of the year he wandered all over the West, setting
out his seeds, caring for them, and giving young trees and seeds to
the settlers.

While he traveled alone for forty years, apple trees sprung up all
around. Some folks thought he was very different from others.
Johnny didn't think so and said, "We are all brothers." One day,
when an old man, he came to the home of a friend to spend the night.
He was tired and his work was done. So Johnny went to sleep by the
fire—and he just never woke up.

Even today, old-timers out there look up at the sky when the snow
begins to fall, and they smile and say, "Old Johnny's shaking the apple
trees up there in heaven."

Motion Pictures   • A • C • GMS • MR • NP • TB •

Equipment: A 16-millimeter portable motion picture projector, motion picture screen, chairs for spectators, 16-milli-
meter film, and electric current.

Secure 16-millimeter film (preferably sound and color)
that is entertaining and beneficial for the participants. Set up
the chairs in a well-ventilated room. Place the screen at one
end of room within range of all viewers. In accordance with
directions printed on the projector, place the film on the reel
arm and then around the sprocket wheels and other mecha-
nisms. Turn the power switch on prior to the light switch.
After following other directions on the projector, the film is
ready for showing. Switch off the room lights and show the
film.

Carefully compare new projectors before purchasing one.
Three well known brand projectors are "Ampro" (Ampro
Corporation), "Bell and Howell" (Bell and Howell Company), and "RCA" (Radio Corporation of America). Purchase a glass-beaded fabric motion picture screen that is wash-
able as well as mildew- and flame-proof. If a manufactured
screen is not available, use a white sheet or white painted wall.

Do not move the projector immediately after showing a film as this can crack the projection bulb filament. Have an extra projection bulb available whenever the projector is in operation. Clean the projector lens only with specially made lens cleaning paper. Do not use water, fingers, or soft tissue for this purpose.

Secure films on a rental basis for school or institutional use. Association Films and other selected dealers have a number of travel and commercially sponsored films available on a lending no-charge plan. Contact your public library regarding 16-millimeter films that they have on loan use for nominal fees or free of charge or rent 16-millimeter film from a regional or local distributor or contact one of the following for information and prices on film rentals that are practical in recreational programs:

Coronet Films
Encyclopaedia Britannica Films
Association Films
International Film Bureau Inc.
McGraw-Hill Book Co.
Swank Motion Pictures, Inc.

If any extensive showing of films is planned, borrow or purchase a copy of the *Educational Film Guide* for a complete listing of 16-millimeter educational films. Eight-millimeter projectors are cheaper than the 35- or 16-millimeter varieties and show only silent film. Do not attempt to run 16-millimeter film on an 8-millimeter projector. Notice that silent film has sprocket holes on both sides of it. Purchase comedies and "shorts" for this "home" type of projector.

If there is a large group of persons that consistently view motion pictures, consider the installation of 35-millimeter motion picture projectors in a specially constructed projection booth. Secure a qualified projectionist to operate this complicated, expensive, nonportable type of equipment. Secure 35-mm. films (same as seen in commercial motion picture theaters) on a rental basis from film companies. This should be a permanent investment for a large institution (500 or more persons).

Preview the film and select those that are most apt to be enjoyable and beneficial for viewing. If advance viewing or clearance of the film is not possible, choose films on the basis of the title and written description. In general, film subjects fall into these ten categories: Adventure, Cartoons, Documentary, Entertainment, History, Instructional, Nature, Newsreel, Sports, and Travel. Exclude long films (over two hours) and films which have as their theme:

1. Ridicule of treatment or of hospitals
2. Plots of a sexual or suggestive nature
3. Crime, punishment, or imprisonment
4. Death or other depressing subjects
5. Battle and war scenes (especially for an audience of war veterans)
6. Pictures that feature phantasy or abnormal behavior.

See *Audio-Visual Procedures in Teaching* by Lester B. Sands for more ideas on the use of motion pictures as well as other audio-visual aids.

Projector Cart: Make a projector cart out of scrap wood, wheels, and other materials for about $35. Make the cart on a pair of front dolly-type wheels. Include a couple of compartments for storage. See "This Projector Cart Is Practical," in *The Modern Hospital*, for more specific directions on how one hospital made such a cart.

Opaque Projection   • A • C • GMS • MR • NP • TB •

Equipment: Opaque projector, beaded-glass picture screen, opaque pictures that fit projector, and electric current.

Read directions on the projector regarding its operation. Place it on a table in middle of room about twelve feet from the screen. Set up the screen at one end of the room. Place any type of opaque picture, one at a time, in the opaque projector. Describe the picture projected on the screen.

Purchase a small projector for small room use. Use 3½ inch by 5½ inch (post-card size) pictures in these. Keep two extra projection bulbs available at all times when showing pictures.

For use in a large room, secure a large projector ($50 to $350) that uses pictures up to 10 inches by 10 inches. Some of the popular models of this more advanced type are made by the American Optical Company, Bausch and Lomb Optical Company, and the Charles Beseler Company.

Remember that there is some light loss in opaque projection. The projected pictures are not as sharp or clear as the transparent projection of slides and filmstrips. Opaque projection does, however, allow the projection of any flat opaque picture that is small enough for convenient insertion in the projector.

Arrange shows on special subjects. Collect pictures or picture post cards on selected subjects, and arrange a sequence of pictures that are appealing and colorful. Plan a script to go along with the numbered pictures. Invite a small group who might be interested in this kind of spectator activity and present the narrated show on the opaque projector along with oral descriptions. Serve refreshments and have a general discussion period.

Invite picture post card collectors (deltiologists) to put on a projected show of their unusual cards. Inquire at the community public library regarding persons in local picture post card collecting clubs.

Slide and Filmstrip Projection

• A • C • GMS
• MR • NP • TB •

Equipment: Combination 35-millimeter slide and filmstrip projector, beaded-glass screen, transparent photographic slides or filmstrip, and electric current.

Set up the screen at one end of the room. Read directions that accompany the projector regarding its safe and efficient operation. Project the slides or filmstrip onto the screen. Describe the scenes or pictures being shown to the group.

Be sure that slides are the right size: 2 inch by 2 inch slides for a 35-millimeter slide projector and 3¼ inch by 4 inch slides for lantern-slide size projector. Obtain new 35-millimeter slide-filmstrip projectors for between $55 and $475. The typical slide-filmstrip projector is approximately the size of a portable typewriter. Procure transparent 35-millimeter slides that have words of songs printed on them. Project these on the screen for a novel community song fest. For a "sound" filmstrip, purchase a record attachment for the projector. Use synchronized records which are made to accompany selected filmstrips.

Purchase filmstrips and slides rather than renting them as this is always more economical in the long run. Purchase black-and-white filmstrips for as little as $2.50 each and color ones for about $4.00 each. Color filmstrips are usually more interesting and appealing than black-and-white ones. Some filmstrips have as few as twenty frames (pictures) in each while others contain as many as a hundred. Purchase filmstrips from local audio-visual companies or camera stores. Several national concerns that sell popular filmstrips are Eye Gate House, Inc., Life Magazine Filmstrips, Popular Science Publishing Company, and the Society for Visual Education.

Film strips are more advantageous than slides in that a self contained and edited story or subject of a number of scenes may be projected in one showing. They tend to be quite durable and are conducive to discussion. Several titles and subjects that are suggested for a well-rounded filmstrip library are:

Cities of Our Country	*Story of Johnny Appleseed*
Some European Neighbors	*Birds, How They Live and*
Children Near and Far	*Help Us*
The Greatest Show on Earth	*Crackling Mountain*
The Night Before Christmas	*Treasure Island*
A Christmas Carol	*Artists of Many Lands*
Emerson's New England	*The Story of America*
The World We Live In	

These and many other subjects may be purchased in filmstrip form.

Purchase 35-millimeter color slides for as little as ten cents each from your local camera store. Ask these concerns for more information on the purchase of color slides: Slide Supply Service or the Society for Visual Education, Inc.

Make slides and filmstrips with a 35-millimeter miniature camera. Urge the advanced camera enthusiast to practice making these in the home or hospital setting. See *Photographic Production of Slides and Filmstrips* (Kodak publication) for detailed information and directions.

Try several 35-millimeter slide games with the handicapped. Select a number of color slides and orally describe the place shown. Have participants guess the location. Use these samples of script (shown here with answers) for typical slides:

1. Foggy, #10 Downing Street, afternoon tea, chimes (London)
2. The "Windy City," home of the Cubs, on a lake (Chicago)
3. Cherry blossoms, Fujiyama, yen (Japan)
4. Oldest schoolhouse in U.S., on Florida beach (St. Augustine)
5. The Latin Quarter, sidewalk cafes, artists (Paris)

Another use for slides is that of showing certain subjects prior to a visit to a scenic area. Show flowers before visiting flower gardens, animals before going to the zoo, and sports shots before traveling to watch a football game. Use these as a means of arousing interest before the journey.

Stereoscopic Viewing • A • C • GMS • MR • NP • TB •

Equipment: Hand stereoscopic viewer and stereographs or stereoscopic reels.

Place the stereograph in the viewer and see a three dimensional view that resembles real life. Hold the stereoscopic viewer toward the light to produce the best visual effect (unless the stereograph or stereoscopic reel is artificially lighted by means of batteries and a light bulb). A new world is provided the participant through stereographs or stereoscopic reels of travel, history, nature, local scenes, and nursery rhymes.

Antique shops and second-hand stores often have stereographs for the older type of stereoscope (sometimes called "Stereographoscope"). These can be purchased for reasonable amounts and are quite durable. Purchase a newer type three-dimensional viewer, sometimes called "Viewmaster," along with a variety of colorful scenes on circular reels. Purchase other accessories such as a light attachment (for viewing slides in dark rooms) and a box for storing reels. Check on the interest of a group in viewing stereoscopic reels. Projectors and

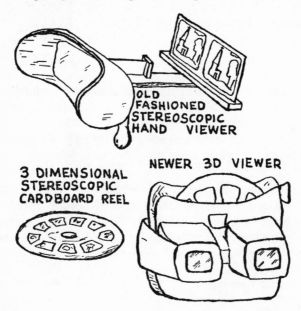

OLD FASHIONED STEREOSCOPIC HAND VIEWER

3 DIMENSIONAL STEREOSCOPIC CARDBOARD REEL

NEWER 3D VIEWER

screens are available for showing reels to a group. These show the reels in two dimensions. Expensive projectors may be purchased for the showing of reels in three dimensions on the screen.

Try out these subjects in a beginner's library of stereoscopic reels:

> Yellowstone National Park
> The Mardi Gras, New Orleans
> Indian Arts and Crafts
> Flowers of Hawaii
> Costumes and Dances of Mexico
> Shakespeare's Stratford-on-Avon, Warwickshire

Snow White and The Seven Dwarfs
A Day at the Circus
The Birth of The Saviour
Wild Flowers

Television Viewing   • *A* • *C* • *GMS* • *MR* • *NP* • *TB* •

Equipment: Television set and electric current.

Turn television set on and adjust picture and sound so that they are visible and audible. Turn on another small light above or to the side of the set so that eye strain will be prevented. Do not allow a viewer to watch television for more than two or three hours at one time (less if so indicated by a physician). Advise the viewer to sit or recline several feet away from the television screen while looking at a program.

Study advance television schedules and try to plan programs for worthwhile viewing. Whenever possible and feasible, try to suggest types of programs for the handicapped to watch. Announce special sports events, public affairs, and educational programs so that one or more persons in various locations may accordingly tune in recommended programs.

Purchase television guide magazines that give summaries of programs on local stations during the day. Call local television stations for advance copies of their telecast programs. Consult these in planning worthwhile programs for the participants to watch. Check with a nearby college or university about any educational television channel that may be operating in the state. Tune in on an educational television station and study their program schedules. Find out if they offer any correspondence courses (see page 137) via television. If so a student may watch and listen to lectures on the television screen. Later on he may wish to take a supervised examination according to arrangements made with the correspondence department of the college or university.

Chapter 6

Dance Activities

Dancing is an activity that does much to encourage socialization and enjoyment in a group situation. An atmosphere of music, gaiety, and rhythm is rewarding for depressed or handicapped minds and bodies. As a physical exercise and psychological release, it is beneficial for men and women. This type of wholesome social contact is necessary in an institutional setting for both sexes. Fellowship, social satisfaction and creative expression are fostered by dancing.

Dance instruction for the handicapped is a personal contact type of learning that requires skilled and understanding leadership. This applies to all dancing and particularly to certain kinds of square and folk dancing. Personal direction and practice are necessary in addition to printed directions and diagrams.

"Live" music is that provided by an orchestra or musicians who are in person near the dancers. "Canned" is recorded music, the second best type of accompaniment. The gay and true spirit of the dance seems more meaningful when supported by proper musical background.

Dances may also combine such program elements as singing, parties, decorations, drama, rhythms, singing games, and refreshments. A theme and plan is a must for a successful evening. Emphasis is, of course, on participation rather than perfection. The reinstatement of confidence, self-respect, and social charm is easily implemented through a planned offering of dance activities. However, some persons have religious objections to dancing. It behooves the leader to respect this wish when it is known.

Healthy social contact is needed more by younger handicapped persons than by older ones. Good judgment and discretion should be the guide in planning dance themes. The mentally retarded need particular observation so that this activity does not facilitate undesirable romances. Sometimes limiting the number of times a participant may dance consecutively with the same partner is a solution.

A major advantage of square and circle dancing is the ease in including larger groups of persons with only limited emphasis upon partners. In a hospital setting, this benefit of involving varied numbers of patients warrants consideration.

Whenever phonograph records are desired for music background, purchase quality records that are, if possible, unbreakable. In general, $33\frac{1}{3}$ and 45 r.p.m. records are the two speeds that seem more popular than the out-dated 78 r.p.m. records. Be certain to have record players that accommodate the $33\frac{1}{3}$ (LP's) and 45's. The records listed in the dancing section are generally available in 45's and $33\frac{1}{3}$'s and are recommended for the hospital-medical, school, or home setting.

In the diagrams accompanying the various dance activities in this chapter, the shaded steps and figures represent the gentlemen and the unshaded ones the ladies.

The dance activities are divided into several sections. These sections define and differentiate to some degree the activities included in them: singing dances, social dances, mixer dances, and folk dances.

Themes for Dance Parties

Plan festive all-hospital dances at regular intervals, perhaps monthly or bi-monthly. Work with patients in the decorating and publicizing of the dance. Follow these themes in organizing a special dance party each month:

January: "New Year's Eve" (hire a dance band—stay up after midnight!)

February: "Valentine Dance" (decorate with cupids and hearts)

March: "Swing Your Partner" (make flameproof crepe paper animals and a barn yard scene for this square dance)

April: "Springtime" (decorate gaily and combine with community singing)

May: "Carousel" (feature a carnival or circus atmosphere; include some "side show" and carnival booths)

June: "Stardust" (use the outdoor concrete tennis court as setting for a real under-the-stars dance)

July: "South of the Border" (follow a fiesta theme along with cactuses and community singing to guitar accompaniment)

August: "Calico Carnival" (a songfest together with entertainment)

September: "Bar-None-Ranch" (make a corral; decorate with cattle brands, boots, camp fires, and horns)

October: "Harvest Festival" (follow County Fair idea with varied displays, booths; highlight folk and square dancing)

November: "Winter Carnival Dance" (precede by ice skating on the rink adjacent to the dance hall)

December: "Sleigh Bell Frolic" (sing Christmas Carols and exchange small gifts)

SINGING DANCES

Bingo Dance   • C • MR • NP •

Equipment: Phonograph and phonograph record with a tune to go with the Bingo dance or other appropriate musical accompaniment.

Lead couples into a circle formation, and have them get in position for marching in a clockwise (right) direction. The gentlemen are on the inside of circle to the ladies' right sides.

Commence music for the dance and lead dancers in singing the verse "Bingo." At the word "bone" (or "name" in second version) in the fourth line, all of the men turn about and go in the opposite direction while ladies keep going in their same previous direction. As the lines move in opposite circle directions, stress a skipping step to the tune of "Bingo." At the start of the first B—I—N—G—O in the last line, each person loudly calls the letters out and steps to a new partner.

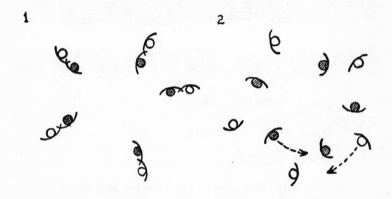

At the letter O, the gentlemen swing (or shake hands with) the ladies opposite them. Upon arrival at the letter O, the new sets of partners are located and the peppy skipping step is repeated to the "Bingo" tune and song.

Bingo

There was a farmer had a dog;
And Bingo is his name.
That farmer's dog's at our back door,
Begging for a bone,
B with an I and I with an N;
N with a G and G with an O;
B—I—N—G—O, Bingo was his name.

Bingo (second version)

A big brown dog sat on the porch,
And Bingo was his name.

A big brown dog sat on the porch,
And Bingo was his name.
B-I-N-G-O B-I-N-G-O B-I-N-G-O,
Bingo was his name.
B—I—N—G—O, Oh!

If a phonograph record is desired for musical background, use the RCA Victor 45 r.p.m. "Bingo" (American) record with "Seven Jumps" (Danish) on the reverse side.

Did You Ever See a Lassie?   • C • MR •

Equipment: Phonograph and phonograph record with music to "Did You Ever See a Lassie?" or other appropriate musical accompaniment.

Lead five or more participants with joined hands into a circle. One player stands in the center. Have the children skip around the circle and sing the first two verses of "Did You Ever See a Lassie?" While the players are doing this, the one in the center is going through some movement which the ones forming the circle are to imitate later. When the third line of the song is reached, the players sing the line, and while standing still, imitate actions of the person in the center. During the remainder of the song, all imitate the movement in rhythm. The center person goes through any action, such as imitating a dog or cat, pretending to dive or swim. If a boy is in the center, sing the word "laddie" in place of "lassie." Choose a new lassie or laddie and repeat the actions.

Did You Ever See a Lassie?

Did you ever see a lassie (or laddie), a lassie, a lassie,
Did you ever see a lassie go this way and that?
Go this way and that way, and this way and that way;
Did you ever see a lassie go this way and that?

Here We Go Round the Mulberry Bush   • C • MR •

Equipment: Phonograph and phonograph record with music to "Here We Go Round the Mulberry Bush" or other appropriate musical accompaniment.

Lead children with joined hands in a circle formation. Have them sing the words and gaily step around the circle to music. Participants are to pantomime the movements in each verse. If desired, after each new verse, sing the first verse or chorus.

Here We Go Round the Mulberry Bush

1. Here we go round the mulberry bush, the mulberry bush, the mulberry bush,
   Here we go round the mulberry bush,
   So early in the morning.

2. This is the way we wash our clothes, we wash our clothes, we wash our clothes,
This is the way we wash our clothes,
So early in the morning.
3. This is the way we iron our clothes, etc.
4. This is the way we mend our clothes, etc.
5. This is the way we sweep the floor, etc.
6. This is the way we bake the bread, etc.
7. This is the way we scrub the floor, etc.
8. This is the way we go to church, etc.

As musical background try the RCA Victor 45 r.p.m. album on *Singing Games for Primary Grades* that includes "Here We Go Round the Mulberry Bush" along with other selections.

Hokey Pokey   • C • MR • NP •

Equipment: Phonograph and phonograph record with music to "Hokey Pokey" or other appropriate musical accompaniment.

To start the dance, tell the participants to get into a circle formation. Follow words of the song and do the suggested actions. Sing the song as actions are executed in the circle dance formation. Upon reaching the last verse, participants get on knees and in a swaying motion lean forward bringing both hands to floor.

Hokey Pokey

Put your right hand in,
Take your right hand out,
Put your right hand in,
And you shake it all about,
You do the hokey pokey,
And turn yourself around,
That's what it's all about.
Put your left hand in, etc.
Put your right foot in, etc.
Put your left foot in, etc.
Put your right elbow in, etc.
Put your left elbow in, etc.
Put your right side in, etc.
Put your left side in, etc.
Put your whole self in, etc.
You do the hokey pokey,
You do the hokey pokey,
That's what it's all about.

If the group is familiar with the words and tune, the phonograph record or musical accompaniment is not necessary. They then sing the words and do the actions.

Looby Loo

• C • MR • NP •

Equipment: Phonograph and record with "Looby Loo" words or other musical accompaniment.

In a circle formation, the participants walk or skip in a counterclockwise direction to the music of "Looby Loo." They sing the verses of the song as they march to the music.

At the second verse, the players stop and extend their right hands toward the center, then back from the circle, and lastly into the circle with a vigorous shake. Each verse is pantomimed according to actions suggested by the words. At the words "whole self," the participants jump a step toward the center of the circle and then jump back to the original circle formation. As they start each new verse of the song the participants move around the circle singing "Here we dance, Looby Loo," and so on.

Looby Loo

Here we dance, Looby Loo,
Here we dance, Looby La.

Here we dance, Looby Loo,
All on a Saturday night.
I put my right hand in,
I put my right hand out;
I give my right hand a shake, shake, shake,
And turn myself around.
(Repeat the first verse, and also repeat it after each of the following verses.)
I put my left hand in,
I put my left hand out;
I give my left hand a shake, shake, shake,
And turn myself around.
I put my right foot in, etc.
I put my left foot in, etc.
I put my whole self in, etc.

The Farmer in the Dell   • C • MR •

Equipment: Phonograph and phonograph record with music to "Farmer in the Dell" or other appropriate musical accompaniment.

Have eight or more participants join hands and walk in a clockwise direction around one in the center who is the farmer. At the second verse, the farmer chooses a player for a wife. The outer circle continues to move while the wife leads the farmer in a lockstep formation inside in an opposite direction. At the third verse, the wife chooses a child who in turn goes inside the circle and in front of the wife. Verses are repeated until all have been chosen. At the last verse all return to the outer circle formation except the one selected as "cheese." The child playing the part of cheese remains as the new farmer for the next game.

The Farmer in the Dell

1. The farmer in the dell,
   The farmer in the dell,
   Heigh Ho! the Derry O!
   The farmer in the dell.

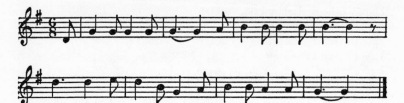

2. The farmer takes a wife,
   The farmer takes a wife,
   Heigh Ho! the Derry O!
   The farmer takes a wife.
3. The wife takes a child,
   The wife takes a child,
   Heigh Ho! the Derry O!
   The wife takes a child.
4. The child takes a nurse, etc.
5. The nurse takes a dog, etc.
6. The dog takes a cat, etc.
7. The cat takes a rat, etc.
8. The rat takes the cheese, etc.
9. The cheese stands alone, etc.

SOCIAL DANCES

Fox Trot   • *A* • *C* • *GMS* • *MR* • *NP* •

Equipment: Phonograph and phonograph record with fox trot or social dancing music or other appropriate musical accompaniment.

Use this step or a modification thereof as a basic one in all social dancing. Encourage participation rather than perfection in exactly following these suggested steps. The gentleman starts in this manner:

1. Step forward slowly with left foot
2. Step forward slowly with the right foot
3. Step sideways quickly with left foot
4. Close right foot quickly and transfer weight to right foot
5. Repeat beginning with left foot again

The lady's part is the reverse (beginning with right foot) of the gentleman's step.

Lead the fox trot in a group situation to medium slow music in 4/4 time (four quarter beats in each measure). Each step requires one and one-half measures (or six beats). Use long,

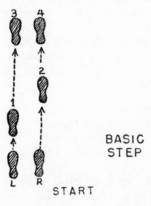

BASIC STEP

START

gliding steps that are smooth and not jerky. First start with the gentlemen in one semicircle and ladies in another semicircle. After some practice, do in the social dance positions (see Waltz on page 100 for description of social dance position). Remember that the gentleman always leads. Use these suggestions in social dancing:

1. Be aware of the rhythm and tempo of music.
2. Practice maintaining balance and timing.
3. Gentleman begins with left foot and lady with right foot. The gentleman always starts and the lady follows his lead.
4. Gentleman gives lead directions through pressure of his hand or arm on lady's back.

Rock and Roll

• C • NP •

Equipment: Phonograph and phonograph record with swing music or other appropriate musical accompaniment.

There are many diversified steps for rock and roll dancing. Follow the style that is current and predominant. One such group of steps for the gentleman (reverse for lady with her starting on right foot) is as follows:

1. First step to the left with the left foot.
2. Bring the right foot up to the left.
3. Take a quick step to the left with the left foot. All of these three steps have two beats of music and are counted "one and two."
4. The next step is a slow step in place with the right foot.
5. Then take a slow step in place with the left foot.

An alternate step is as follows:

1. Do steps one, two, and three (as described above), but go to the right with right foot.
2. Step back with the left foot.
3. Step forward on the right foot.

Use "jive" and "rock-and-roll" music for fast dancing. Allow the expression of rock and roll to come from the group (rather than the leader actively encouraging it). Younger men and women and teenagers are the most avid fans of rock and roll.

Watch for signs of fatigue in those who may become so engrossed with this dance that they forget their physical limitations. The steps of "rock and roll" are constantly changing. The dances are done to fast-paced rhythms which appeal chiefly to adolescents and others who are well coordinated. Musical selections for this kind of dance vary from week to week. Consult the younger set who are interested in rock and roll for their suggestions as to current records and music for background effect.

Encourage rock and roll dances that feature small circular groups of dancers. This brings variety to the couple arrangement of dancing.

Waltz   • A • GMS • NP •

Equipment: Phonograph and phonograph record with waltz music or other appropriate musical accompaniment.

Assume a social dance position. In a social dance position, the partners face each other. The gentleman places his right arm around the lady's waist with his right hand on her back just below her shoulder blades. His left hand holds the lady's right hand out to his left side. The lady places her left hand on her partner's right shoulder and looks over his right shoulder. Use the count of "one-two-three" and follow the direction:

Gentleman

1. Step forward on left foot (count of "one")
2. Step to the right on right foot (count of "two")
3. Close left foot to right foot and transfer weight to the left foot (count of "three")
4. Step back right (count of "one")
5. Step left foot to left of the right (count of "two")
6. Bring right foot to the left and transfer the weight (count of "three")

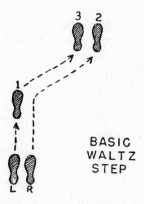

BASIC
WALTZ
STEP

Lady

1. Step back on the right foot (count of "one")
2. Step sideways left (count of "two")
3. Step right foot to the left and transfer the weight (count of "three")
4. Step forward left (count of "one")
5. Step sideways right (count of "two")
6. Step left foot to right and transfer weight (count "three")

First teach the step to an individual before partners are selected. Have dancers line up in a straight line. Draw a chalked square on the floor and tell them to imagine they are standing in the lower left hand corner of the square. Let dancers go through the waltz step (as previously outlined in the six movements) so they step in all four corners of the square. Have them practice this several times alone and then repeat the action with partners.

After the basic waltz-box step is understood, try the waltz turn. Gentleman steps forward (lady backward) on count "one," makes a quarter turn counterclockwise on count "two," and close on count "three."

MIXER DANCES

Grand March   • A • NP •

Equipment: Phonograph and phonograph records with march music or other appropriate musical accompaniment.

Have gentlemen line up on one side of auditorium or dance floor. Have ladies line up on other side of floor. A leader is at the head of each line. Direct all to face the wall opposite the location of the phonograph. At the start of music the two lines march near the walls to back of the hall and at the middle of this end meet their partners. They march in couples in opposite direction from where they came and up middle of floor. Upon reaching the front hall end near the phonograph the head couple goes to the right, second couple to left, third couple to right and so on around edge of room back to the opposite end of hall. Follow same procedure in fours and then in eights. Encourage a peppy marching rhythm to the music. As the marching groups split into fours and eights, assist them around the corners and in joining groups at back of room.

Have each group of eight form a set for square dancing or have each person dance with his original partner.

Select peppy march music as appropriate background for

the grand march. Try RCA 45 r.p.m. album *America's Favorite Marches*.

As a variation, when the groups of four reach the front of the room, divide them into twos, one file of couples turning to the right and the other to the left. As the two lines of partners meet at the back of room, they continue marching toward each other. The line of partners to the right (to the right facing front of room) form "bridges" by joining hands and holding them high; the other line of partners march through. Both files of couples continue marching forward.

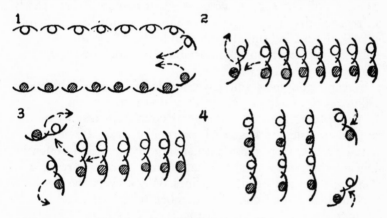

Try the snail march in which the two lines meet and form a large single circle. Have the ladies and gentlemen alternated as much as possible in the circle formation. Take any person and lead him (and the whole circle after him in a circle line formation) around the inside of the circle. In effect, the long line is wound in a corkscrew manner of many circles, but all holding hands. At any given point unwind the circle by doubling back. March gaily in circular manner until the original circle line is unwound.

Other Mixer Dances   • A • C • NP •

Equipment: Phonograph and phonograph records or other appropriate musical accompaniment.

Try some of these program helps in mixing up dance partners and assisting in the get-acquainted process. The only equipment needed for each (in addition to music background) is indicated in parentheses after the title:

Broom Dance (one or two old brooms): Give a broom to one of the dancers to be used as his partner. Commence the music and stop it once or twice during each selection. When the music stops whoever holds a broom gives it to a nearby person of the same sex in exchange for his partner.

Partner Sharing (wrapped candy or miniature cardboard phonograph records): Give each gentleman an object (candy or record) that he can present to another gentleman. When he wants to "cut in" on another couple, he hands the object to another gentleman on the floor and then dances with his lady partner.

Reverse the roles and have the ladies present objects to ladies on the floor on whom they desire to "cut in."

Multiplying Dance: Ask several couples to begin dancing. Stop the music and have each partner of those dancing select a new partner from those not dancing. Stop music frequently. During the pauses each partner on the floor secures a new dancing partner from the sidelines. When everyone has been included, play one complete number so that the last chosen partners have a longer dance together.

Suggestion: Try the Grand March as another way of getting new partners. See page 102 for directions on the Grand March.

FOLK DANCING

Polka   • A • NP •

Equipment: Phonograph and phonograph record with polka music or other appropriate musical accompaniment.

Have partners face each other with the gentleman's hands on the lady's waist and her hands on his shoulders (with lady using opposite foot as described):

1. Hop on right foot
2. Step forward on left foot
3. Bring right foot up to the left foot
4. Step forward on left foot
5. Hop on left foot
6. Step forward on right foot
7. Move left foot up to right foot and step forward right

The couple turns on the "hop" in a clockwise motion. Teach carefully and start with the hopping step. Use a count of "one-two-three-four" with the hop on "one," step forward on "two," feet together on "three," and step forward on "four." Allow the gentleman to lift the lady off the floor at the turn. Seek older patients who are sometimes very skilled in the polka to teach others.

A very good polka phonograph record is the "Emilia Polka," RCA Victor. Here are two 45 r.p.m. records for use with the polka: RCA Victor "Polka Time" and RCA Victor "Kinder-polka" record. See *The Country Dance Book* by Beth Tolman and Ralph Page for directions and ideas on the "Heel-and-Toe Polka" as well as the "Polka Mazurka."

Schottische   • A • NP •

Equipment: Phonograph and phonograph record with schottische music or other appropriate musical accompaniment.

Assume a social dance position (as outlined in description of the waltz, page 101). Use the count of "one-two-three-four." Follow these steps in practicing the schottische.

1. Move left foot to side (count "one")
2. Slide right foot to left one (count "two")
3. Close left foot to side (count "three")
4. Move left foot in to left with weight still on the left foot and raise and lower heel of left foot (count "four")
5. Repeat steps 1 through 4 with the right foot to right side
6. Do four step hops turning, starting with left foot and alternating

Purchase selected phonograph records for use with the schottische. Two 45 r.p.m. record selections to include are RCA Victor "Bummel Schottische," and RCA Victor "Highland Schottische."

Refer the advanced folk dancer to a detailed manual on folk dance patterns. See *Handbook of Couple Dances* by Martin H. Trieb.

Square Dancing   • A • C • GMS • NP •

Equipment: Square dance caller, phonograph, and square dance records, or square dance caller and other musical accompaniment, or phonograph and square dance records with calls on them.

Any number of "sets" (four couples) may participate. The sets are "squared" in dance formation. Number the couples counterclockwise with number three being opposite number one and number two to the right of number one.

The dancers should follow, but not anticipate in movement, the calls of the leader. Some important key words and phrases and their meanings in square dancing are:

1. *Honor Your Partner:* Facing their partners the gentlemen bow, bending slightly from the waist, as the ladies curtsy. The bow can be deep and formal or merely a quick nod of the head.
2. *Balance:* The caller should take care to explain which of the two possible meanings of "Balance" he wishes to convey.
   a. *Balance and Swing:* The gentleman takes his partner's left hand in his right and steps back for a second. The two Honor each other and then step forward and swing.
   b. *Step Swing Balance:* The gentleman takes his partner's right hand in his right hand, facing her. They simultaneously step forward with their right feet and swing their left feet across and in front. Then they step on their left feet and swing their right feet across and in front.

3. *Circle Left:* All couples in the set join hands in a circle formation and step in a clockwise direction for eight steps, then take eight steps in a counterclockwise direction which returns them to their original positions.

4. *Allemande Left:* All the dancers face their corners. They give their left hand to the left hand of their corners and walk around the corner. Returning to place, they drop the corner's hand and face their own partner. This is usually followed by the Grand Right and Left.

5. *The Grand Right and Left:* All dancers face their partners, the gentlemen facing in a counterclockwise direction and the ladies facing in a clockwise direction. Each gentleman gives his right hand to his partner and walks by her, passing right shoulders. Releasing his partner's hand, he gives his left hand to the next person. He walks by her passing left shoulders. Each gentleman continues to walk around the square in the same direction—gentlemen counterclockwise, ladies clockwise—without turning, alternating right and left hands, until he meets his partner again. Each gentleman then takes his partner in a promenade position and promenades in a counterclockwise direction until they return to their original position.

6. *Promenade:* Each couple faces to the right and walks in a counterclockwise direction around the square until they reach their home position. They may hold hands in a skating grip with arms crossed in front.

7. *Home:* This is the original position of the dancer at the beginning of the dance.

8. *Do-si-do:* Facing his partner, each dancer walks forward. He goes around his partner and returns home. Both the gentleman and the lady move at the same time and do not turn as they walk around. They pass right shoulders as they move forward and go past one another. They pass left shoulders as they walk backwards to home. Arms may hang loosely at sides or be folded in front of the dancer.

9. *Swing:* The most common swing is the buzz step. Partners put their right feet forward with the outside of the foot almost touching the partner's foot. Then, pushing

steadily with the left foot which is kept back, and pivoting with very short steps on the right foot, which is kept forward and on the floor, they begin to swing. This is something like being on a scooter. The dancers should swing slowly at the beginning; when they gain grace and confidence, they can begin to swing faster.

10. *Elbow Swing:* A variety of swing that may be done as part of certain squares is the elbow swing. The partners link right elbows and swing in a clockwise direction. This may be done either with a walking step or a buzz step.

11. *Indian Style:* The dancers walk in a counterclockwise direction with the ladies preceding the gentlemen.

Follow the key words and phrases in executing these dances.

Divide the Ring

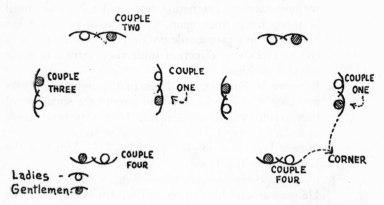

COUPLE TWO

COUPLE THREE

COUPLE ONE

COUPLE ONE

COUPLE FOUR

CORNER

COUPLE FOUR

Ladies -
Gentlemen

(Calls of the leader)	(Movements of the dancers)
1. First couple bow, first couple swing.	1. First couple bows and swings, once or twice around.
2. Down the set and divide the ring.	2. First couple walks down the center of the set and "splits" the opposite, or third couple, which separates to let them through.

Step 2

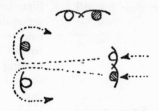

3. Lady go gee and gent go haw.

3. The first couple now separates. The lady goes around the outside of the set to the right and back to her home position while the gentleman goes to the left and back to home.

4. Swing when you meet as you did before.

4. First couple meets in their home position and swing.

5. Down the set and cut off four.

5. First couple goes down the set again. The gentleman cuts to the left between the third and fourth couples, as the lady goes to the right, between the second and third couples.

Step 5

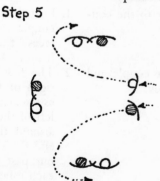

6. You swing her and she'll swing you.

6. They meet and swing in their home positions.

7. Down the set and cut off two.

7. First couple goes down the set again, the gentleman cutting to the left dividing the fourth couple and the lady cutting right dividing the second couple. Both return home.

Step 7

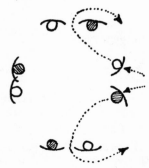

8. Everybody swing.

8. All four couples swing.

The leader then repeats the call but substitutes "second couple," then "third couple," and finally "fourth couple," until all couples have divided the ring.

Take a Little Peek

(Calls of the Leader)

(Movements of the Dancers)

1. First couple out to the couple on the right.

1. First couple walks to the couple on the right and faces them, not holding hands.

2. Go around that couple and take a little peek.

2. The first lady steps to the right of the second couple as the gentleman steps to the left of them. Without going around them the first lady and the first gentleman lean out past them and peek at each other.

3. Back to the center and swing your sweet.

3. First couple goes back to the center of the set and swings there.

4. Go round that couple and peek once more.

4. First couple repeats action 2.

5. Back to the center and swing all four.

5. First couple returns to the center, and both first and second couples swing.

6. On to the next.

6. First couple now goes to the third couple and repeats the same action, then goes on to the fourth couple and repeats the same action.

The leader repeats all the calls for the second, third, and fourth couples, substituting the appropriate words for "first couple." The two calls described are known as patter calls. Use the calls to any type of square dance patter music. Use the RCA Victor 45 r.p.m. record, "Blackberry Quadrille," which is one of eight selections in Victor 45 r.p.m. record album entitled "Square Dance" by Woodhull's Old Tyme Masters. Also, try the RCA Victor "Oh, Susanna!" 45 r.p.m. record, or similar 33⅓ r.p.m. versions.

People sometimes shy away from square dancing because they fear to make mistakes. Never talk down to square dancers nor strive for perfection in dancing techniques. Mention that mistakes are a part of the enjoyment and fellowship. Stress that mistakes are a part of square dancing and are to be expected of all participants from time to time.

Secure a skilled caller (possibly a patient) who will move the dancing along at a pace in harmony with the group's skill, ability and experience. If a caller is not available in person, use square dance records with beginning calls and instructions. Two of several recommended album groups are as follows:

1. Columbia Album Set on square dances by Carson Robison, his Old Timers and Lawrence V. Loy.

2. Honor Your Partner Albums 1, 2, and 3 (including introductory steps and calls) by Ed Durlacher, Square Dance Associates.

Purchase booklets with words and music to selected square dances, such as the variety of titles on country and square dancing available from the Cooperative Recreation Service. See *Square Dances of Today* by Richard Kraus for more detailed information on steps and square dance programming. If there is considerable interest or participation in square dancing in the hospital, consider purchasing or renting square dance instructional films in color. Write to Indiana University for more information.

Selected Veterans Administration Hospital general medical and surgical patients in wheelchairs have successfully square danced. Have interested patients in wheelchairs assume regular dance positions and follow suggested steps. Of course, this is done in a slower tempo. Be on the alert for overexertion of any patients. Provide ample ventilation, periodic breaks in the dance routine, and refreshments. Introduce other dances (grand march, hokey pokey, schottische, and polka) during the evening for variety.

Virginia Reel   • C • MR • NP •

Equipment: Phonograph and phonograph record with fast and peppy music for the Virginia Reel dance or other appropriate musical accompaniment.

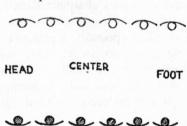

HEAD   CENTER   FOOT

Ladies
Gentlemen-

Direct dancers to form two lines with ladies and gentlemen facing each other. Allow six to seven feet between the lines. The basic action to music is as follows:

1. Head lady and foot gentleman go diagonally forward to center. Here they bow and curtsy to each other. They return, stepping backward to their original positions.

Step 1

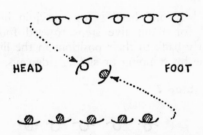

2. Head gentleman and foot lady then go forward diagonally to center and bow. They return to their positions.

3. In same order (first, head lady and foot gentleman, then head gentleman and foot lady) go to center and do a right hand swing. To do a right hand swing, the lady and gentleman join right hands at shoulder height and make one complete turn.

4. Do same procedure as in number three, but with a left hand swing. The left hand swing is reverse of right hand swing.

5. Do same procedure as in number three, but with a two hand swing.

6. Do same procedure as in number three, but with a right shoulder do-si-do. In order to do the do-si-do, the lady and gentleman face each other and walk forward, passing right shoulders, go around each other back to back. They return to place passing left shoulders, moving in a back-to-back motion, and still facing in the same direction.

Step 6

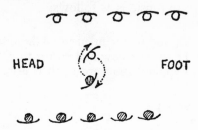

7. Head lady and head gentleman join both hands and chassé for about five steps toward foot of line and similarly back to their positions in the line. The chassé is done by stepping or sliding sideways.

Step 7

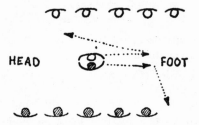

8. The head couple hooks right arms and turns one and a half times around until the gentleman is facing the lady's line and the lady facing the gentleman's line. The gentleman gives his left arm to the second lady and swings with her halfway around in a counterclockwise manner. At the same time, the head lady extends her left arm to the second gentleman and swings with him halfway around in a counterclockwise manner. The head couple then meets in the center, hooks right arms, and turns halfway around in a clockwise direction. This process is repeated down the line, the head couple alternately turning dancers with the left arm and turning each other in the center with the right arm until all have been turned. When reaching the end of the line,

the head couple turns one and a half times around so that the lady and gentleman are near their respective lines. The head lady and gentleman then slide (chassé) up to the head of the lines.

Step 8

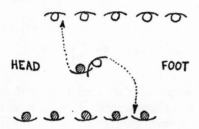

9. The gentleman turns outward and leads his line of gentlemen toward the foot of set in a marching manner. At the same time, the head lady turns outward and leads the ladies toward the foot of set with the same step.

Step 9

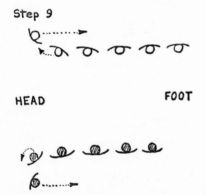

10. At the foot, the head couple meets and joins hands, and holds them high in an arch formation. The rest of the couples go under the arch and back to their places. The second couple is now the head couple. Repeat the dance until all couples have served as head couples.

Step 10

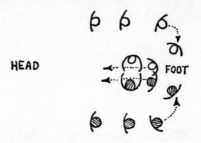

HEAD   FOOT

Variation: Instead of the head lady and foot gentleman dancing while all others watch, change the directions so that each lady and *opposite* gentleman do the regular dance steps of the head and foot couples. This will involve more persons at one time instead of their waiting and watching others.

Chapter 7

Dramatic Activities

DRAMATIC ACTIVITIES feature projected actions and voices in play-acting situations. Most drama activities for the handicapped are of the impromptu and informal type. Achieving participation and some active expression is probably just as significant as refined thespian art. The group leader in hospital settings will undoubtedly find a more receptive response to the casual types of drama such as charades and group stunts.

Some dramatic activities include other areas of endeavor such as arts and crafts and writing. The making of marionettes certainly necessitates a good amount of craft ability. An important by-product of drama is that of vocal and speech expression. Handicapped persons will be helped in gaining self-confidence and assurance through participation in story-telling, choral reading, and plays.

INFORMAL DRAMATICS

Charades   • C • GMS • TB •

Equipment: Slips of paper, two pencils, and a watch with second hand.

Divide the group equally into two teams. Each team in private chooses book titles, motion picture titles, song titles, or sayings that they want the other side to act out. Each team writes out on slips of paper one saying or title for each member on the opposing team. Then the teams assemble. A person on the team selected to start draws a slip of paper from the other team and shows each member of that side the word or words stated on it. He then attempts to act out for his own team the title or saying. A person appointed as time keeper keeps the time that each participant takes before his side correctly guesses the charade. No props are used. Parts of words, syllables, or groups of words are pantomimed. Team members may raise questions as to the correctness of the acted-out movements. The one doing the charade may answer by shaking his head for "yes" or "no." The team which guesses the correct titles or sayings in the shortest length of time is declared winner.

Variations: Play drawing charades. These differ only in that each player draws a picture on a blackboard or sheet of paper for his team to guess, rather than acting out the charade. Two or more bed patients may also play charades. Limit action to the use of hands and expression of faces. Some suggestions for charades are:

Songs

"Stardust"	"John Peel"
"Row, Row, Row Your Boat"	"Tell Me Why"
"I Love You Truly"	"Tea for Two"
"Bicycle Built for Two"	"Green Eyes
"Down in the Valley"	"After the Ball Is Over"

Advertising Slogans

"Ask the man who owns one"
"LS/MFT"
"Breakfast of champions"
"The pause that refreshes"
"Body by Fisher"
"Good to the last drop"
"When it rains, it pours"

Book Titles

Inside U.S.A.
Gone With the Wind
A Tree Grows in Brooklyn
How to Win Friends and Influence People
The Wizard of Oz
Uncle Tom's Cabin
Alice in Wonderland

Proverbs

Haste makes waste.	Two heads are better than one.
A miss is as good as a mile.	A rolling stone gathers no moss.
He who laughs last laughs best.	Don't cry over spilled milk.

Creative Dramatics   • C • GMS •

Tell some of the younger children (about five to ten years of age) about the plan to act out a story and encourage them to think about how it should be done. Read two stories to the group and let them decide which they would like to dramatize. Divide the story into scenes. Decide where the first scene will take place, who the characters are, and what happens. Select those to play in the first scene. Call the word "curtain" at the beginning and closing of each scene. After the scene has been acted out in pantomime (acting while someone reads story, or without reading a story), discuss and evaluate it with the actors. If the children seem satisfied with their performance (or if interest declines), start another scene. Play the scenes until the story is finished. In evaluating the session, have the children refer to the characters' names rather than their own real names. Bring out the good points first: the actors' ability, how they carried the roles, and how the story progressed. Do not (as a leader) step into the dramatization process unless it appears necessary in order to keep it going. Do not let visitors observe until the group has worked out the story.

Among many, two stories which are easily adapted for children's dramatics are the universally known "The Three Bears" and "The Three Billy Goats Gruff."

Musical accompaniment may be used in place of dialogue as a variation. Try other stories for older children (eleven through fifteen years of age). Some suggestions are: "Rumpelstiltskin," "Robin Hood Stories," "The Legend of Sleepy Hollow," and "Rip Van Winkle." See *Playmaking with Children* by Winifred Ward or *Creative Play Acting* by Isabel B. Burger for additional ideas on creative dramatics.

Group Stunts   • C • GMS • NP •

"Casey at the Bat"

Select a group stunt that is on the interest level and maturity level of the particular group. Have a responsive, articulate, and skillful person serve as narrator. He assigns specific parts to members of the group. Those persons perform or speak the role of their character or characters when they are reached in the narration.

Use the popular poem, "Casey at the Bat" as a group stunt. Divide the group into four sections. One section will play the role of Casey, and each of the other three sections will respectively play parts of the Crowd, Pitcher, and Umpire. As the leader slowly reads the poem, each group section acts out the appropriate lines spoken by the reader. Each line in the poem requiring group action is indicated and italicized:

"CASEY AT THE BAT"

by Ernest T. Thayer

The outlook wasn't brilliant for the Mudville nine that day;
The score stood four to two with but one inning more to play.
And then, when Cooney died at first, and Barrows did the same,
A *sickly silence fell upon the patrons of the game. (Crowd)*

A *straggling few got up to go in deep despair. (Crowd)* The rest
Clung to the hope which springs eternal in the human breast;
They thought if only Casey could get a whack at that—
We'd put up even money now with Casey at the bat.

But Flynn preceded Casey, as did also Jimmy Blake,
And the former was a lulu and the latter was a cake;
So *upon that stricken multitude grim melancholy sat, (Crowd)*
For there seemed but little chance of Casey's getting to the bat.

But Flynn let drive a single, to the wonderment of all,
And Blake, the much despised, tore the cover off the ball;
And when the dust had lifted, and the men saw what had occurred,
There was Johnnie safe at second and Flynn a-hugging third.

Then, *from 5,000 throats and more, there rose a lusty yell; (Crowd)*
It rumbled through the valley, *it rattled in the dell; (Crowd)*

It knocked upon the mountain and recoiled upon the flat,
For Casey, *Mighty Casey, was advancing to the bat. (Casey)*

There was *ease in Casey's manner as he stepped into his place; (Casey)*
There was *pride in Casey's bearing, and a smile on Casey's face.*
  (Casey)
And when, responding to *the cheers, (Crowd) he lightly doffed his*
  hat, (Casey)
No stranger in the crowd could doubt 'twas Casey at the bat.

Ten thousand eyes were on him (Crowd) as he rubbed his hands with
  dirt; (Casey)
Five thousand tongues applauded (Crowd) when he wiped them on
  his shirt. (Casey)
Then while the writhing pitcher *ground the ball into his hip,*
  (Pitcher)
Defiance gleamed in Casey's eye, a sneer curled Casey's lip. (Casey)

And now the leather-covered sphere came hurtling through the air,
And *Casey stood a-watching it in haughty grandeur there. (Casey)*
Close by the sturdy batsman the ball unheeded sped—
"*That ain't my style," (Casey)* said Casey. "*Strike one!" (Umpire)*
  the umpire said.

From the benches, black with people, there *went up a muffled roar,*
  (Crowd)
Like the beating of the storm waves on a stern and distant shore.
"*Kill him! Kill the umpire!" (Crowd)* shouted some one in the stand;
And it's likely they'd have killed him had not *Casey raised his hand.*
(Casey)

With a *smile of Christian charity (Casey)* great Casey's visage shone;
He stilled the rising tumult; he bade the game go on; (Casey)
He signalled to the pitcher, (Casey) and once more *the spheroid flew;*
  (Pitcher)
But *Casey still ignored it, (Casey)* and the umpire said: "*Strike two!"*
  (Umpire)

"*Fraud!" (Crowd)* cried the maddened thousands, and the *echo*
  answered "fraud!" (Crowd)
But *one scornful look from Casey, (Casey)* and the *audience was*
  awed. (Crowd)
They saw *his face grow stern and cold, (Casey)* they saw *his muscles*
  strain, (Casey)
And they knew that Casey wouldn't let that ball go by again.

The *sneer is gone from Casey's lip, (Casey)* his *teeth are clenched in
hate; (Casey)*
He pounds with cruel violence his bat upon the plate. (Casey)
And now the *pitcher holds the ball, and now he lets it go, (Pitcher)*
And now the *air is shattered by the force of Casey's blow. (Casey)*

Oh! somewhere in this favored land the sun is shining bright;
The band is playing somewhere, and somewhere hearts are light,
And somewhere men are laughing, and somewhere children shout;
But there is no joy in Mudville—mighty Casey has struck out.

Use another procedure which does not require splitting the
group into several parts. The audience sits facing the leader
and mimics and repeats everything he does and says. The
leader should know the words and action by heart.

"The Lion Hunt"

"Wouldn't you like to go on a lion hunt?"
"Good."
"Are you sure you're not afraid?"
"Let's get started!"
"Let's open the door and walk out." *(Pantomime opening of door and
clapping of hands on knees in a slow alternating tempo.)*
"Up the hill." *(Slow the beats and begin to pant.)*
"Whew! Gosh, that was steep. Now let's look around." *(Shade eyes,
peer into distance and point.)*
"There it is!" *(point)*
"See that cave?"
"That's the lion's den."
"Let's go." *(Clap hands on knees, quickly moving downhill.)*
"Now we're on level ground again." *(resume normal handclapping.)*
"Through the wheat field." *(Brush hands together to make a swish-
ing noise.)*
"Here's a fork in the road. We'll go left." *(Tilt body and head to the
left.)*
"Another fork. Go right."
"Here's a creek. Think we can jump it? Let's back up." *(Hands on
thighs, patter quickly forward, rise in air, hold for a moment, and
down on knees hard.)*
"Made it!"
"Let's keep walking. We're not far from the lion's den now. Sure
you're not afraid? Then let's keep moving."

"Through the swamp." *(Lift hands slowly up and down from knees.)*

"Look! Blueberries growing on this bush! Let's eat 'em." *(Pick and eat.)*

"We're almost there."

"First, let's go through the covered bridge." *(Hit chest with palms of hands slowly for hollow bridge sound.)*

"Now we're in the open! Creep up slowly. Quiet. . . ." *(Suddenly clap hands together and back up.)*

"What's that? Maybe it's the lion. Let's go in the cave and see, but be quiet." *(Creep forward slowly. Suddenly clap hands again.)*

"Look! It's the lion! Quick, shoot him!" *(Make horrified facial expression. Pantomime the shooting.)*

"We missed! Run!" *(Repeat all actions in reverse, at a very fast pace.)*

"Through the bridge."

"No time to pick blueberries."

"Through the swamp."

"Jump the creek."

"Go right! Go left! Through the wheat field."

"Up the hill! Down hill!"

"Into the house! Slam the door!"

"Whew! Safe at last!"

Memorize the stunt so that full attention may be given to the group and their appropriate actions in keeping with the game. See *Handy* by Lynn Rohrbough, "Handy Stunts," Kit I for additional stunt ideas such as "The Toy Shop," and "The Fatal Quest." Remember that some stunts (like "The King with a Terrible Temper" in *Handy*, Kit I) include parts possibly offensive to certain handicapped persons.

Story Telling   • A • C • GMS • MR • TB •

Carefully choose a story that is geared to the needs and interests of the particular age group. Study the story so that it can be told without the necessity of reading it. Prepare in advance the plan, timing, setting, and any needed props. Arrange the room or area so that it is free from distractions and comfortable.

Bring the group into the place where the story is to be told (or take the story where the group is located). Be certain to speak in a clear, audible voice and stand or sit in a location visible to all listeners. Tell the story with props or objects to illustrate it. See "Flannelgraphs" on page 77 for more ideas on storytelling and the use of felt pieces for story illustration purposes. Let the story tell itself without philosophical side comments or other material that does not contribute to the meaning. Confine the length and number of stories to the interest span of listeners. Stop at a high point of interest rather than overworking the period just to fill up time. Remember when telling stories to boys and girls to respect their world of make-believe and adventure. Do not talk down to them, but be a part of their group even to the point of sitting in the audience while telling the fable.

Variation: Introduce progressive stories whereby one participant (or leader) starts a story and talks for about two minutes. The next person in circle then continues with the story, telling it in accordance with his own imagination of how the plot or content should progress. After his turn, the third person carries on and so on until the last one has had a chance to speak.

Do not use ghost stories or any that unduly excite children, especially before bedtime. Tell a variety of stories to children. Some topics which children find interesting are legends, fairy tales, Indian stories, historical tales, and stories with a moral. Include in the repertory large story books with colored illustrations to assist in holding attention and conveying the story. Always *tell* the story unless it is so lengthy or adventurous that the true meaning could not be portrayed other than through reading. Use volunteers or students in the program as a corps of trained storytellers.

Purchase story records for a welcome change in the program for children. Play the phonograph record and hold up the book accompanying the record. Turn the pages as the tale is told on the record. When there is only one individual, let him play the record and look at the book at the same time. Several RCA Victor 45 r.p.m. story records to check when buying are the following: *Cowboys and Indians, Johnny*

Appleseed, The Little Engine That Could, and *Peter and the Wolf.*

When using props or objects to illustrate the story, use some of these ideas: An orange or grapefruit for a story about the world or sun, and toy animals for any stories that feature animals (like "The Three Bears"). Tell these stories that may be secured from any nearby library.

Children—one to ten years of age
"The Three Bears"
"Billy Goats Gruff"
"Peter Pan"
Stories of Presidents (Washington, Lincoln, and others)
Bible Stories
"Johnny Appleseed" (See "Flannelgraphs" on pages 77-80)
"Tom Sawyer"

Children—eleven to seventeen years of age
"Robin Hood"
"A Christmas Carol"
"King Arthur and Knights of the Round Table"
Stories of Service to Man, or Adventure

Children and Adults—eighteen years and over
"Gulliver's Travels"
"The Gold Bug"
"The Swiss Family Robinson"
Travel Stories

FORMAL DRAMATICS

Choral Reading   • A • GMS • NP •

Equipment: Selections to be read by the group.

Review selections that might be easily presented by a group. Study voice qualities and speech skills of individuals who will be in the choral reading group. Divide parts according to the timbre of voices and speech qualities of participants. Commence group reading. Permit solo readings within the total selection when these add to the effectiveness of the performance. Practice the solo parts and responses between various members of the group. Perform for others. Use choral reading (or choral speaking) in connection with religious services in the hospital. Discuss with hospital chaplain the values and problems in this type of activity. Seek his assistance or leadership. The Bible (especially the Psalms and story of Elijah) is an excellent source of material. Try poetry and prose. Use the following selections: The symbols used are S—Solo part; G—Group part; L—Low voice; H—High vice; P—Pause.

The Twenty-Third Psalm

(G)   The Lord is my shepherd;

{G)   I shall not want.

(L-S)   He maketh me to lie down in green pastures:

(L-S)   He leadeth me beside the still waters.

(S)   He restoreth my soul:

(H-S)   He leadeth me in the paths of righteousness for His name's sake.

(G)   Yea, though I walk through the valley of the shadow of death, I will fear no evil:

(G)   for Thou art with me;

(G)   Thy rod and Thy staff they comfort me. (P)

(L-S)   Thou preparest a table before me in the presence of mine enemies:

(H-S)   Thou anointest my head with oil; my cup runneth over.

(G)   Surely goodness and mercy shall follow me all the days of my life:

(G)   and I will dwell in the house of the Lord forever.

Use the Nineteenth Psalm also in choral reading.

"Snowflakes" (Author Unknown)

(S)   See the pretty snowflakes

(S)   Falling from the sky;

(L-G)   On the walk and housetop

(L-G)   Soft and thick they lie.

(H-S)   On the window ledges,

(L-S)   On the branches bare;

(L-G)   Now how fast they gather,

(S)   Filling all the air.

Try "Afternoon on a Hill" by Edna St. Vincent Millay or "Fog" by Carl Sandburg for interesting reading effects.

Plays   • GMS • NP •

Equipment: Stage, curtains, stage equipment, and scripts.

Secure cooperation of any institutional departments that are necessary for successful performance of play. Discuss play with those who may be interested in dramatics. Read several plays and have a committee determine which play is most suitable for production. After there is general consensus on the one chosen, proceed with tryouts for various parts. After careful study and review, asssign parts in the performance. Also select persons to fulfill these tasks: director, assistant director, stage manager, lighting director, sound director, costume technician, prompter, stage hands, and publicity committee. Consider a staff person for director or assistant director so that good care and judgment is always uppermost in decisions relative to progress of the play. Select handicapped persons to assist in details on the stage and for nonspeaking parts. Include staff members for some of the parts so there is support and intrinsic leadership within the cast. Schedule rehearsals and encourage regular attendance and promptness. Make the rehearsals joyous occasions that build *esprit de corps* among the cast members.

After sufficient rehearsal have a performance for other groups. Perform for the staff, and if the dramatic quality warrants it, go to hospitals or schools in the community for additional performances. Publicly thank the cast for their cooperation and fine work in presenting the play. Definitely plan on more than one presentation, and encourage the cast regardless of how well the first performance went over.

In a formal play, have skilled direction. In order to justify the time spent on this kind of dramatic production, involve as many players as possible. Have some make programs, costumes, and props. As a variation, try operettas as a means of combining play-acting with musical content.

Avoid old-fashioned melodramas, tragedies, and psychological studies as these are too difficult to put on with patients as actors and do not generally evoke a warm and favorable response from an audience.

See pages 94—121 of *The Recreation Program* for specific ideas, diagrams, and suggestions in staging, lighting, props, costumes, and make-up and follow these hints:

1. Secure participation of hospital electrician in lighting problems.
2. Light the stage center more brightly than the corners.
3. Use crepe paper extensively for flowers, wigs, mustaches, and background color.
4. Use such scrap materials as burlap bags, old curtains, sheets, and scarves.
5. In simple productions, label items for props; use simplicity and humor where appropriate.
6. Try shredded crepe paper for beards or hair.
7. Cast persons wisely and apply make-up carefully in terms of their personal identification with the parts.

Post and make known to the cast these backstage rules:

1. Keep those away from backstage that are not involved in some way in the play.
2. Have actors backstage thirty minutes before curtain time.
3. Do not smoke backstage.
4. Do not allow unnecesary talking backstage during performance.
5. Do not allow actors to go into the auditorium (or audience) in costume before or after the performance.

Chapter 8

Hobbies and Special Interests

INDIVIDUALIZED interests and activities provide a start for self-confidence, absorption, and enjoyment in the handicapped person's relatively empty hours. Continuous return to a pursuit over a period of time characterizes the hobby. These special and personal outlets are not only engrossing, but also of value to environmental adjustment and possible vocational preparation. The special interest is something engaged in during available time that is recreational and informally educational. Because these activities are important to many, they deserve to be ranked as a key area in recreation and require a special approach in their administration.

Repeated interest in any area during leisure time may be properly classified as a hobby. An important kind of hobby is one in which the enthusiast acquires and systematically preserves unusual or rare articles. The hobby which involves collections of various items is worthwhile for the patient confined at home who has considerable time, space, and attention. Avid interest in a hobby may come from previous exposure to it, such as in the aged individual who as a child collected postage stamps. The hobby "bug" may also bite after a person has observed the enjoyment others gain from hobbies or after he has read hobby magazines.

Self improvement can easily come through determined effort in correspondence course study, magic shows, photography, and affiliation with programs of national organizations. The intellectual, introverted, or quieter person may comfortably engage in thought-provoking special interests.

A balanced recreation program features the restrained and individualized approach. Handicapped persons are individuals

129

and may derive ease or solace in entering the group situation with the fortification of a hobby. Hence, although it is desirable to read, it is even more beneficial to read and become a part of a book club or discussion group. The carry-over values of hobbies and special interests are considerable and worthy of close scrutiny in any recreation offering for the handicapped.

"COLLECTING" HOBBIES

Collecting   • A • C • GMS • NP • TB •

Equipment: Whatever items are necessary for the collection.

Urge the handicapped person to further explore any demonstrated interest he now has. Use this consistent and repeated interest in an activity as a creative outlet for filling empty hours. Suggest advanced study and investigation of a hobby. Consider the prevocational skills that are developed through participation in a collecting hobby.

Assist the participant in devising an efficient manner for cataloging or arranging whatever he has in the collection. Encourage hobbies that do not require considerable space, facilities, or noise. Some of the items most often collected are:

Art pieces	Minerals
Autographs	Model trains
Badges	Nature objects
Books	Paintings
Buttons	Pencils
Circus tales or pictures	Phonograph records
Clocks	Picture post cards
Coins (see page 131)	Playing cards
Dolls	Rocks and minerals
Fans	Scrap books
Jewelry	Sea shells
Match covers	Spoons
Miniature animal replicas	Stamps (see page 131)
Miniature slippers and shoes	

Subscribe to a hobby magazine such as *Hobbies, The Magazine for Collectors*, Lightner Publishing Corporation. Read a book for additional hints on starting a hobby. See the *Complete Book of Collecting Hobbies* by William Bricker and *Handicrafts and Hobbies for Pleasure and Profit* by Marguerite Ickis.

Coin Collecting (Numismatics)   • A • C • GMS • NP •

Equipment: Coins and coin folders in which to mount coins.

First discover a means of assembling several interesting coins as a nucleus for a collection. Solicit friends to aid in saving old, unusual, or foreign coins.

Purchase coin folders (display cards) for about thirty-five cents each. Select folders for commoner coins (pennies, nickels) that the collector is apt to have. Mount coins in the folders according to the printed descriptions and dates. Start a collection of the United States coins with these folders:

> Indian Eagle pennies—1856 to 1909
> Lincoln Head pennies—starting 1941
> Liberty Head nickles—1883 to 1913
> Buffalo nickles—1913 to 1938
> Jefferson nickles—starting 1938
> Roosevelt dimes—starting 1946

Look for coin folders that contain spaces without date and printed description, captions for pennies, nickles, dimes, and quarters. Consult a local hobby dealer for more ideas and prices of supplies.

Purchase any of the better known guide books on United States or foreign coins. Several well known titles are published by the Whitman Publishing Company.

Stamp Collecting (Philately)   • A • C • GMS • NP •

Equipment: stamps, postage stamp album, one package of stamp hinges, stamp tongs (or tweezers), and small magnifying glass.

Encourage the collector to handle the stamps carefully with stamp tongs. Have him study the stamps and notice finer detail on them through the magnifying glass. He should locate the proper places in the album for the stamps according to countries of origin, moisten and affix a part of hinge near top of stamp back and bend hinge, moisten balance of hinge and mount stamp in its proper place on album page.

Secure stamps from stamp dealers or volunteers for collections. Try Wildlife Conservation Stamps which are purchasable along with special albums and binders from the National Wildlife Federation. Also collect Easter Seals or tuberculosis Christmas Seals. Contact a local county Easter Seal Committee or Christmas Seal Committee for information on how to secure these seals. When working with handicapped or sick children, look over albums which feature seals of animals, automobiles, nature study, and birds. These are available in most ten-cent and department stores.

Begin a stamp club if there are enough interested persons. Invite a philatelist from a community stamp club, or a commercial stamp dealer to speak to the stamp club. Suggest the trading of stamps and discussion of rare stamps.

For the advanced collector secure stamp catalogs which describe the value and present details about all postage stamps. One popularly accepted catalog is Scott's *Standard Postage Stamp Catalog*, Vol. I and Vol. II (issued annually). Subscribe to one of the postage stamp newspapers or magazines. Note much information therein on the sources of stamps and philatelic supplies as well as recent news in philately. Two stamp newspapers are "Mekeel's Weekly Stamp News" and the "Western Stamp Collector." Some postage stamp collectors are particularly interested in United States stamps. Purchase *Postage Stamps of the United States, 1847-1955*.

Use old postage stamps as a "philatelic" craft project. Collect small frozen orange juice cans (or other cans) that have had their tops neatly cut off without any jagged edges. Use white glue to affix old postage stamps of different countries over the can's outside. Arrange the stamps in an overlapping and slanting formation. Cover all exposed sides of the can. Use ample glue so that all of the stamp backs are firmly glued on the can. Shellac the completed project. Use it as a colorful container for pencils, letters, and other miscellaneous small objects on the dresser or desk.

Hobby Show • A • GMS • NP •

Equipment: Tables, hobbies, and awards.

The hobby show is the climax of a year's activity in hobbies for a hospital. Plan for several active hobbies (collections which lend themselves to display) and an area where they can be displayed. Sketch a floor plan of the hobby-show room after it is known which hobbies are available for display. Have participants mount the displays so that they are easily observable.

Tell each hobbyist to fill out a form describing the hobby when entering the show. Display along with the hobby the name of its owner and other information.

Open the show to visitors, handicapped persons, staff, and possibly members of the community at stated hours. Have various persons serve as guides if the show is on a large scale. Take measures to safeguard the exhibits overnight. If prizes and awards are given, minimize the quantity of these or handle so each entry gets some tangible recognition.

Variation: Make a "traveling hobby show" mounted on movable carts which make the rounds of the school or hospital. Many will then have a chance to see the displays in their own rooms. Do not rush this touring show from one area to another. Move it slowly so that everyone will have an opportunity to inspect it thoroughly. See ideas on how to make a cart on page 285.

SELF-IMPROVEMENT ACTIVITIES

Book Club   • A • C • GMS • NP •

Equipment: Books of interest to the club.

Secure the cooperation, interest, and possible leadership of the librarian or staff member responsible for the library.

Circulate books and reading material to those who are interested in this quiet type of activity.

Invite those who are interested to the library or other accessible meeting spot and discuss good reading materials. Make the general organization and plan of the club simple so that interest in books is of primary consideration. After having several meetings, and being assured of an interested group, select officers and formal procedures for more efficient club organization. (See hints on starting clubs on page 142.)

Urge club members in their weekly readings to critically evaluate and review books. Have them ask themselves if they are favorably or unfavorably impressed by the book. Suggest that they follow an outline similar to the following in their critical description of the book:

1. Introductory paragraph: author, title, length of book and reading time.
2. Description: the setting, characters, plot and theme.
3. Style of writing: vocabulary and general structure.
4. Conclusion: objectives of author, particular value of book and hints to readers.

Use this outline in book reviews made by readers to the club. During the first meeting or so have a book review and discussion of a current best-seller or one of interest to those in attendance. Serve refreshments at end of meetings.

Variations: Review and encourage reading of The National Geographic Magazine. Secure back issues from volunteers and organizations. Have book club meetings in settings convenient to the handicapped. Use volunteers or others to read aloud to participants. Invite any volunteers who are skilled in book reviewing to meet with club.

Suggestions: Write to the American Library Association or the Children's Book Council for information on National Book Week. Stimulate special interest of others in reading books as self-improvement activity during this week. Obtain through the local librarian or above organizations book reading aids such as posters, book marks, and leaflets.

Charm School   • GMS • NP • TB •

Equipment: Cosmetics, clothing, or other accessories necessary for demonstration or instruction.

Enlist the help and leadership of someone skilled in facial make-up, hair-dos and general dress styling. Be certain that this person is sympathetic to the limitations and needs of handicapped people. Check with a local community beauty operator regarding suggestions and possible assistance with demonstrations. Talk to others who are experienced in clothing design and color.

Select those persons who would benefit from one or more demonstrations. In an atmosphere of informality, have the leader or specialist commence the facial or dress design lessons. Include color charts, mirrors, posters, and other visual aids to make the instruction more appealing and understandable. Include, in some of the sessions, content on table manners, posture (only if working with those whose posture is not physically impaired), and sewing of clothing.

Borrow hair styling charts and facial outlines from stores or libraries. Look for books on personal care that include this information. Seek information on social etiquette, manners, personal hygiene, body carriage, posture exercises, and health. Study the use of rouge, lipstick, powder, and coloring that blends in with complexion and hair style. Discuss figure proportions and skin care. Consider diet and exercise as important features of self-training.

Plan regular meetings that stress personal body care and neat appearance. Use care in not advocating any diets, exercises, or procedures that conflict with medical care of the handicapped. Include some of these visual aids in aiding the lectures and demonstration: measurement charts, food charts, vitamin information, hair style drawings, dress and color contrasts, and courtesy posters.

Invite select volunteers to assist in leading the charm school.

Seek these specialists from the community: Beauty shop operators, home economics teachers, physical education teachers, women's apparel buyers, and homemakers.

Include only demonstrations that are strictly for the benefit of the handicapped with no ulterior motives such as required cosmetic purchases or other sales gimmicks. In dealing with clothing and dresses, utilize only that attire which is practical for the handicapped to wear. Good taste and common sense are principles to use in the demonstration of proper dress.

Variations: Put on a style show with handicapped persons serving as models. Use a seasonal theme, or have the show as the culmination of a series of charm school sessions. Invite both men and women to attend. Serve light refreshments.

Use the charm school idea with bed patients. Isolation techniques will in some cases limit the manner in which these ideas are presented.

Correspondence Courses   • A • GMS • NP •

Secure from the National Home Study Council in Washington, D.C., or any accredited college or university, a list of correspondence course areas for study. Carefully scrutinize the correspondence course literature and be sure that it is a legitimate school that does not promise degrees, jobs, or other misleading enticements. Make arrangements with the school for the payment of fees and procurement of materials when it has been determined what field of study to pursue. Provide a typewriter if it is necessary for doing the lessons. Make arrangements for any required supervision in completion of examinations. Encourage regularity in returning written lesson assignments to the school, and provide a study atmosphere which is quiet. Be sure a dictionary and other source books are available. Many universities have correspondence courses in art, education, handicrafts, languages, music, speech, and other subject areas.

Discussion Groups • A • GMS • NP •

Equipment: Large table, comfortable chairs, paper, and pencils.

Publicize or make known plans for a discussion club. Encourage individuals who are mentally alert, curious, articulate, intelligent, and cooperative to attend the first meeting. Conduct an interesting program with a skilled speaker or leader during the first meeting. Briefly discuss values and advantages in group consideration of current, meaningful topics.

In subsequent meetings, use audio-visual aids to assist in maintenance of members' attention. Select an advance plan of program topics for future meetings. Tell the participants to study and explore subjects which will be considered in meetings yet to come.

Avoid in all cases topics of discussion that are likely to end in tense emotional conflict or considerable controversy. Avoid lengthy discussion of religion or politics as some differences of opinion turn into discord.

Consider some of these topics for meeting program plans:

Athletics	Literature
Advertising in radio	Metric system
Book reviews	Modernistic furniture
Celebration of the Fourth of July	Music
	Nature study
Conservation	Newspaper management
Current news events	Patent laws of the United States
Dress designs	
Foreign languages	Reading improvement
Forest rangers	Symphony music
Great Books program	Theater
History	Television and radio
Hobbies	Travel
Lie detectors	Vocational education

Suggestion: Form a club dealing with speech improvement and parliamentary procedure similar to the program of Toastmaster clubs. Consult community representatives of Toastmaster or other service clubs about help in organizing discussion groups. Study and practice discussion methods. Read the chapter on group discussion in *Leadership in Recreation* by Gerald B. Fitzgerald.

Patients' Council · A · GMS · NP ·

Equipment: Large table, comfortable chairs, paper, and pencils.

Secure medical and psychological sanction and approval of a patients' council. Publicize the purpose of a patients' council and recruit members through one of these methods:

1. Ward nurses or physicians select representatives from their wards
2. Patients vote for their representatives
3. Recreation or other staff select the members
4. Patients volunteer to serve as members

After the group has been formed, another method of selection is to ask the members to choose their own successors. A definite term of membership such as one or two months has the advantage of passing to others this group discussion opportunity as well as bringing new ideas and opinions into the council. A limited membership of from fifteen to twenty is best for most groups of this sort.

Include a physician or psychologist in the council meetings along with a recreation staff person. Elect a chairman and secretary from among the patient members. Work out in advance with the chairman an agenda and plans for meetings. Use parliamentary procedure and order whenever possible. Make arrangements for light refreshments after meetings.

Stimulate discussion on means for improving patients' activities and services in the hospital. Allow democratic expression of opinion, being careful not to give assurance that any or all patients' requests will be granted. Remember that the hospital physicians and administration still are responsible for management and decisions in policies and procedures regardless of the council's recommendations. When possible, and within reason, satisfy and solve problem situations that are raised in council meetings. Utilize ideas of patients in changing and improving the recreation program.

Invite special staff guests to council meetings for the purpose of explaining or clarifying questions on hospital policy (for example, a dietitian speaking on food, a gardener speaking on flowers and gardens).

Form committees of council members for consideration of special problems. Urge full democratic participation and the group process.

SPECIAL INTERESTS

Chess   • A • GMS • NP •

Equipment: One book of chess rules, one checkered board for chess, and two sets of sixteen pieces that include eight pawns, two rooks, two knights, two bishops, one queen, and one king to a set.

Have each player place his set of pieces (black or white) in the two rows of squares parallel and closest to the player. A row of squares extending from one player's side of board to the other side is a file. The rows parallel to the players are called ranks. A description of the pieces is as follows:

King—tallest, with a central spike or cross on its crown
Queen—second tallest, with a crenellated crown
Bishop—next tallest, with a cleft head like a miter
Knight—next tallest, with a horse's head
Rook—next tallest, a cylindrical tower with a flat and castellated top
Pawn—smallest piece with a simple knob at top.

The object of the game is to capture the enemy king. If it is attacked and cannot escape, it is said to be checkmated or mated. This ends the game. On making any move that attacks the enemy king, the player must say "Check." His opponent must avert the check or lose the game.

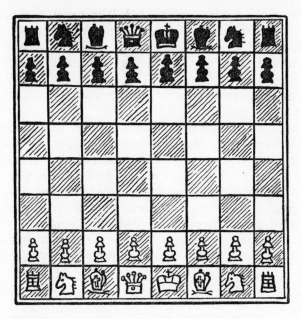

In brief, the moves taken alternately by the players are as follows for these pieces:

King: moves in any direction on rank, file, or diagonally, one square at a time.

Queen: moves in any direction, on rank, file, or diagonal, and any distance as far as the line is unobstructed.

Rook: moves along rank or file any distance as long as line is unobstructed.

Bishop: moves on any diagonal and any distance so far as the line is unobstructed.

Knight: moves to the nearest squares of opposite color that are not adjacent to its starting square.

Pawn: from home square on second rank, moves one or two squares forward on the file. Thereafter the pawn moves one square at a time forward on the file.

Any piece other than a pawn can capture an enemy piece standing on the square to which it can legally move. The captured piece is removed from the board and the captor is placed on the square just vacated. The pawn may take any piece which stands on either of the two squares diagonally ahead of it. Consult a rule book for additional methods of capture and other moves (castling and *en passant*). Secure the *First Book of Chess* by I. A. Horowitz and Fred Reinfeld for the beginner who wants additional help and ideas on moves in the game.

Enlist volunteers who are chess players to serve as partners for any who play the game. Attempt to work out arrangements with chess players elsewhere for exchange games via the mail. This method by mail involves a long time for each game with plays written down according to numbers (last numbered square to the next). A number of games may be played simultaneously this way with several opponents. If there are several chess players, consider a tournament. The tournament, of course, is a time-consuming event.

Clubs   • A • C • GMS • NP •

Equipment: Any hobby or other necessary items for special interest of the group.

Seek several persons that are avidly interested in any one hobby, activity, or cause. Suggest the advantages of sharing their enthusiasm for their pursuit with others. The beginning of a club program is the meeting of interested persons regularly for the purpose of sharing ideas and fellowship.

Some of the key factors to remember in advising a club in its meetings are as follows:

1. Utilize the leadership of participants. Elect officers, but on not too extensive a plane. Allow for changes in officers and programs.
2. Open membership to all, including personnel and volunteers.
3. Include any confined to beds in the membership with visitations scheduled from the ambulatory membership.
4. Make the formal framework, constitution, and parliamentary procedure brief and simplified.

5. Select an attractive meeting place that is quiet, well ventilated, and conducive to the pursuance of the club's special interest.
6. Keep to a minimum or eliminate any prerequisites for club participation such as dues and age limits.
7. Publicize the club's program and activities through bulletin boards, patients' newspapers, signs, and word-of-mouth.
8. As long as there is interest, keep the club going.

Here are some special interest items or activities around which to organize clubs:

African violets
Airplanes
Art appreciation
Birds
Books
Chess
Coins
Creative writing
Drama
Gardens
Language study
Magic
Minerals and gems

Music appreciation
Nature study
Needlework
Philosophy
Photography
Post cards
Radio
Sports
Square dance
Stamps
Storytelling
Travel

Contest Participation   • GMS •

Equipment: Pencil, paper, contest information, pen, and ink.

Search for nationally advertised contest information through magazines, newspapers, radio, and television. Secure any needed box tops or labels from volunteers for the contest entries.

Some contests require the completion of sentences on various commercial products while others necessitate the completion of crossword puzzles and drawings. Remind the contestants that the larger contest prizes are not frequently won by beginners. Stress participation in contests for the enjoyment derived rather than the sole objective of winning prizes.

Emphasize that contest entries must be submitted in exact accordance with stated rules. Many contest entries are rejected by judging companies because the contestants do not follow precise directions. Purchase from hobby dealers or news stands some of the magazines that deal exclusively with contest hobbyists and the science of entering contests. Follow these rules when sending in entries:

1. Make the entry neat and clear, yet not flowery and decorative in appearance.
2. Carefully study the rules and follow them to the word!
3. Gather material and information about the product that the contest describes and then study it well.
4. Make entries logical, original, but not so far out of the ordinary that they are too lavish and overly flattering.
5. In Limerick and name contests, stress the positive features of a product.

Creative Writing   • A • C • GMS • NP • TB •

Seek out those persons who have skill in literary and writing pursuits. Encourage free writing on current topics, history, nature, legends, philosophy, and other subject matter. Have possible outlets for verses, poetry, or stories such as the patients' newspaper, holiday greetings, or even the sale of suitable written material to magazines and commercial publishers. When a number of creative writers are located, assist in the formation of a discussion group for purposes of exchanging views on written works.

Consider some of these topics as ideas for creative writing:

In the Locker Room Before the Game
The Last Hour of the Mountain Climb
A Ride in the Fastest Streamliner
In the North Woods in the Winter
After the First Horseback Ride

Variation: Write letters to pen pals in other parts of the country or world. Describe life in any locality to another in a far-off country. Two sources of correspondence friends are columns in magazines such as *Together* or, for children, in *The Children's Plea for Peace.*

Magic   • A • C • GMS • NP •

Equipment: Book on magic, deck of playing cards, paper, pencil, and supplies or articles needed for specific magic tricks.

Encourage the handicapped person who is quick and alert in hands and mind to investigate the fun of mastery in magic tricks. Provide him with playing cards and other articles necessary for performance of the tricks. Emphasize the importance of practice and self-assurance. If the participant is sufficiently skilled, make arrangements for his handling magic shows for different groups.

Have the magician practice the development of gestures and "patter" talk while tricks are being performed. Such action and conversation keeps the audience's attention from wandering, but still prevents them from paying too much attention to the actions.

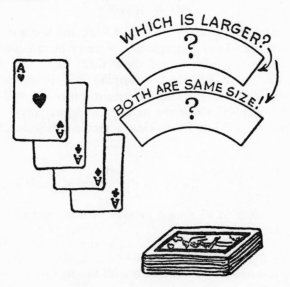

Try some of these simple magic tricks that require little equipment:

Number Guess

Tell a person to think of a number and have him jot it down. Have him double it, add four, multiply by five, add twelve, and multiply by ten. Ask him to tell you the last number thereby produced. You subtract 320, then cross out the last two ciphers and the resultant figure is the number originally guessed. Here is a specific example of how it works:

1.	The number	9
2.	Doubled	18
3.	Add four	22
4.	Multiply by five	110
5.	Add twelve	122
6.	Multiply by ten	1220

When 320 is subtracted from 1200 by the magician, the resulting number is 900. With the last two ciphers crossed off, the original nine is found.

Magic Writing

Secure a small quantity of lemon juice and use a clean pen point to write a brief message on a piece of plain white paper.

Assemble the audience and show them the blank piece of paper. Let them individually examine it if they wish. Tell the group that through magical means a message will appear on it and heat will cause the message to appear mysteriously.

Follow these hints in making a magic program effective and interesting:

1. Be cheerful, informal, and chatty.
2. Do not tell audience all the secrets of magic nor repeat tricks.
3. Practice in advance a number of times and occasionally in front of a mirror.
4. Try to capture an audience's attention with your eyes and mannerisms.
5. If a mistake occurs, laugh with the audience.

Model Hobbies • A • C • GMS • MR • NP •

Equipment: Model kit or miniature vehicle set.

Seek out those who are intrigued with model trains, automobiles, or airplanes and have some skill and patience in detailed work with knives. Purchase kits that have vehicles to assemble. See more information about carving on page 60. Arrange space for display or use of sets such as model trains and tracks for the advanced hobbyists.

Urge additional reading about the vehicle upon which the participant is working. Attempt to broaden his interest in the hobby through further reading or consideration of various aspects of it. Stress neatness in storage of model kits and supplies when not in use.

Model cars, airplanes and boats are often described as "solid scale" models. "Flying model" airplanes are also available. The flying model is a delicate balsa fuselage covered with paper that actually flies by a rubber band mechanism. Ascertain first whether or not a solid model is desired, then proceed with construction plans.

Purchase model kits from nearly any department store, arts and crafts store, or hobby dealer. Prices range from ten cents per kit on up to about three dollars each. Make any of these models from kits: airplanes, boats, locomotives, old-fashioned cars, racing cars, sailboats, ships, sports cars, submarines, and totem poles.

National Organization Programs • A • C • GMS
• MR • NP • TB •

Equipment: Whatever is deemed necessary according to the specific interest, organization, and program.

Investigate the possible values of a group affiliating with a national organization and program. Initiate correspondence with such agencies as to the feasibility of a handicapped group being a part of their cause and program. If the organization is fully receptive and interested, pursue ways of further implementing such a plan in the school or institution. Discuss this with physicians and other staff. Talk to persons about their interests and willingness to join an organized program like scouting or conservation.

Take steps to welcome and unite a group into the activities of the organization. Secure clear directions and advice of the national group before commencing activities. Anticipate this program with long-term objectives, even though the membership may fluctuate and change. Use only those uniforms, badges, and emblems that are economical and reasonable in terms of local financial resources. Some of the national organizations that may have programs for handicapped persons are:

> American National Red Cross
> Boy Scouts of America
> Camp Fire Girls, Inc.
> Girl Scouts of America
> National Audubon Society

Newspaper   • A • C • GMS • MR • NP •

Equipment: Paper, pencils, typewriter, mimeograph machine, mimeograph supplies, mimeograph paper in quantity sufficient for the number of newspaper pages desired, staples, and stapler.

Start with a nucleus of persons interested and somewhat skilled in journalism or writing. Meet and discuss the advantages and problems in commencing a school or institutional newspaper. If there is sufficient interest for newspaper distribution, confer with the proper authority on permission to inaugurate the publication. With all clearances made, take steps to locate necessary materials.

Solicit contributions of articles and writings for the newspaper. Secure a staff of reporters, editor, and writers from handicapped persons. Type the paper, mimeograph, and assemble it. Staple the paper on the left-hand side. Distribute the newspaper in some manner so that there is assurance of it

actually getting in the hands of all readers. Exchange newspapers with other institutions and schools.

Keep these principles in mind when writing and editing the newspaper:

1. Use color in newspaper reproduction when possible.
2. Feature illustrations and drawings freely throughout the paper.
3. Include frequent contributions of as many writers as possible.
4. Use names often in the newspaper, if in keeping with local policy.
5. Incorporate the work and activities of all departments in the news columns.
6. Highlight a variety of columns in newspaper. Examples are editorial, interviews, announcements, sports, puzzles, and general news.
7. Do a good duplication, assembly, and stapling job.

Start the publication with a few pages and increase the size of paper gradually. Put it on a firm and permanent basis before expanding the contents. Be consistent and dependable in the date that it reaches the readers. Publish it on a weekly or monthly basis, depending upon the interests of readers as well as the needs and sizes of the buildings that are supplied. Have all newspaper material cleared in advance with a staff advisor to the newspaper staff.

Maintain newspaper suggestion and contribution boxes in accessible spots about the halls and areas. Receive news contributions in these boxes and screen out material for consideration in the paper. Conduct a contest to determine the best title for the new newspaper after the first week or so of its publication.

Type even right-hand as well as left-hand margins on the pages. First type a dummy copy and determine to what point on the page the right-hand margin is to reach. If a word does not reach that exact point, type a star or some other symbol in each vacant space until the specified right hand margin is reached. Continue similarly until arriving at the end of page. In re-typing the page, allow the number of extra spaces between words in any one line according to the number of "extra" spaces indicated by symbols that are left on right end of line.

Consider other means of duplication in addition to mimeograph such as ditto, multilith, and printing. Contact a local stationery store, A. B. Dick Company, or Ditto, Inc. for additional information or help on mimeographing or ditto processes.

Mentally retarded persons enjoy reading and looking at a newspaper of their own. Their journalistic and writing assistance may be limited, but they can help in simpler ways such as preparation or distribution of the paper. Feature for them frequent illustrations for easy comprehension.

Pet Animals   • A • C • GMS • MR • NP •

Equipment: Pet, home for pet (if needed), food, and water.
Seek interests of the sick or disabled prior to consideration of any pet. Do not make promises or assurances as to the pro-

curement of pets. Check with the physician as to the types of pets that do not conflict with treatment procedures.

Read about pets and their care and obtain one through purchase or volunteer sources. Be certain that the animal or animals will not disturb persons nearby.

Some of the more satisfactory pets to place in homes, schools, or sick rooms are birds or fish. Tropical fish, gold fish, parrots, parakeets, and canaries are species that are seen on some hospital wards.

Suggestion: Purchase a parakeet in a pet shop or pet department of a department store for about three dollars. Buy one that is healthy looking and not too fat. Secure a good quality cage for about six dollars. Buy a wide swing to hang from the cage top or get a better cage equipped with one. Be sure to get a cage that has wire sides all the way around and on top. This permits maximum climbing and playing surface for the bird. Feed the bird daily with parakeet seed. Also include specially prepared parakeet "treat," parakeet "gravel," and water. Clean the cage regularly and watch the playful antics of the parakeet. Ask the pet shop for sources of inexpensive booklets on how to care for parakeets and the technique of teaching them to "talk." Parakeets live for several years and tend to be hardy birds that take on many human traits.

Photography   • A • C • GMS • NP •

Equipment: Camera and film.

Check with the physician or other appropriate person to see if there are any rules forbidding the use of cameras on grounds and nearby. With such approval, investigate the many potentialities of photography as a hobby for handicapped persons.

Select a camera that is practical and not too expensive. Following the camera instructions, insert the film. Urge patients to take pictures that do not clash with hospital policy. Take pictures on excursions around and away from the premises. Make use of still and portraiture photography as special undertakings.

Procure one or several of these five types of cameras for a photography program:

1. Box cameras—economical; limited distance (8 or 10 feet) from camera to subject
2. Simple folding cameras—like box, but have folding feature
3. Folding cameras—more expensive; convenient
4. Miniature cameras—portable; low operating cost; very small negative; desirable for color photography; make 35-mm. color slides
5. Reflex cameras—bulky; focusing screen that shows preview of image to be shown on negative

Use this sequence in taking a picture:

1. Focus camera (adjust distance between lens and film).
2. Set shutter speed (regulate length of time shutter is open).
3. Adjust aperture (regulate size and circular hole through which the lens admits light).
4. Aim camera (compose view through view finder).
5. Press shutter-release lever (control duration of exposure).
6. Advance film (turn new film section in place for next picture).

Suggestions: Purchase several cameras as a part of recreation supplies and have them available on a check-out basis. Give careful thought to purchasing miniature cameras. Their portability and general economy (particularly in regard to color film) stand out as prime advantages. Set up a darkroom for the developing and printing of snapshots. Assure adequate lighting and water supply in the room. Purchase only basic chemicals and supplies for beginners. Set up a system for efficient and economical use of supplies.

Let handicapped persons and volunteers use the darkroom in developing, printing, and enlarging pictures. Start out with the purchase of a darkroom developing and printing kit for about ten or twelve dollars. When purchasing darkroom equipment separately, include these items: printing frames, roll-film tank, trays, paper for prints, film clips, darkroom bulb or lamp, graduate (glass measuring cup), funnels, print roller, and ferrotype plate. Enlargers (for enlarging prints) are expensive, but useful in the fully equipped darkroom.

Inquire about written materials on photography, developing, printing, enlarging, and camera clubs. Two sources are Ansco Company and Eastman Kodak Company.

Start a camera club. Feature as some of the activities photographic courses, picture exhibitions, and picture competitions. Plan on certain costs in properly maintaining a camera club. Select a regular meeting space or studio that is adjacent to a photographic darkroom. See hints on organizing clubs on page 142. Visit a local camera store or write to the Ansco Company or the Camera Club and School Service of Eastman Kodak Company for more help on starting a camera club.

Chapter 9

Musical Activities

Music is a basic part of any activities program for the handicapped. Music is a means of facilitating contact and rapport with many persons who are mentally or physically disabled. This area of activity can be a valuable adjunct to treatment under skilled direction. The various moving tones and feelings found in certain selections can be soothing, stirring, exciting, or dreary. The leader of handicapped persons should therefore understand the variety of moods that can be created by music.

The resourceful director of an activities program will carefully review the equipment expenses and individualized instructional needs that are typical of many organized instrumental programs. In institutions of all types the music activities are appropriately placed and fit in as a part of balanced program offerings. However, individual music instruction, while beneficial for selected persons, may be time-consuming and not completely justifiable in a large hospital.

Certain groups like the mentally retarded respond remarkably well to rhythmic activities. Younger adults and adolescents may particularly enjoy musical quizzes and contests. Many persons of young and older age will engage in group singing. The knack of song leading is a valuable tool to be had in any recreation situation.

Music is sometimes a part of other activities like dancing and parties. In certain cases (community singing) music can profitably be made a part of other activities in any one period or session.

Various persons will show wide ranges of musical tastes all the way from jazz to classical renditions. The discriminating leader does not let his own personal musical tastes markedly affect or influence the particular style of musical appreciation interest expressed by any other listeners. Jazz music is just as absorbing to one person as are symphonic melodies to another.

Music, when carefully used, can be a vital and stirring part of an individual or group activities program for handicapped persons.

The musical activities in this chapter are highlighted in four sections: listening, music games, instrument playing, and singing.

LISTENING

Folk Music   • A • GMS • NP •

Equipment: Phonograph, phonograph records, radio, music, and literature about country music.

Satisfy the requests of some who are very interested in folk tunes and music of certain country types. Make available literature and perhaps a guitar for those who want to participate in folk and western music. Stimulate group singing around the avid guitarist who particularly enjoys this kind of music.

Suggestions: Bring into the hospital country music volunteer entertainers to put on shows for patients. Often on Saturday nights and week ends, there are country music programs on television. Recommend these programs to those who desire this kind of music.

Examples of country music and other folk music varieties are as follows:

> Folk songs of various nations
> Western "cowboy" pieces
> American folk ballads
> Square and folk dance music

Choose recorded selections of probable interest to those liking folk tunes. Check these suggestions and many other titles at local music stores:

"Turkey in the Straw"
"Volga Boatman"
"Londonderry Air"
"Irish Washerwoman"
"The Arkansas Traveler"
Negro spirituals

Purchase an album of varied folk music such as the RCA Victor 45 r.p.m. Album, "Music for the Nostalgic Traveler."

Music Appreciation   • A • GMS • NP • TB •

Equipment: Radio, phonograph, appropriate phonograph records, television set, and books about well-known musicians.

Provide an opportunity for expression of music appreciation in those so inclined. Use various media such as phonographs, books, radio, and television to make this kind of music available to listeners. Certain radio stations (especially the noncommercial educational stations) broadcast numerous recorded symphonic music programs.

Tune in the few television programs that feature classical music and opera arias. Look for those programs that are now rendering foreign language opera arias in English for greater ease in audience understanding.

With medical permission, take several handicapped persons to a symphony, opera, or concert in a nearby city. Study composers and read about their lives. Purchase a collection of pictures of famous composers for about ten cents from local record dealers or The RCA Victor Educational Services.

Build a record library of selections that appeal to novice listeners. Include music with pleasant melodies such as Grieg's "A Minor Concerto" and Mozart's "Eine Kleine Nachtmusik." Do not store records near radiators or window sills, or wherever the temperature is unusually high.

Try these pieces that are quite easy to listen to and successfully used with listening groups:

Beethoven, "Symphony No. 5, in E. Minor"
Brahms, "Lullaby, Hungarian Dances"
Debussy, "Reverie, The Little Shepherd"
Dvorak, "Humoresque"
Gershwin, "Rhapsody in Blue"
Grainger, "Country Gardens"
Grieg, "Concerto No. 1, in A Minor"
Kern, "Showboat"
Liszt, "Liebestraum"
Ponchielli, "Dance of The Hours"
Rimski-Korsakov, "Scheherazade"
Strauss, Johann, Jr., "The Beautiful Blue Danube," "Tales from the Vienna Woods"
Tschaikowsky, "Nutcracker Suite"

See *Recreation Through Music* by Charles Leonhard for additional helps on music appreciation.

MUSIC GAMES

Musical Athletics   • GMS • NP •

Equipment: Phonograph and appropriate phonograph records or band, musicians, or pianist and a sufficient number of prizes for all contestants.

The object of this music game is to guess various sports that are suggested by certain song titles. Arrange in advance the specific order of songs to be played by whatever type of accompaniment is desired. Divide the participants into two even-numbered groups. Have the song played by the band, musicians, pianist, or record player or hummed by someone. Have each person take turns and guess the sport represented in the song. Award four points for any sport so correctly identified. Award two points to the participant if he only guesses the key word descriptive of the sport. Award one point to him if he guesses the correct song title. No one participant in any one turn earns more than four points (*not* four points for the sport, plus two points for the descriptive word about the sport, plus one point for the song title).

Some song titles along with the descriptive sports words and sports are these:

1.	"*Green* Eyes"	Golf or Bowling
2.	"I *Love* You Truly"	Tennis
3.	"Brighten the *Corner* Where You Are"	Boxing
4.	"I Get A *Kick* Out of You"	Football, Kickball, Soccer and others
5.	"*Tea* for Two"	Golf
6.	"I'm *Falling* in Love With Someone"	Wrestling
7.	"I Don't Want to *Walk* Without You Baby"	Baseball, Walking
8.	"*Tramp*, Tramp, Tramp"	Walking
9.	"*Row*, Row, Row Your Boat"	Crew
10.	"After the *Ball* Is Over"	Baseball or other ball game
11.	"A Tisket, A Tasket, A *Green* and Yellow *Basket*"	Basketball, Golf or Bowling
12.	"*Skater's* Waltz"	Ice Skating or Roller Skating
13.	"One O'Clock *Jump*"	Track
14.	"*Boots* and *Saddle*"	Horseback Riding or Fishing
15.	"A *Ring* Around A Rosie"	Boxing or Wrestling

Musical Contests and Quizzes   • GMS • NP •

Equipment: Phonograph and appropriate phonograph records or band, musicians, or pianist and a sufficient number of prizes for all contestants.

The object of this game is to test musical knowledge in a game setting. Arrange in advance the specific order of songs to be played by whatever musical accompaniment is utilized.

Divide the participants into two even-numbered groups. Have the song played by the band, musicians, phonograph record, or pianist or hummed by someone. Have everyone on the sides and in turns, guess the song title. Keep score as to which side receives the greatest number of correct titles. After approximately three-quarters of an hour, award head prizes to members of the winning team and consolation prizes to members of the losing team.

Use musical quizzes such as these:

I. What color is mentioned in these songs?

1. "Old *Gray* Bonnet"
2. "Deep *Purple*"
3. "*Red* Sails in the Sunset"
4. "My Wild Irish *Rose*"
5. "*Blue* Skies"
6. "*Green* Eyes"
7. "Mood *Indigo*"
8. "*White* Cliffs of Dover"

II. What girls' names are in these songs?

1. "*Alice* Blue Gown"
2. "*Dinah*"
3. "*Rose Marie*"
4. "*Margie*"
5. "*Jeannie* With the Light Brown Hair"
6. "K-K-K-*Katy*"
7. "*Annie* Laurie"
8. "Sweet *Rosie* O'Grady"
9. "My Darling *Clementine*"
10. "*Ida*"
11. "When You and I Were Young, *Maggie*"
12. "*Juanita*"
13. "*Rosalie*"
14. "Seeing *Nelly* Home"

III. What boys' names are in these songs?

1. "*Reuben* and Rachel"
2. "I'm Just Wild About *Harry*"
3. "*Elmer's* Tune"
4. "My *Bill*"
5. "Oh, *Johnny*"
6. "*Harrigan*"
7. "*Danny* Boy"
8. "*Jim*"
9. "Steamboat *Bill*"

IV. What musical instruments are in these songs?

1. "Sweet *Potato* Piper"
2. "Two *Guitars*"
3. "The *Bells* Are Ringing For Me and My Gal"
4. "McNamara's *Band*"
5. "When the *Organ* Played O Promise Me"
6. "Sam the *Accordion* Man"
7. "Little Boy Blue Come Blow Your *Horn*"

V. What kinds of transportation are suggested by these songs?

1. "Chattanooga *Choo-Choo*"
2. "Row, Row, Row Your *Boat*"
3. "*Bicycle* Built for Two"
4. "*Ferry Boat* Serenade"
5. "In My Merry *Oldsmobile*"
6. "I've Been Working on the *Railroad*"
7. "Swing Low Sweet *Chariot*"
8. "*Sailing*, Sailing"

VI. What kind of wildlife is suggested in these classical selections?

1. "Song of the *Swallows*" (Mignon)
2. "Flight of the *Bumble Bee*" (Rimski-Korsakov)
3. "Dance of the *Grasshopper*" (Massinet)
4. "The *Cat* and the *Mouse*" (Copland)
5. "The *Swan*" (Saint-Saëns)
6. "Song of the *Flea*" (Moussorgsky)
7. "Hark Hark the *Lark*" (Schubert)
8. "The *Nightingale*" (Delius)
9. "White *Peacock*" (Griffis)
10. "I Danced with a *Mosquito*" (Liadov)

INSTRUMENT PLAYING

Bands

• C • MR • NP •

Equipment: Band instruments and music.

Refer this specialized kind of activity to a staff member who is versatile and skilled in musical direction. If the interested persons do not own their own instruments, these will have to be secured. Be certain that there will be continued use made of the instruments over a period of time before purchases are made out of hospital funds because instruments are considerably expensive.

Bring together those who play instruments such as the piano, violin, saxophone, drums, or others. Organize a band around this nucleus and have regular practices. Select a room that is at a distance from others who desire quiet so that the band sounds will not be disturbing. Provide instruction for those who need additional help. Put on musical entertainment for groups.

Determine what type of an instrumental program is desired and feasible. Consider a dance band for dances. Plan to include one of these three groupings of instruments and players in a dance band:

1. Three pieces: piano, string bass, and banjo
2. Five pieces: piano, drums, guitar, cornet, and saxophone
3. Eight pieces: piano, drums, string bass, trumpet, trombone, a tenor, and two alto saxophones

Consider orchestral music for playing and listening. In such event start with a nucleus of a piano, drums, clarinet, trumpet, and three violins. Plan regular rehearsals and occasional performances.

Investigate other types of specialized bands. Kazoo bands work particularly well with mentally retarded persons. Think about these possibilities for a group instrumental program:

1. Harmonica band
2. Kazoo band
3. Marching band
4. Stringed ensembles (combination of piano, violins and/or cellos)
5. "Sweet potato" band (ocarinas)

For sources of written information on musical instruments and bands that is available free or at modest costs write:

1. American Music Conference
2. National Association for Music Therapy
3. National Federation of Music Clubs
4. National Recreation Association

See a separate section on *Rhythm Bands* on page 163.

Drum and Bugle Corps   • NP •

Equipment: Drums, bugles, drum sticks, and batons.

Select those persons who have medical approval and appear best qualified as well as in need of this kind of experience.

Place the drum and bugle corps under the leadership of a musically inclined person who has had contact with music and marching events.

Plan practice sessions of an hour and a half at a time. Include rudiments of drumming and bugling. Stress methods of holding the sticks, beating, and accent. Try playing the drum sticks on a table top at the start. Arrange the outdoor marching periods with the thought of conditioning in mind so that some of the less physically adept will have a chance to get into marching shape and acquire poise.

After sufficient rehearsal put on a performance in or near the hospital grounds. Arrange for possible participation in nearby community festival or special holiday celebrations.

Study carefully the need of uniforms for a skilled drum and bugle corps. Remember that with any turn-over of patients there will be a uniform-fitting problem. Try to make any adopted uniform one that is economical and takes into consideration varying sizes and fits as well as that of a snappy looking drum and bugle corps. In public appearances avoid any public announcement that patients are from a neuropsychiatric hospital.

Instrument Instruction   • C • GMS • NP •

When medically advised, allow consideration in the program for individual or small group instrumental instruction. Plan for instruments that are economically available and in harmony with the musical tastes of the player. The piano is probably the most popular and certainly one of the more available instruments.

Examine various time-consuming problems before commencing individualized music instruction for the handicapped. If it is feasible and medically advisable, start music lessons for those who have some talent or ability. Assign a staff person to this who is particularly qualified in instrumental music. Seek practice rooms where there is no chance of the somewhat repetitious sounds disturbing others. Maintain a schedule of regular practice sessions with as many persons as possible. Use the silent keyboard method or other similar helps in teaching piano.

Consider the possibility of recitals or performances of those pupils who have had continued instruction over a period of time.

Rhythm Bands   • C • MR • NP •

Equipment: Rhythm instruments.

Enlist the services of any recreation staff member who is musically inclined or has a sense of rhythm. Select a "rhythm room" that is away from populated areas so that the band sessions will not disturb others. Purchase instruments or have them made by the handicapped.

Bring together those persons who might benefit from this type of group response and distribute the various instruments. Practice the handling of instruments and keeping time. Have the leader also actually use a rhythm piece while leading the group. Maintain a peppy tempo and occasionally go from player to player assisting in proper motion and rhythm. Stress band direction with gestures, rhythm, and spirited action. If a piano is accessible, have it played for the purpose of providing timing and background.

Use a combination or a few of these instruments in the rhythm band:

Bells

Bottles or jugs (played by blowing into them)

Combs and tissue paper

Cymbals and a wire brush

Drums made out of cylindrical cereal boxes with a piece of stiff paper stretched over the top

Harmonicas

Ocarinas

Piano

Sand blocks

Shakers (seeds in tin cans attached to a handle

Tambourines

Ten penny nails strung together on a holder and struck with a nail

Toy snare drums

Triangle

Two spoons to click together

Two sticks to hit together

Washboard

Wood blocks and drum sticks

For program variety in any recreation offering with the mentally retarded or regressed neuropsychiatric, start a rhythm band.

Solo Musical Performances   • A • C • GMS • MR • NP •

Periodically there will be a child or adult observed who has real singing talent. Encourage such a person to further explore and contribute his musical talent. Check with medical authority on the wisdom of the talented patient performing before a group. Refer the solo singer in some cases to the chaplain, dance band, or other individuals and groups who can accompany or advise in selected kinds of performances.

First let the skilled singer or instrument player perform informally. When the beginner is ready, let him sing before larger groups.

SINGING

Choral Groups · A · NP ·

Equipment: Music and words, piano accompaniment.

Secure a skilled vocalist or choral director to assist in leading this type of activity. Select a core of interested and able singers for the choral group. Practice selections with the piano as accompaniment.

If desired, let the vocal group become a glee club, chorus, or choir. If a choir, cooperate closely with a chaplain or religious leader for maximum benefit and purpose. Use selections that are generally appealing and easy to render.

Try a mixed chorus as a popular form of group singing. Invite fifteen or twenty men and women to join in starting this satisfying kind of vocal presentation. Secure specially written music for mixed choruses. Note the broad range of pitch in combined male and female voices. When there are not both men and women available, try a glee club for men *or* women.

Consider the enjoyment of trios and quartets for the handicapped. See that choral groups and others give public performances. Check with local music stores about appropriate music.

Community Singing · A · C · GMS · NP ·

Try community singing as a change of pace in the auditorium or other gathering places along with scheduled activities. Lead singing in an impromptu manner at any time or place that seems logical and beneficial to the group's morale. Keep the songs from becoming too boisterous or disturbing to others.

Work community singing in with events like dances, parties, motion pictures, and other entertainment. Prolonged group singing by itself soon loses the interest of participants.

Secure piano accompaniment and song sheets for a more formal and complete community singing atmosphere. Engage a song leader who is demonstrative and skilled in community singing. Use gestures and a loud melodic voice to inspire the singing of others. Include solos and group renditions for variety.

Choose songs that are not too depressing, too reminiscent of home, nor too overcharged emotionally. Terminate the period when participants are observed to tire.

Occasionally feature rounds or motion songs. Rounds generally require skilled leadership. Some rounds are "Three Blind Mice" and "Row Your Boat." Motion songs are particularly enjoyed by children. Some selections for children or adults are: "Down By the Old Mill Stream," "I'm a Little Teapot," "Little Red Caboose," and "My Hat."

"My Hat"

My hat it has three corners;
Three corners has my hat;
And if it didn't have three corners,
It wouldn't be my hat.

(Motions to above verses)

On "hat" touch top of head. On "has" hold right elbow out to right with hand to right shoulder. On "three" touch left hand to right hand, right elbow and right shoulder, in that order.

Use these and other similar songs in the group singing program:

"Alouette"
"America the Beautiful"
"Are You Sleeping?"
"Bicycle Built for Two"
"Comin' Round the Mountain"
"Dinah"
"Down by the Old Mill Stream"
"East Side, West Side"
"God Bless America"
"Goodnight Ladies"
"I'm Looking Over a Four Leaf Clover"
"John Brown's Baby Has a Cold Upon Its Chest"
"Oh! Susanna"
"When You Wore a Tulip"

Chapter 10

Nature and Outing Activities

THE APPRECIATION and understanding of natural phenomena is indeed an economical and creative phase of recreation for the handicapped. Activities that take place indoors or outdoors with growing things or any phase of the natural environment constitute nature recreation. Outings or excursions such as fishing, picnicking, and orienteering may involve additional skill or related pursuits, but basically depend upon natural habitat and are therefore classified in this major activity area.

Nature recreation can make a unique contribution to the recreation program for the handicapped. A developing plant, even if it is only a weed, can provide a spark of life and renewed faith for the tubercular, neuropsychiatric, and general medical and surgical patient. The convenience of gardening, bird study, and star viewing from the bedside makes them worthy of consideration in any recreation program for the hospitalized. The prevocational values of gardening further justify this pursuit in some form for various disabled groups.

Nature activities probably require the least amount of financial outlay as compared to most events in a recreation program. This practical aspect further warrants inclusion of nature and outings in the recreation program.

Unfortunately some persons think that nature activities can interest only the effeminate and the childish. This misconception further encourages the attitude that adults should not be bothered with "delicate" and "dainty" things like bird watching and dish gardening. Such an approach represents lack of mature understanding. Personnel who work with the handicapped will encounter this kind of fallacious thinking by some, but should endeavor to include nature as an integral part of the program. The program possibilities in nature are so vast and broad that nearly every individual should have an interest in some facet of nature.

The wise naturalist does not claim to have a complete academic command of every fact that concerns birds, flowers, gardening, insects, rocks, stars, and trees. It is best for him to be honest in admitting the lack of knowledge on some specific phase of nature rather than to bluff an uncertain answer to a question. Honesty will be respected more than unsure answers. However, the nature leader should learn as much as he can about the fundamentals in natural life.

Nature and Outing Activities is divided into the following activity classifications: nature crafts, nature games, nature activities indoors, and nature activities outdoors.

NATURE CRAFTS

Bird Feeder   • A • C • GMS • TB •

Equipment: One piece of soft wood, ¼ inch thick by 2 inches by 12 inches, and two pieces of soft wood, ¼ inch thick by 2 inches by 8 inches (or venetian blind slats); one piece of soft wood, 2 inches thick by 8 inches by 12 inches (platform); two pieces of soft wood, 1½ inches by 10 inches (supports); nails; hammer; saw; and bird feed mixture of crushed corn, sunflower seeds, and other seeds. Try cut-up apple, buckwheat, coconut meat, dog biscuit, and suet for a variety of feed mixture. Instead of the typical bird feed seed mixture, purchase all sunflower seeds. Secure this from a local feed dealer and buy a large quantity (entire winter's estimated supply) for a proportionately lower price. Sunflower seeds are a bit more expensive than usual bird feed mixtures, but are large and seem to last longer than other types. Sunflower seeds are preferred by some of the favorite garden birds (chickadees, nut-hatches, woodpeckers, cardinals, gold-finches, juncos, and others) and are not as popular with sparrows.

Nail the two ¼ inch by 2 inch by 8 inch pieces of wood (or venetian blind slats) to the two ends of the platform so that an edge is ½ inch to 1 inch above the platform. Similarly nail the one ¼ inch by 2 inch by 12 inch piece of wood (or

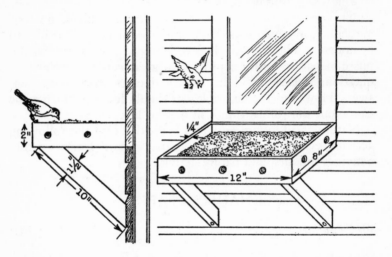

venetian blind slat) on the long side of the platform. Saw the supports so that they will smoothly attach to the platform and the side of house or building. Nail the supports to the bottom of the platform and then place it in position under-neath and outside window. Nail the platform complete with supports to the window ledge. Place in it a supply of bird feed mixture and enjoy birds that come to the window sill. Once feeding is commenced in winter months, never stop it as birds become dependent on a source of food and might die if this supply is suddenly removed.

This can be a source of real joy to one confined to a bed. Exercise patience in viewing and moving around so that birds do not become frightened. If possible, select a window ledge that is not near a tree branch so that squirrels will be unable to reach the feeder and devour its contents.

Leaf Spatter Prints   • A • C • GMS • NP •

Equipment: Old toothbrush, any color of ink, leaves, straight pins, old table knife, white paper, and newspaper.

Place a large sheet of newspaper on a flat surface. Select a leaf and put it on a sheet of white paper over the newspaper. Pin the lobes of the leaf so that it is as flat as possible on the sheet. Have the pins bend slightly toward the center of leaf. Insert the toothbrush into the ink. Hold the inked toothbrush near the leaf stem and slowly pull the knife blade across the bristles toward the body. Spatter several times over and around the leaf outline on the paper. Let the ink dry and remove pins, thereby exposing the outline of a leaf on the spatter print.

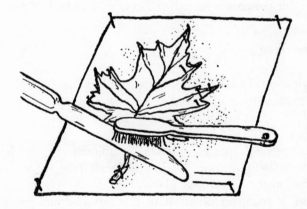

Variations: Use any colored liquid instead of ink, and use several colors on parts or all of the same print. A small piece of screen may be used in place of the table knife to draw the brush over. Make a scrapbook out of spatter prints.

Place leaf underneath a piece of onion skin paper and lightly color over it with a green crayon. Create interesting effects with pencils also.

NATURE GAMES

Bird, Beast, or Fish   • C • GMS • TB •

Have the players sit in a circle formation with one designated as "it" standing in the center. It points to a player and says the word, "bird," or "beast," or "fish." This person must then name an animal in that category before it counts to ten. If this player does not succeed he may be eliminated or placed into another game. The player called upon may not name an animal that was named before in the same game. The last one in the game serves as "it" for the next game.

For variety, add or use such groupings as flowers, rocks, insects, trees, fruits, vegetables, planets, or cars. Play this game with patients who may be confined to beds.

Lollipop Tree   • C • MR •

Equipment: One or two lollipops with safety paper handles per person, a string of thread about 6 to 9 inches long each for each lollipop, and large trees or bushes with low-hanging branches.

Select several species of trees on adjoining grounds. Tie threads to lollipop loop handles and carefully hang on low branches in inconspicuous places.

Invite a group of children to this out-of-doors game and use the lollipop tree activity as a culmination of or in conjunction with another event. Use some of these activities along with the lollipop tree for children: Low organized games, picnic, rock hunt, treasure hunt or nature scavenger hunt.

Tell the children that there is one lollipop (or two, as case may be) to each and that they are to look for them on certain kinds of trees.

Nature Scavenger Hunt   • C • GMS • NP •

Equipment: A list of nature articles for each participant, two containers, and prizes for all participants.

Make up in advance a list of common nature articles that are found in the nearby area. Specify the names of articles that can be conveniently carried. Remember proper conservation principles and do not encourage the destruction of vital or valuable wildlife. Consider these items for inclusion on a nature scavenger hunt list:

Piece of basalt	Spruce needle
Elm tree leaf	Oak tree twig
Maple tree leaf	An acorn cup
Box elder tree leaf	Four leaf clover
Dandelion green	Pine cone
Agate	Piece of granite
Clover in bloom	

Duplicate enough lists so there is one for each participant.

Divide the people into two teams. Give a container for the articles to each team. Distribute the scavenger hunt lists to participants and tell them that they are to go out by teams within a certain area and look for articles described on the list. The nature articles are to be collected by teams and returned within a specified length of time to the same point.

Each team upon return displays the articles they located. A final count of correctly collected articles is made with the team who has the highest number declared as winners. Distribute prizes to the winning and losing groups. Use the nature scavenger hunt as a culmination to discussions dealing with nature study and identification.

Variations: Try a scavenger hunt with players (instead of two teams) competing against one another, or have this activity indoors with a greatly modified list of objects that have been hidden in advance about a gymnasium or day room floor.

Nature Scrambles   • GMS • NP • TB •

Equipment: A pencil and sheet of paper with scrambled words for each participant.

List some of these nature scrambles on sheets of paper. Pass out the slips to persons and tell them to rearrange the letters so that a nature word (bird, animal, flower, or vegetable) is formed. Allow a limited length of time and note the ones who have correctly completed the most words. Applaud the winners and compliment them for their abilities.

Bird Scramble I

1. calaindr
2. weehot
3. pipchign woarrsp
4. yllowe haeedd bribckald
5. rete wlslawo
6. anbr llawswo
7. akwthgihn

Bird Scramble II

1. meynhic wfits
2. parowsr akhw
3. rpuple aritmn
4. diekrlel
5. lubiderb
6. yswno low
7. imreaadwokl

Animal Scramble

1. eiuopprcn
2. ooccnar
3. rvbaee
4. erab
5. amuksrt
6. nkmi
7. britab
8. rede
9. lrsrquei
10. ksukn
11. xfo

Vegetable Scramble

1. noino
2. bbcaaeg
3. dpsu
4. ttmooa
5. ape
6. abne
7. tebe
8. ptiunr
9. rrcota
10. rebmucuc

Flower Scramble

1. wefosnlur
2. oers
3. ypopp
4. weest eap

5. offaddil
6. bubellel
7. rcnatanio
8. strutanmiu

The correct answers to the puzzles are as follows:

Bird Scramble I

1. cardinal
2. towhee
3. chipping sparrow
4. yellow headed blackbird
5. tree swallow
6. barn swallow
7. nighthawk

Bird Scramble II

1. chimney swift
2. sparrow hawk
3. purple martin
4. killdeer
5. bluebird
6. snowy owl
7. meadowlark

Vegetable Scramble

1. onion
2. cabbage
3. spud
4. tomato
5. pea
6. bean
7. beet
8. turnip
9. carrot
10. cucumber

Animal Scramble

1. porcupine
2. raccoon
3. beaver
4. bear
5. muskrat
6. mink
7. rabbit
8. deer
9. squirrel
10. skunk
11. fox

Flower Scramble

1. sunflower
2. rose
3. poppy
4. sweet pea
5. daffodil
6. bluebell
7. carnation
8. nasturtium

Variation: Divide the players into two sides. Pass out scramble sheets and have sides compete against each other in a specified period of time.

Nature Treasure Hunt
• C • NP •

Equipment: Treasure hunt direction notes and treasure for group consumption or interest.

Scout the adjacent outdoor area for an itinerary that is in a nature setting, not far from the home base nor full of natural hazards and rough terrain. Write out in advance a group of notes that require identification of some specimen in nature. Fold notes, place them in envelopes, and hide them near selected nature objects. Examples of the first three notes are as follows (directions to leader in parentheses):

1. "Go to the big elm tree at the fork of the road." (Hand first note to the group.)
2. "Stop at the first zinnia garden on the road." (Place this note at base of big elm tree mentioned in number one.)
3. "Walk in an easterly direction to the first pile of several basalt stones." (Place this note inside of and near edge of zinnia garden mentioned in number two.)

Place ten to twenty notes about the grounds. Have last note read something like this:

"Go to nearest lilac bush, underneath which you will see a treasure. Quietly bring the treasure to the recreation director."

Have a treasure located at the end of the hunt. Put a variety of leaves, a box of caramels, or fruit in a box for the treasure.

To commence the activity, have the group start out together. Tell them to go individually or in small groups from note to note, being sure that they replace notes exactly where they were found. When the treasure has been located and the whole group finally reassembled, have them identify tree leaves from the treasure box.

Tree Tag   • C • MR • NP •

Equipment: Several different species of trees in the same general vicinity.

Choose someone to be "it." Tell the group that a certain type of tree (box elder, red oak, maple, poplar) is the "safe" tree. Explain that no one can be tagged when in contact with the kind of tree (not necessarily all players touching the same tree) that has been so designated by the leader. The object is to be tagged "it" as few times as possible. Commence the game after the rules have been explained.

Periodically change the kind of tree so that players will have to get to a tree that is "safe." If the player is caught by the one indicated as "it" while he is away from a "safe" tree, he is then the new "it."

Variation: Use objects other than trees as the "safe" places. Examples are large rocks, telephone poles, corners of buildings, and bushes. This variation works very satisfactorily with mentally retarded children.

NATURE ACTIVITIES INDOORS

Box Gardening • A • C • GMS • MR • NP • TB •

Equipment: Pumpkin and gourd seeds; two softwood boards, ¼ inch thick by 18 inches by 4 inches; two softwood boards, ¼ inch thick by 5 inches by 4 inches; one softwood board, ¼ inch thick by 18 inches by 5½ inches; 2 dozen small nails; hammer; four cups sand; four cups small pebbles; fifteen cups rich black dirt, and water. Prior to assemblage of box sides, measure the window sill where box is to rest. If necessary, rearrange sizes of the box pieces so that the completed window box will exactly fit the sill.

Place the pieces of wood together so they make a box. Pound nails into the wood edges so that a sturdy box is formed. Cover the inside bottom of box with sand and the small stones for good drainage. Place the black dirt over this. Plant two rows of the gourd and pumpkin seeds. Place box of dirt and seeds on the window sill outside of patient's window and watch the blossoming vines over a period of days. Periodically water the planted seeds.

Try herb gardening in a box with these herbs: basil, lavender, mint, parsley, rosemary, sage, savory, sorrel, sweet marjoram, and thyme.

Organize discussions of the gardens of different patients. Suggest study and reading about flower origins (tulips from Turkey, poppies from China).

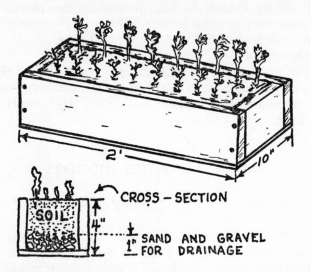

CROSS – SECTION

SOIL

4"

SAND AND GRAVEL
FOR DRAINAGE

Variation: Obtain a variety of flower seeds. Place the varieties of seeds in small bottles (easily obtainable in hospital settings) or flat-bottomed paper cups.

Some handicapped persons are interested in the color, aesthetics, and arrangement of flowers. Centerpieces and table decorations can be made out of flowers by patients. Secure flowers, branches, leaves, and vases for those who show an interest in flower arranging. See *Flower Arrangement, A Hobby for All* by Matilda Rogers for additional ideas and plans to follow in arrangements.

Dish Gardening   • A • C • GMS • MR • NP • TB •

Equipment: Large sauce dish, small sponge, water, flax or radish seeds, small pebbles, and small amount of rich black dirt.

Place the dampened sponge and a small amount of water in the dish. Sprinkle flax seed over the sponge. Notice that within several days the seeds will be green.

Cut off the top two inches of a carrot. Place the top in a dish and surround carrot with small stones. Cover with water.

Watch the small fern like branches that soon appear from top of carrot.

Collect seeds from various citris fruits (oranges, lemons, and grapefruit) along with apple seeds. Plant them in rich black dirt. Water soil periodically and watch the appearance of small plants in several days. Use these as centerpieces for dining tables.

Plant a sweet-potato half in a jar of water. Watch the plant growth that soon comes from the sweet potato. Place an avocado seed on top of a jar of water. Watch it shoot into growth.

Try bottle gardens for such plants as small begonias, philodendron, African violets, and others.

Fish Aquariums   • A • C • GMS • MR • NP • TB •

Equipment: Rectangular tank aquarium, selected fish, several small snails, plants for aquarium, fish food, and water.

Fill tank with clean water and place the plants in water. Put the snails and fish in the water. The plant life adds to the beauty, absorbs carbon dioxide, produces oxygen, and helps in hiding small fish from any cannibalistic adult fish. The snails clean up uneaten food.

Choose the more common fish like goldfish or guppies at first. Later on, select sword-tails, mollienisia, platys, and others.

Place the aquarium on a sturdy, shaded (from the direct sunlight) table underneath a light bulb in a reflector shade. This aids in better viewing of the fish and provides additional needed heat in the aquarium water.

Feed the fish commercially purchased fish food in strict accordance with directions on the container regarding quantity and frequency of feeding. Secure a variety of fish food for some change. Try these possibilities:

> Worms
> Ant larvae
> Egg yolk (finely crumbled, cooked)
> Green vegetables (boiled)
> Insects (not those killed by insecticides)

Variation: Make a terrarium out of a rectangular glass tank. Place rich black dirt, varied plant life, and possibly some small animals (lizards, toads, and worms) in the tank. Observe growth of the plant life and activity of the land animals. Water the plant life and provide some food for the animals. After the terrarium has served its purpose, be sure to return any animals to their natural habitat.

Lapidary Work   • C • GMS • NP •

Equipment: Lapidary machine, stones, and electric current.

In a geographical area that has various rocks and minerals, this activity is a natural culmination of rock collecting. First, cut the stones on the diamond-toothed wheel of the lapidary machine in a shape desired for mounting or other display. Be certain that the participant has a steady hand and good eyesight before allowing him to work at this rather time-consuming activity. Affix the newly cut stone to a short stick and smooth off, as well as polish, the stone on a lapidary wheel. This activity is one that requires patience and an avid interest in rocks. It provides hours of enjoyment for the "rockhound."

Carefully study the directions that come with various lapidary outfits as the methods of operation sometimes vary. A lapidary machine will occupy a 30 inch square table top. Be sure that it is securely bolted to a heavy table top before operating it. The initial investment for a lapidary outfit is fifty dollars and up (including motor) but represents an investment that only need be replenished with cutting wheels. Some manufacturers call their lapidary outfits "gem makers." Purchase one of the better known lapidary outfits through Sears, Roebuck and Company stores or from the B and I Manufacturing Company. Purchase cutting wheels (sometimes called diamond blades) from the same sources. A few of the larger hobby stores carry lapidary outfits in stock or know where to procure them.

Nature Notebooks   • A • C • GMS • MR • NP •

Equipment: Scrapbook, paste, transparent gummed tape, and articles or items about nature.

Color and finish the cover. Make plywood covers for additional sturdiness and natural appearance. Decide upon the best manner in which to mount the articles in the scrapbook. Include any of the following nature items:

Bird pictures	Nature observation notes
Conservation stamps	Nature stamps
Crayon leaf prints	Newspaper clippings
Diaries of hikes	Photographs
Mounted leaves	Poetry
Nature clippings	Pressed flowers
Nature drawings	Spatter prints

Use nature notebooks as means of arranging and displaying nature articles and interests.

Weather Forecasting   • A • C • GMS • NP • TB •

Equipment: A weather station kit; pencil; paper; five 12-inch white cloth squares; five poles or dowel sticks 2½ feet long; roll of heavy string; staples; stapler; scissors; black crayon; red crayon; blue crayon; and a view of the out-of-doors and sky.

Purchase a weather station kit with parts and instructions for construction of a weather vane and barometer. Make these weather pieces in accordance with directions in the kit. Place the weather vane outside the bedroom or nearby window along with a thermometer.

Make a weather chart with spaces for daily recordings of the climatic conditions. Insert daily figures and statements as to the status of the weather and estimates of forecasts.

Use additional helps in predicting weather conditions. These conditions tend to indicate either fair or stormy weather:

Fair Weather

Cloudless skies   Steadily rising barometer
Heavy dew at night   Red sunset

Stormy Weather

No dew at night   Falling barometer
Atmosphere muggy and sticky   Red sunrise
Smoke not rising straight in air   Gray or dull sunset

WEATHER FLAGS

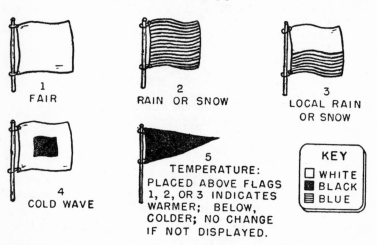

Color the cloth squares with crayons like weather flag diagrams. Tie each cloth square with string to the flag poles. Use staples and stapler to more permanently affix the cloth square to each pole. Display the correct weather flag (announcing weather for the day) outside of window or other spot for benefit of others. Explain or publicize in the school or institutional newspaper the meaning of various weather flags. Following are three sayings about weather. Those interested might collect others:

"Rainbow at night—Sailor's delight.
Rainbow at morning—Sailors take warning."

"A ring around the moon means rain.
The larger the ring, the nearer the rain."

"When the clouds appear like rocks and towers,
The earth's refreshed by frequent showers."

Secure for the advanced weather enthusiast copies of daily weather maps from local newspapers or through the United States Weather Bureau. The latter weather maps are available for a subscription cost from the Superintendent of Documents, United States Government Printing Office, Washington, D.C.

NATURE ACTIVITIES OUTDOORS

Bait Casting (Angling)   • GMS • NP •

Equipment: Fishing rod, reel, and wooden weight (one outfit for each participant). Seek the assistance of volunteers in procuring bait casting equipment.

Mark or place a target on the ground or in a large room within casting distance of the participant. Make the target about thirty inches in diameter, like a rubber bicycle tire.

Talk to those men and women who appear to be interested in fly fishing. If they are real fishermen, seek their enthusiasm and participation.

In testing (angling) for accuracy, select five rings and place them about five feet apart. Let the caster have two casts at each circle. Allow eight minutes for this series of ten casts. Count up the number of bull's-eyes (bait in center of ring) made by casters.

Test for distance casts by placing target at ordinary range and moving it farther out as any caster exceeds the distance. "Ordinary range" may be 125 feet from the casting spot. The weight used by each caster will determine distances which could go as far as 125 to 375 feet away.

Bird Watching   • *A* • *C* • *GMS* • *TB* •

Equipment: Bird book, bird card, pencil, and field glasses.

Have the participant read over the descriptions of birds and their habits in a colored, illustrated bird book. After the bird watcher is familiar with some of the common local birds, he is ready to view birds more extensively in their natural habitat. Go to a garden or bird trail in a somewhat wooded area for best results. If the participant is unable to go out-of-doors, have him view birds through clean windows. Use a set of field glasses of three to eight power for viewing of birds either through windows or outside. Keep track of all observed birds in any one observation by checking their names off on a bird card. Study the birds so that they may be identified through color, size, and habits.

Birds seem to be especially prevalent in spring months and during the early morning and afternoon hours. Tree leaves are not full-sized in the early spring, and do not obscure the viewing of birds.

Organize a bird hike during the early morning (5 to 7 A.M.) and secure permission to go on such a walk with an informed leader. Eat lightly and dress warmly prior to departure. Emphasize the importance of patience and quietness in waiting for and observing birds. Movements on the ground or in the brush or noise of any kind can frighten birds away. Expect to see twenty-five or more different species of birds during an early morning bird hike in the spring of the year. Look for varied landscape that has ponds, streams, swamps, bushes, berries, trees, and hills for best results. The use of field glasses, pencil, bird check list, and a bird identification book makes the observation trip more enjoyable.

Learn more about birds through drawing birds and building bird replicas. Select a concise bird book in color such as *Birds* by Herbert Zim and Ira Gabrielson. For clear, understandable pictures, look for those that are hand painted in color and produced in books like *Birds*.

Take an artificial bird call along on bird hikes. Buy these for approximately one dollar each from larger stationery stores. They are small round wooden pieces that contain a pewter center which squeaks like a real bird when the metal key is turned. If these are not available for purchase locally, contact an organization such as the National Audubon Society for information on their procurement.

Fishing   • A • C • MR • NP •

Equipment: Bamboo pole, fishing line, bobber, hook, live minnows or angleworms for bait, and fishing license.

Look over any fishing licenses of the persons who are going fishing and be certain they comply with local or state fishing and conservation laws. Locate a lake or stream that is stocked with fish. Ascertain whether fishing can best take place from a boat or shore. Shore fishing is by far the safer and wiser when handicapped persons are involved. If handicapped persons are taken on water in a boat, secure demonstrated proof that they can swim proficiently. Check to see that the staff person in the boat has qualified in senior life saving with The

American Red Cross or other similar national agency. Place a life jacket on everyone who goes in a boat on the water. Let the fishermen bait their hooks and place them in water at the appropriate depth. Keep only those fish that are within the legal catch limit. Have a fish fry upon return from a fishing expedition.

Check with the State Department of Conservation about any special fishing laws. Some states provide free fishing licenses for persons over sixty years of age and those living on relief funds.

Orienteering   • C • GMS • NP •

Equipment: Small compass, map of local area, prearranged signals, orienteering sheets of directions, paper, and pencil.

Study nearby grounds and outdoor wooded areas. Make a map of the area in which the orienteering experience is to take place. If stone or stick signals are to be used, place them in the logical places for the orienteering hike. Allocate between one-fourth and one mile for the planned hike. Determine directions, starting point, and destination as well as any treasure (refreshments, cigarettes, or other acceptable prizes in sufficient quantity for all participants) that is deemed necessary. Mimeograph or write on sheets of paper any sig-

```
       ORIENTEERING  DIRECTION
                SHEET
        1.  N 2 Pines
        2.  E Cross path-dandelions
        3.  S 1st Maple
        4.  SE 10 yds-rock pile
        5.  Pick up basalt-retain
        6.  N 1st Boxelder
        7.  SW Lilacs
        8.  N Poplar
        9.  Hospital is E
       10.  SE side of creek
       11.  E largest Oak
       12.  Face hospital entrance
       13.  Write compass reading
       14.  Return to leader
       15.  Finis !
```

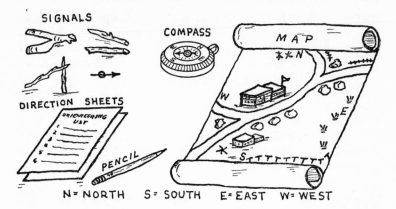

nal symbols that are to be used together with their meanings. Also include any directions, compass readings, signals, or landmarks that are necessary for the orienteering hike. Prior to orienteering, explain how to read a compass. Schedule practice readings on natural terrain around hospital grounds.

Assemble the group and explain rules for the hike. Indicate that they are to follow the compass readings, signals, and landmarks to destination, the first one there being the winner. Pass out orienteering direction sheets, maps, and compasses, if such are to be used. At a given signal, start group out on the orienteering trip.

Adapt orienteering to the needs of the general medical and surgical patient by conducting similar contests and walks in a limited yard area (three hundred square yards or less), using modifications of orienteering and much shorter distances.

Write to American Orienteering Service for additional information on orienteering. Illustrations of map symbols, signs, and trail marks are located in the official Boy Scout *Handbook for Boys*. Make up an orienteering direction sheet. Note this sample plan with guides for the participant to follow. Vary the direction sheet according to local terrain and geographic conditions.

The letters N, S, E, and W, when used separately or in combination with one another, mean: North, South, East, and West. Start at the institution's main entrance and walk N to 2 Pine trees. Head E. Cross pathway and look for group of dande-lion plants. Go S until first maple tree is encountered. At this point go SE approximately 10 yards to a small pile of rocks. Pick up a small piece of basalt and retain the same. Go N to first box elder tree. Go SW to clump of lilac bushes. Head N to poplar tree. Hospital is now directly E of you. Walk to the SE side of creek and then E to largest oak tree near red brick building. Stand directly facing the main entrance. Jot down compass reading at this point and return to recreation office or group leader at starting point.

Picnicking   • A • C • GMS • MR • NP • TB •

Equipment: Refreshments or sufficient food for a meal, an appropriate out-of-doors location for a picnic, and any needed equipment for selected games.

Select a date, place, and time that is appropriate for the size and kind of group. Be certain that there are toilets and drinking water at the picnic site. Check with personnel re-garding clearance for specified persons to attend the picnic. Arrange for suitable transportation to the picnic spot. Publi-cize facts about the picnic location, time, and other features. Check with the dietitian or food department about refresh-ments or the meal to be eaten at the outing. Work out a plan of activities to be followed at the picnic. A logical sequence of events from start to finish might be in this order: arrival; get acquainted and mixer period; races, relays and games; re-freshments; community singing or quiet activity; and de-parture. Secure permission from the owner of the picnic site to use the grounds. Permission assures the necessary space and facilities for the number in the group. If in doubt as to where to go, check with nearby community park departments.

Look on the specified pages for program ideas to use in planning a picnic:

Bean Bag Throw (page 238)   Charades (page 117)
Bird, Beast, or Fish (page 172)   Community Singing (page 165)
Bird Watching (page 184)   Croquet (page 240)

In the event that the picnic includes the noon lunch hour, plan for an outing period of five hours or less. Vary the time according to the different needs of the type of handicaps. Plan on a longer time period for the neuropsychiatric. Schedule picnics over the evening meal hour for not more than four hours.

If a full meal is not planned, arrange for light refreshments such as a weiner roast or desert. Allow handicapped persons to cook weiners and marshmallows over a fire. Secure dry wood, paper, and matches for a fire.

After all arrangements have been made and checked, take the picnickers, food, and needed equipment to the picnic site. Request physicians, nurses, teachers, or ward personnel to accompany the group to the picnic in addition to necessary recreation leaders. Carry out preplanned activities. Afterwards clean up the grounds area.

In case of rain, plan an alternate indoor event or set-up for eating, or have an alternate date in mind for the picnic.

Try this menu for a different and interesting cook-out: punch, shish kabobs, rolls and butter, salad, and sumores.

Shish Kabobs

Make shish kabobs out of one-inch cubes of beef, veal, liver, ham, apple or tomato wedges, bacon, mushrooms, or onions in any combination. Fish may be substituted for meat. Alternate favorite combinations on a skewer or long green stick and broil over the campfire. Slip the cooked shish kabob onto a hot buttered roll.

Sumores

Place a square of plain milk chocolate on a graham cracker. Roast a marshmallow on a long green stick (or a straightened-out wire coat hanger) over the fire. Slip the roasted marsh-mallow off stick and onto the chocolate square. Place another graham cracker over the marshmallow and press together like a sandwich. The hot marshmallow tends to melt the choco-late between the crackers. This produces a rich and tasty desert.

Remember to use special care during summer weather with all food that should be refrigerated to prevent spoilage and food poisoning.

Try to include as many persons as possible in a picnic activity. This group occasion is festive and invariably repre-sentative of a good time in the picnicker's mind. When plan-ning a special picnic consider these ideas:

1. *Box social:* each patient bring a box of lunch and eat with a partner of the opposite sex. Partners may be determined by names drawn from a hat.
2. *Corn and potato roast:* roast corn and potatoes in jackets underground, covered and surrounded by hot coals and stones.
3. *Holiday picnic:* celebrate a holiday such as Independence Day or Memorial Day.
4. *Pow-wow:* have an evening weiner and marshallow roast around the campfire.
5. *Watermelon feed:* Feature quantities of ice-cold water-melons.

See *Social Games for Recreation* by Evelyne Borst and Elmer D. Mitchell for additional suggestions on picnics.

Rocks and Minerals   • A • C • NP •

Equipment: A book on rocks and a cloth bag for collecting purposes.

Visit roadsides, sand piles, gravel pits, or other places where rocks are found in or outside grounds. Look for unusual varie-ties of rocks and collect them in the cloth bag. Search for agates (orange, brown, red, or white with bands, stripes, and dots). Seek new specimens after rains when new rocks have been uncovered. Study the rocks located and try to identify them according to descriptions in the rock and mineral book.

Purchase model airplane colorless cement or other strong glue and affix selected rocks to a cardboard or wood board. Identify the small mounted rocks and glue the appropriate labels beneath the specimens. Also try mounting rocks in flat boxes (ask volunteers to secure stocking cardboard boxes, possibly from department stores). Use the box cover to enclose the mounted specimens for more permanent preservation.

Go on a rock hunt in an area that has varied quantity of different rocks. Use this as a follow-up on the study of common rocks. Provide each patient with a small cloth bag or heavy paper bag for collecting the specimens and the list of rocks to be found. Use rocks that are common to the local area. One sample list is cited:

1. Basalt 2. Porphery 3. Agate 4. Quartz 5. Limestone
6. Sandstone 7. Conglomerate 8. Fossil

Cut and polish selected stones on a lapidary outfit (see "Lapidary Work" activity on page 180). Purchase a rock tumbler for the experienced enthusiast. Place agates and other attractive smaller stones along with the proper proportion of tumbling compounds into tumbler. Operate the turning tumbler in accordance with directions for about five full days and nights continuously. Observe beautiful polished stones after the tumbling process. Secure more information on tumbling from mineral and gem publications. Prices for tumbling machines (less the necessary electric motor) average between sixty-five and one-hundred dollars. Check with local dealers as to sources of tumbling machines. Ask them for literature describing them along with facts on various kinds.

Write to the United States Geological Survey or the United States Bureau of Mines for surveys and publications on rocks and minerals.

Star Gazing   • A • C • GMS • NP • TB •

Equipment: An area suitable for viewing skies, a book on stars, and a pair of field glasses (six to eight power), or a small telescope.

Check with the proper authority regarding the possibility of star gazing for any handicapped person who expresses an interest in natural phenomena. If this does not conflict with treatment schedules, proper rest, or comfort, procure additional resources. Make a colored illustrated book on stars available to the patient. Encourage his study and review of it.

During an evening when the sky is clear, suggest a star viewing period from the home, school, or hospital window or out-of-doors, if this is practical. A range of fifty to one-hundred and sixty degrees of sky can be seen from the average window. Stress comfort in viewing such as a reclining chair, couch, or several pillows on the bed, or a blanket spread on the ground if out-of-doors. Wear warm clothing if the activity is taking place outside.

Start first with learning about ten stars and ten constellations (groups of stars in sky that form imaginary pictures). Some of the constellations to look for in certain seasons are:

Spring	*Summer*
Boötes, the Herdsman	The Eagle, Arrow, and Dolphin
Gemini, the Twins	Hercules
Leo, the Lion	Scorpio, the Scorpion

Autumn	*Winter*
Andromeda	Canis Major and Minor
Auriga, the Charioteer	Orion, the Hunter
Perseus	Taurus, the Bull

Schedule a trip to a nearby observatory (where there are large telescopes and professional astronomers) or planetarium (where images of planets and stars are projected on a darkened dome). Take only individuals who have demonstrated interest in astronomical subjects.

Form an astronomy club of those who are especially interested in stars and planets. Pursue with this group such projects as telescope making, museum trips, astronomy lectures, and stellar photography.

Read astronomy publications about eclipses, comets, meteors (shooting stars), and aurora borealis (northern lights). Publicize the occurrance of any of these phenomena and urge observation by as many as is feasible.

Purchase a fully illustrated guide on the stars. One recommended source book is: *Stars*, by H. S. Zim and R. H. Baker. For those interested in photography get R. Newton Mayall and Margaret L. Mayall's book *Skyshooting: Hunting the Stars with Your Camera*. Purchase a star chart. This cardboard device gives the position of major stars and constellations according to times of the day and month. Purchase one from the American Nature Association for approximately a dollar or less. See *Nature* Magazine for practical program helps in star study.

Check with a local public library or science museum for information they may have on astronomy clubs in the area of the hospital. Inquire if planetariums or observatories are located nearby that interested handicapped persons might visit.

Chapter 11

Social Recreation Activities

ONE REASON FOR the existence of recreation programs for the handicapped is to provide socialization. Cooperative understanding and socially acceptable habits can be enhanced through a group activities program. Activities of a game and social nature that do not involve strenuous physical effort may be defined as social recreation. Often these pursuits stress participation of groups of both sexes.

The gregarious and carefree spirit of recreation is often best captured in parties and table games. "Losing one's self" can be accomplished in a social atmosphere in which there is absorption and fascination in the activity. It is here that therapeutic climate is realized and a degree of receptivity observed toward other medical treatment.

There are many card games and quizzes that might be suitable for certain individuals. As additional activities are introduced, the leader is urged to use care in adapting them to the intellectual and comprehension levels of the handicapped.

In activities like bingo, bunco, and playing card games, the elements of chance may give rise to gambling. Consider the policy of the home or institution before commencing games involving the element of chance. Gambling and participation merely for the sake of winning prizes or money make recreation into a business and not creative pleasure.

Mixers, guessing contests, and quizzes can often be used along with other events. One of the tasks of a leader is to get persons acquainted and relaxed in a social situation. Well-directed mixers and ice-breakers can help the disabled gain courage and self-confidence in a group. This feeling of ease in the presence of others is especially needed by some types of neuropsychiatric and general medical and surgical patients.

Social recreation for the handicapped requires skillful direction and vivacious leadership. Activities at a party include mixers, quizzes, and a combination of other games. Mature and personality-building recreations contribute to growth and adjustment.

Materials within this chapter are divided into four categories: contests, mixers, party activities, and table games.

For additional games and parties see *Social Games for Recreation* by Evelyne Borst and Elmer D. Mitchell and *The Book of Games for Boys and Girls* by Evelyne Borst.

CONTESTS

Guessing Contests   • A • C • GMS • NP • TB •

Equipment: A large jar full of hard beans, book, sheet of newspaper, large piece of poster board, black crayon, gummed colored stars, ball of yarn, and a small card and pencil for each participant.

Make a star chart in advance by carefully drawing a large star with crayon on poster board. Paste the many gummed colored stars within the large drawn star. The leader should count in advance the number of beans in the jar, pages in the book, words in the newspaper, stars or yards in the yarn ball.

Tell the participants to guess the number of items included in whatever is held before them. Pass out the pencils and cards and instruct all to write out their names. Allow a set period of time (one to two minutes) for each item that is guessed. Collect the cards. Determine who has the largest number of correct guesses, and announce the winner.

Use these six ideas as possibilities for guessing contests:

> Guess how many beans are in the jar.
> Guess how many pages are in this book.

Guess the number of words on this newspaper.
Guess the number of small stars within the large star.
Guess how many yards are in this ball of yarn.

Try this activity in a ward where there are a number of persons. Consider a guessing contest along with some other longer activity.

Nail Driving Contest   • GMS • MR • NP •

Equipment: Two or three dozen nails each of several sizes (about one to three inches long), five to ten wood blocks at least three inches thick or more, and a hammer for each participant.

Lightly tap nail into wood so it is held in place ready to strike. Tell the participant that he is to pound the nail all the way into the wood with as few strikes as possible. Whoever pounds the nail into the wood with the least number of strikes is the winner. Use nail driving contests at picnics, carnivals and special events.

Quizzes   • A • GMS • NP • TB •

Equipment: Two dozen or more quiz questions, scissors, and one dozen sheets 8½ inch by 11 inch construction paper of assorted colors.

In planning a quiz for the handicapped, always keep in mind the intellectual ability of those who are participating. Allow a wide range of difficulty in the questions, with more easy ones than hard ones. Have several extra questions available for each quiz session. Keep in mind the fun aspect rather than the examination one in constructing questions.

Some of the subjects to include in quizzes are:

Abbreviations	History
Bands	Motion pictures
Famous couples	Music
Foreign countries	Nicknames
General questions	Song titles
Geography	Sports

Prepare twenty to thirty colored construction paper blank tickets. Have each participant get into a circle formation. Start by asking a question of one participant. If he answers the question correctly, give him two tickets. If he misses, pass onto the next one with the same question and so on around the circle. Whoever answers that same question correctly receives one bonus ticket. Return to the first contestant and follow the same procedure. Whoever holds the most tickets is the winner. Try this special type of quiz:

Baseball Quiz

Equipment: Quiz questions and four chairs.

Have a sizable number of general quiz questions ready for the game. Place the four chairs in a baseball diamond formation to indicate the home plate, first base, second base, and third base. Divide the players into two even teams. Teams take position on either side of the diamond.

Toss a coin to determine which team comes to bat first. Have first player "come to bat" at home plate and face the leader (standing on the pitcher's mound) who asks the first question. If the first man at bat answers the question correctly, he goes to first base. The second player then comes to bat. If he also correctly answers the question, he goes to first base, thereby advancing the first batter to second base. Have players move from base to base as in a regular baseball game. If a question is missed, call an out for the team. With three outs, the team retires and the opposing team comes to bat.

Keep score as in a regular ball game. Play baseball quiz for about an hour depending upon the available time. The allotted time determines the number of innings with the same number being played by each side.

Variations: Classify questions according to difficulty with some being "one base" questions, some "two base" questions and others "home run" questions.

Play a musical variation. Have players guess songs played by a pianist. Have the player advance to bases according to these answer-steps:

Guessing song title—First base
Singing first line—Second base
Singing second line—Third base
Singing whole song—Home run

Give credit for orally repeating the song words for those who cannot sing. Have proxies (substitutes) serve for any restricted to bed. These ambulatory "runners" move from base to base according to correct answers made by those in beds.

Use these sample questions for all types of quiz sessions:

Q. What is curling? A. A game played on the ice in which the opposing players slide large circular stones toward a mark at either end called the tee.

Q. What is the name of the only President of the United States who served two terms but not in succession? A. Grover Cleveland (22nd and 24th President).

Q. By what name are the first ten amendments to the United States Constitution known? A. Bill of Rights.

Q. How many squares are there on a checkerboard? A. 64. 32 black and 32 red.

Q. Give the proverb suggested by these lines: "A single piece of a certain fruit every time the earth revolves on its axis restrains one licensed to practise the science dealing with the alleviation of illness from coming to the door." A. "An apple a day keeps the doctor away."

Q. In the event of the death of the President and Vice-President of the United States, who would become President? A. Secretary of State.

Q. How many keys are there on a standard piano keyboard? A. Eighty-eight.

Q. Name one walled city in North America. A. Quebec.

Q. How many carats are contained in pure gold? A. Twenty-four.

Q. Which of the United States is farthest north? A. Alaska.

Q. Name a square ring. A. Boxing ring.

Q. What is the capital of Alaska? A. Juneau.

Q. What coat is finished without buttons and put on wet? A. Coat of paint.

Q. When a mosquito bites you, is it a male or female? A. Female.

Q. What nut is shaped like a comma, sounds like a sneeze, and grows on the end of a fruit tree in South America and India? A. Cashew.

Look for written sources of quizzes. One very helpful book containing selected quizzes is: Esther M. Hawley, *Recreation Is Fun, A Handbook on Hospital Recreation and Entertainment.*

MIXERS

Cooperative Spelling   • A • GMS • NP •

Equipment: Two 4 inch by 5 inch blank cards, pencil and straight pin for each person, and a black crayon.

Print each letter of the alphabet (except the letters Q, X, and Z) with black crayon on the blank cards. Each card has one large letter plainly printed on it.

As each person arrives in the auditorium or dayroom, give him a lettered card, blank card, and pencil. Have someone pin the lettered cards to the front of the guests' clothing. Tell the people that they should reassemble according to letters assigned to them so that they can spell out words. As each word is constructed, the persons who own the letters in the newly made word write it down on their blank cards. An example would be those persons owning C, A, and T getting together and each writing on their cards the word "cat."

After about five to fifteen minutes call the entire group together. The person with the longest list of words is the winner.

Irish Stew   • A • GMS • NP •

Equipment: Fourteen slips of paper and fourteen pins, pencils, and slips of paper for each participant.

Print in advance each of the following ingredients on a separate slip of paper:

Seasoned flour	Cubed potatoes
Hot fat	Bay leaf
Boiling water	Minced parsley
Cut-up carrots	Thyme
Diced turnips	Celery leaves
Sliced celery	Lamb
Whole tiny onions	Marjoram

Have fourteen players selected and available in advance to the arrival of the group. Pin one of the slips on each of their backs, each slip describing by name one ingredient for Irish stew. Tell them to move about and avoid as much as possible letting anyone see the slips on their backs.

As the guests or larger group arrive, give them paper and pencil. Tell them to try and assemble in ten minutes a complete list of the exact ingredients, as described on the other persons' backs, used in making Irish stew. Whoever turns in the most complete list wins.

Picture Guessing   • A • GMS • NP •

Equipment: Several old magazines, scissors, black crayon, ten 8½ inch by 11 inch or larger pieces of assorted colored construction paper, and paste.

Search through old magazines for pictures of places, people, or things. Carefully remove key words, phrases, or portions of the pictures in such a way that the content of the picture becomes difficult to identify. Choose eight or ten of these pictures to fit the theme of the forthcoming activity. Number these with a black crayon and mount them on construction paper and place around the room in prominent places.

Give the guests pencils and paper upon arrival. Ask them to guess the names of the places, people, or things. Award the winner a small prize or other type of recognition.

PARTY ACTIVITIES

Birthday Party   • A • C • GMS • NP • TB •

Equipment: Birthday cake, cake knife, a paper plate for each person, coffee or milk, paper cup for each person, and any other equipment needed for selected birthday activities.

As the guests enter the room (or shortly thereafter) informally sing "For He's a Jolly Good Fellow," "Happy Birthday" or some similar song. Use these words and music for the occasion:

"For He's a Jolly Good Fellow"

For he's a jolly good fellow,
For he's a jolly good fellow,
For he's a jolly good fellow,
Which nobody can deny!
Which nobody can deny!

Change the line "For he's a jolly good fellow" to "For she's a jolly good lady" if the party is for a lady.

"Happy Birthday to You"

Happy birthday to you, Happy birthday to you
Happy birthday, God bless you,
Happy birthday to you.

Also substitute in place of "God bless you" the word *dear* and the name of the person whose birthday it is.

Encourage informal conversation and friendly chat. Make the participants comfortable and at ease. Pass out candies and nuts. Furnish cigarettes to adults if such practice has medical approval. Play any or all of the following games and activities:

> Battleship (see page 206)
> Bean Bag Toss (see page 219)
> Guggenheim (see page 215)
> Playing Card Toss (see page 220)

If possible, have honored guest cut the cake. Serve it to the others. Make the coffee or milk available at this time.

Suggestions: Invite several volunteers to assist with birthday parties. Let them help with many of the individualized services and refreshment serving.

In a large hospital where a separate party for each patient is not practical, use the plan of having one birthday party on a stated day of each month (same day of each month). Invite all to the party who have a birthday during that month.

Suggest to a volunteer organization the project of sending birthday greetings to long-term (ninety days or longer in the hospital) patients. Collect the names of these patients along with the anniversary day of the year that commemorates their birth. Do not provide information about the age of the patient (unless a child patient).

Coffee Hours   • A • GMS • NP •

Equipment: Refreshments (coffee, tea, milk, and/or soft drinks), cups or glasses, and crackers, cookies, or crumpets.

Plan a coffee hour regularly or periodically. If refreshments cannot be obtained without charge, collect contributions or devise some other means of defraying the cost. Provide for occasional coffee hours some musical entertainment. Use phonograph records, harmonica players, vocalists, pianists, "combo units," or radio as musical background.

If the coffee period plan is in accordance with established policies and is sanctioned by proper authority, invite staff members to the recreation building or ward dayroom for this occasion. Include as many as possible in the coffee hour activity. Encourage social friendliness with the handicapped guests.

St. Patrick's Day Party   • A • GMS • NP •

Equipment: Ticket and pencil for each guest, one small prize, one-quarter pint green paint, two small paint brushes, rock one foot or more in diameter, several packages of green and white flameproof crepe paper, straight pins, one quarter pint of tempera paint, five or more golf club putters, five or more potatoes of similar size, refreshments consisting of cookies, cake, and coffee.

In advance of the party paint the rock green and allow it to dry thoroughly. Note the rock's exact weight. Place it on a sturdy pedestal near the entrance of the dayroom or auditorium where party is to be held.

Select a decoration committee and have them decorate the room on the day before (March 16th) the party with crepe paper and pins.

Hand each person a ticket and pencil as he enters the party room. Tell him to guess the weight of the Blarney Stone (painted green rock) and place his or her guess along with name on ticket. Collect the marked tickets and have an employee or volunteer locate the ticket with the most correct guess. Award a small prize to the winner sometime during the party.

Play Playing Card Toss (See page 220). Have the waste baskets trimmed with green crepe paper.

Next announce Potato Golf. Have participants try to knock a potato with golf clubs (putters) into one of four circles about twenty feet away. Have circles painted in advance on the floor with tempera paint.

Try this "Green Quiz" with applause for any who correctly answer these questions aloud.

1. A valuable piece of paper (greenback)
2. Tree that grows in Minnesota (evergreen)
3. A very cold country (Greenland)
4. A house in which flowers are kept (green house)
5. A beginner (greenhorn)
6. An internationally famous village (Greenwich)
7. A fruit that can give a tummy ache (green apple)
8. A town in Kentucky (Bowling Green)
9. Not quite as good as blue cheese (green cheese)
10. Name of a song once popular ("Green eyes")

Suggest several songs that the group might sing. Start out with "When Irish Eyes Are Smiling" and include some of the following:

"America the Beautiful"
"When You Wore a Tulip"
"I'm Looking Over a Four Leaf Clover"

Invite volunteers to assist in the leadership of the St. Patrick's Day Party. Serve refreshments at the end of the party.

Valentine Party   • C •

Equipment: Two or three dozen sheets of red construction paper, several pairs of scissors, several pencils, spools of thread, jar of paste, large glass jar, one-half to one pound small red candy hearts, Valentine cookies, and ice cream.

A day or two in advance of Valentine's Day (February 14), suggest to the children that they cut out hearts to be used as decorations or invitations. Use the red construction paper, scissors, and pencils for this. Cut the paper into various size squares. Fold the squares diagonally and draw half of a heart to cover most of the triangular-shaped folded paper with one side of the drawing on the sheet fold. Cut out the one half heart (except along the fold) and unfold the sheet into a full heart shape. Write an invitation on each heart and have children send these to their friends. If the hearts are to be used as decorations, hang or affix them with thread or paste to bedposts or windows. Ask children to make paper square dishes for the party (see page 44), and draw red hearts on them.

Plan to have a lollipop tree (see page 172) adopted to an inside setting. Let the children select their lollipops.

Sing several songs to accompaniment (if available). Sing some of the action songs suggested on page 166. Try "My Hat" with the motions described on page 166. For variety sing "My Hat" in German to these words:

Mein hut er hat drei Ecken,
Drei Ecken hat mein Hut,
Und hat er nicht drei Ecken,
(Denn) das ist nicht mein Hut.

Substitute the word "heart" for "hat" as a variation.

Play a quiz game which involves the making of smaller words from "St. Valentine." Print "St. Valentine" on one of the pieces of construction paper and let the children guess the answer words to these nine question-statements. Each answer is one word made up of letters in "St. Valentine."

1. Number following eight
2. A small body of land
3. Used to hold a fish hook
4. Stories
5. Egyptian river
6. Material for roofs
7. Sometimes used to catch fish
8. Same as tardy
9. Home for birds

The quiz answers are:

1. Nine		6. Tile or tin
2. Isle		7. Net
3. Line		8. Late
4. Tales		9. Nest
5. Nile		

Bring into the room a glass jar filled with small candy hearts. These have been counted before the party by the leader. Ask the guests to guess individually how many pieces of candy there are in the jar and write the figures down with their names on paper hearts. Collect the written guesses and announce the winner who came closest to guessing the actual number of hearts in the jar.

Play a "famous couple" guessing game! The leader calls out one name of the following couples and anyone in the group may call out the other person in the famous couple. See who can guess the most couples correctly.

1. Jack—Jill
2. Abraham—Sarah
3. Romeo—Juliet
4. Samson—Delilah
5. Mickey—Minnie
6. Anthony—Cleopatra
7. Adam—Eve
8. Joseph—Mary
9. Jacob—Rachel
10. Isaac—Rebekah

Tell the story of *Johnny Appleseed* (see page 79) to the group when they are in a circle formation.

TABLE GAMES

Battleship   • A • C • GMS • NP •

Equipment: Four enemy battleship charts, four home battleship charts, and two pencils. Some call this game "Salvo" rather than "Battleship" since a series of shots is sometimes called a salvo in military parlance.

Study the battleship game rules and procedure. Distribute an enemy battleship chart, home battleship chart, and pencil to each participant. Explain the rules to players and go through a trial game with them. Suggest this game to adults who have favorable recollection of naval life.

Instruct each player to place his four ships independently on his own home chart. Place two S's in adjacent squares for the location of the submarine. Similarly place the three D's in a line somewhere on the chart for the destroyer. Allocate four spaces for the cruiser (four C's) and five spaces for the battleship (five B's). Tell opponents not to let each other see their home charts or reveal locations of their ships.

To start a game have the first player "fire" five successive shots at the squares in which he thinks the enemy's ships might be located. In order to "fire" a shot, name the letter and

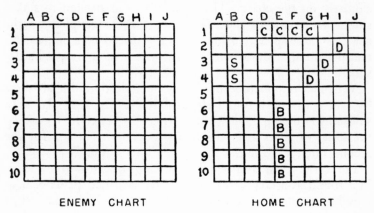

ENEMY CHART   HOME CHART

Score

Submarine — 2 squares S [ ][ ]

Destroyer   — 3 squares D [ ][ ][ ]

Cruiser   — 4 squares C [ ][ ][ ][ ]

Battleship — 5 squares B [ ][ ][ ][ ][ ]

number that identifies a square. The first player might say A-3. Both players then write a 1 (for the first round of shots) in the third square of column A. The attacker puts the number in his enemy chart and the opponent writes it in his home chart. The opponent remains silent while the whole round of five shots is being fired. They record each shot by placing it in the proper place on the appropriate chart. After the fifth shot, the opponent is asked if any ships were hit. In the event that a ship was hit, the opponent answers with the type of ship (submarine, destroyer, cruiser, or battleship) and the number of times hit. Have the attacker record on the score diagram a number 1 in each square for any ship that he has hit. While the attacker does not know the exact total squares locating the hit ship, he has a hint as to its location and may try next turn to place the shots to again hit the same ship. The opponent fires his five shots. These are located similarly on the charts. The number of hits needed to sink a ship corresponds to the number of spaces occupied by the ship (for example, two hits properly placed can sink a submarine, three, a destroyer, four a cruiser, and five, a battleship).

When an opponent's ship has been sunk, diminish his shots by one (now only four instead of five). The first player to sink all of his opponent's ships wins the game. In recording the series of shots after the first group, write in a 2 for the second ones, a 3 for the third ones, and so on.

For variety, use a larger fleet of ships or allow more shots in a round as a change of pace. Have two bed patients who may be separated by screens or partitions play this game. The only additional game requirement in this case is that they be able to hear each other in calling out the shots. Prepare mimeographed or dittoed sheets in advance for players to use. If there is a shortage of game charts, have players record their shots lightly with pencils. Erase the marks after a game and use the sheets over again.

Bingo   • A • C • GMS • NP •

Equipment: Two or three bingo cards for each player, approximately sixty wooden card markers (or pieces of corn) for each player, caller's numbered sheet, numbered markers for caller's sheet, shaker box, and prizes.

Arrange the bingo cards and card markers for the players' convenience. Have each player select the cards that he desires for playing the game. Select a person to serve as the caller, and instruct him on rules of the game.

Inform the players on how the game is played and see that all are ready for the start. Place the caller's numbered markers in the shaker box. Shake box and draw the first numbered piece out. Call the letter and number out clearly so that all players can hear. Place the number piece in its same numbered and lettered place on the caller's numbered sheet. Any players who have that number in the column under the same letter in their card cover it with a card marker. Continue to draw

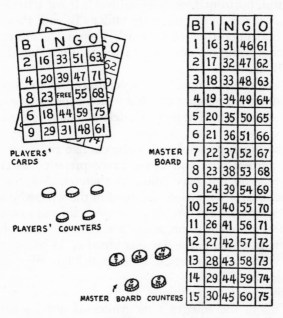

PLAYERS'
CARDS

MASTER
BOARD

PLAYERS' COUNTERS

MASTER BOARD COUNTERS

the numbered markers out of the shaker box. The players cover numbers on their cards as the calls are made by the caller. Whenever a line of numbers on any card is consecutively covered vertically, horizontally, or diagonally, the player owning the card calls out "Bingo." At this point halt the calling of numbers, and have players retain the markers in place on their cards.

Check the bingo card which has the straight line of filled spaces on it with the caller's sheet. Call back each number in the line and see if it is similarly covered on the caller's sheet. Declare the card owner as winner if the card does not have any mistakenly placed markers on the line of covered squares. Have players clear the markers from their cards in preparation for the next game. Award a prize to the winner.

In ensuing games, allow the players to each use two or three cards at a time.

Variations: Announce that a certain letter formation must be made on the cards in order to reach "Bingo" (instead of the vertical, horizontal, or diagonal line). If the letter selected is an "L," cover all the numbers under "B" and those in the bottom horizontal row on the card. Try an "X" instead with the solution being the covering of the two crossing diagonals under "B" and "G."

Try "stand-up" bingo. All players stand at the beginning of the game. As a number is called which appears on a player's card, he sits down. The last one left standing is declared as winner.

Use the bingo principle with objects like trees, vegetables, animals, automobiles, and birds. Have prepared sheets with squares that do not have numbers thereon. Ask players to fill in the squares with names of items in the selected category. Examples for trees are birch, oak, maple, elm and so on. Then read off a previously prepared list that contains the best known items in the particular classification. Whoever reaches bingo (a vertical, horizontal, or diagonal line filled in) first is the winner.

Use the previous technique in "pocketbook bingo." Have players fill in the squares with names of articles that they think would be in a woman's pocketbook. Call out items drawn from a woman's pocketbook (prepared beforehand with a variety of typical items).

Purchase special bingo cards for persons confined to beds. These cards do not require separate markers or playing pieces and can therefore be played in a sitting or reclining position. These cards feature movable sliding shutters that cover up the numbers. The Bingo King Company is one company which produces automatic bingo cards. The added expense of automatic bingo cards is generally justified by the added convenience and durability.

Vary the kind of prizes given to winners. Use small and insignificant ones so that games are not played for the prize only. Money used as bingo prizes encourages players to view the game as a money-making activity rather than one for enjoyment or therapeutic benefit. When dietary conditions permit, hold a bakery or ice-cream bingo with bakery goods or ice cream bars as prizes.

Use a portable microphone when playing bingo in a ward where patients are spaced here and there or separated by partitions. If this is not practical, use a couple of assistants for relaying numbers around corners or to sections of ward where patients are not in a position to hear.

Bunco • A • GMS • NP •

Equipment: A card table, two dice, pencil and four sheets of paper for every four players, and prizes.

Have players (four or any multiple of four) find places with partners at tables, four to a table. Play the game in about an hour as a progressive card party where players move from table to table. Place two dice, a pencil, and paper at each table.

During the first round of play, all players shoot for "ones" on the dice. Use "twos" during second round and so on each round up to six, then repeating the "ones" again until "sixes" are again reached. Determine the length of a round by the head table. Upon reaching a score of 21 at the head table, "Bunco" is called out thereby stopping play at all tables. Have all players total the scores on their sheets according to the total achieved by partners. Winners progress to next tables except the head table where winners remain. The head table losers go to the foot table. Playing at any table (except the head table) is not limited by 21 in score. Therefore the scores at tables other than the head table mount in some cases above 21.

Use these numbers in tabulating scores within each round:

Number that is being rolled (one, two, three, four, five or six): 1 point for each appearance made in throw

Number that is being rolled appearing as a double (on both dice): 21 points

A double of any other number: 5 points

Have each player around the table take turns in shaking and rolling the dice. Each player rolls the dice once (at a turn) unless he scores and then there are successive rolls for each time scored. Have players delegate one at each table to act as scorekeeper.

Determine when game is to end and then have players add up their points. Award one or two head prizes and one for the lowest score.

Have each player switch partners at the table after each new round. This adds variety to the game.

Card Games   • A • C • GMS • NP • TB •

Explore the many types of games that can be played with playing cards. Procure quantities of card decks so that these are consistently available to those who desire to play cards at varying times during the day. Suggest types of games that might interest nonplayers or beginners. Do not attempt to alter the playing habits or games of seasoned players. Discourage card games that feature gambling.

When there is an intellectual group interested in cards, try the game of bridge. Secure in local stationery stores the rules of contract bridge and information on the "Goren count method." Teach a group the fundamentals of contract bridge over several lessons. Make this a social situation that includes small prizes for the top scores and refreshments for all.

Play these games for the stated number of participants:

> Canasta (2, 3, or 4)
> Casino (2 or 3)
> Contract Bridge (4)
> Five Hundred (4)
> Honeymoon Bridge (2)
> I Doubt It (4 or more)
> Pinochle (2, 3, 4)
> Pig (4 or more)
> Rummy (2 or more)
> Whist (4)

Write to the United States Playing Card Company for additional information on how to purchase or secure official rules for these ten popular playing card games (and many others). Also check local stationery stores for rules on these and similar games.

Cootie   • GMS •

Equipment: A pencil and cootie sheet for each participant, and two dice.

Pass out a cootie sheet and pencil to each player. The drawing is a louse with seven parts: one body, one head, two eyes, four feelers, one mouth, five legs, and two arms. Have each player assign a number (one through seven) in the upper right-hand corner of the cootie sheet to each of the seven louse parts. Let each player make his own decision as to which number to assign to the various parts.

When players are ready, have a designated leader throw the dice and call out numbers. Players consult their diagrams and draw in whatever parts of the louse that they have assigned to the called numbers. In the case of duplicate louse parts (two eyes, four feelers, five legs, and two arms), only one such part can be drawn for each number called (if eyes are assigned number 3, then draw in one eye for a number 3 called, and the second eye only when a second number 3 is called).

	BODY ——— HEAD ——— EYES ——— FEELERS ——— MOUTH ——— LEGS ——— ARMS ———			BODY — 3 HEAD — 2 EYES — 7 FEELERS — 6 MOUTH — 5 LEGS — 4 ARMS — 1	
GAME 1	GAME 2	GAME 3	GAME 1	GAME 2	GAME 3
GAME 4	GAME 5	GAME 6	GAME 4	GAME 5	GAME 6
GAME 7	GAME 8	GAME 9	GAME 7	GAME 8	GAME 9
GAME 10	GAME 11	GAME 12	GAME 10	GAME 11	GAME 12

Whoever completes the drawing first calls out "Cootie" and wins.

Award points (or a prize) for each game with a high score. If desired, have an assistant record throws made by the leader. Read back the number of throws against the completed louse on anyone's cootie sheet. For example, a number has to be thrown five times for anyone to draw in the five legs.

Variation: Play Cootie at tables of four with each player in turn rolling his own dice. No player starts to draw his cootie until the number assigned for the body has been thrown. Follow a standard system of numbering the parts for every participant.

Donkey   • A • C • GMS •

Equipment: Deck of standard playing cards and one less checker (or similar pieces) than there are players in the game.

Shuffle the cards and deal four cards, one at a time, to each player. Each player therefore has a total of four cards in his hand. Place the balance of playing cards to left of the dealer. The object of the game is to collect a group of four cards of a kind in one's hand, and not to be the last to notice when someone else does similarly. Place three checkers in the center of the table (if there are four players).

Have dealer start game by picking a card from the stock pile (deck) and passing any one of his five cards to the left. Each player picks up the card passed to him and uses it if he can. A player never holds more than four cards in his hand at any one time, passing the extra cards from person to person. When a player does hold four cards in his hand of one denomination (such as four queens or four sevens) he stops passing or picking up cards and steals one checker from the table. The other players immediately stop passing and each take a checker. The player failing to get a checker is the "donkey."

There are numerous other playing card games that handicapped persons will be interested in playing, among them casino, hearts, and rummy. More complicated games include pinochle, whist, canasta, cribbage, and bridge. See section on Card Games on page 212.

Guggenheim
• A • GMS •

Equipment: A Guggenheim chart and pencil for each participant.

Pass out the Guggenheim charts and pencils. Ask the group which of the following names they prefer to place on top of the columns, with one letter to a column: (IRMA, LOIS,

	L	O	I	S
BIG CITIES				
RIVERS				
BIRDS				
STATES				

WORKED OUT GUGGENHEIM	I	R	M	A
BIG CITIES	Indianapolis	Rochester	Minneapolis	Aberdeen
RIVERS	Illinois	Rhine	Mississippi	Amazon
BIRDS	Indigo Bunting	Robin	Martin	Arctic Owl
STATES	Indiana	Rhode Island	Michigan	Alabama

CORA, MAUD, OLGA, OPAL, or FRAN). Similarly have them place classifications of objects in the left hand verticle column such as vegetables, rivers, girls' names, big cities, states, and birds. The purpose of the game is to fill in the spaces with words that begin with the letter at the top of the column, and are in the class of nouns indicated to the left. For example, if IRMA is used at the chart top, the first boxed-in square under I might have cities beginning with I (like Indiannapolis or Istanbul). Impose a time limit on the activity and have the one with the largest and most correct list of names declared as winner.

Variations: Use longer names than those of only four letters. Add other categories such as countries, boys' names, universities, or fruit. Another variation is to play Guggenheim in a team formation with teams competing against each other.

Chapter 12

Special Events

THE MORALE and conduct of handicapped persons is so often dependent upon holiday and special events that typically reflect normal community life. The hospital, institution, or home that disregards Christmas, Independence Day, birthdays, and entertainments is taking immeasurable pleasure away from those who live there. Special events are those occasions, seasons, or celebrations that recall or commemorate some festive experience or tradition. The great worth in these group events is in the warm attitudes and good feelings that are sparked in the minds of those who are handicapped.

The haven for the handicapped that neglects these seasonal and regular activities may operate, but it neglects an area which may bring much joy to its occupants. A person who is eventually to return to community life and occupation needs some duplication of community living that is embodied in special program events. Recreation includes the joyous and pleasurable participation in mass holiday and seasonal activities.

In such major events as Christmas and the Fourth of July, particular care is needed in the delegation of special duties and efficient direction. Volunteers, committees, and other staff personnel should be included in over-all direction of these programs. Mass activities tend to minimize the individual needs of patients for the majority's benefit. However, with adequate staff assignments and thought-out program plans, the single handicapped member need not be lost in a large group.

Decorations and atmosphere do much to carry holidays and special events a long way in the minds of participants.

Wise use of facilities, props, decorations, climate conditions, and equipment lend value to the carnival or entertainment show.

The chapter on Special Events is divided into two categories: group events and holiday celebrations.

For additional ideas about special events, affairs, and parties see *Social Games for Recreation* by Evelyne Borst and Elmer D. Mitchell.

GROUP EVENTS

Carnivals   • GMS • NP •

Equipment: Chairs and tables for making booths; decorative flameproof crepe paper; pieces of poster board, nine that are 17 inches by 22 inches; assorted colored crayons; balloons; portable microphone or several megaphones; a blank 2 by 4 inch card for each participant; two dozen pencils and several prizes.

Plan with school or institutional personnel a time of the year that is appropriate for a carnival or "county fair." Secure medical approval for this community type of event, if it involves the total hospital. Set the date sufficiently in advance so that preparations for activities and promotion may be adequately made. Consider having the carnival in conjunction with some special holiday or season such as the Fourth of July or autumn (perhaps calling a carnival at this time a "Fall Festival"). If the carnival is to take place out-of-doors, make arrangements for substitute activities in the event of rain.

A check list of advance preparations for a carnival is suggested for the leader:

1. Attractively print with crayons the names of the booth activities on posterboards along with numbers (a number for each booth activity).
2. Have blank cards made into score cards with spaces for participants' names as well as numbers listed for each

activity. Allow two or three blank spaces for the participant to use as he pleases at any booth.

3. Assign handicapped persons or volunteers as operators for the various booths. If the handicapped are employed, be sure to arrange for relief periods so they, too, can visit the booths.
4. Set up tables, chairs, and decorations in such a manner as to indicate clearly the locations of booths.
5. Arrange for advertisements and other promotional devices for the forthcoming carnival.
6. Check with electricians and dietitians regarding any problems involving electricity, lighting, or food.
7. Instruct those in charge of booths how to record scores of participants on the score cards.

When the guests arrive, give them each a score card and tell them to try their luck and skill at the activities. As the people mingle around the carnival area, use the portable microphone or megaphones to "talk up" the various activities. Urge persons in booths to act as "barkers" in attracting patients to their activities. Remind persons behind the booths to mark the achieved score of each contestant on his score card after every participation.

At the end of the day or carnival event, collect score cards and tabulate the scores. Award prizes to the several top winners.

Try these booth activities at the carnival:

Bean Bag Toss

Equipment: Chalk and eight bean bags.

Hand the contestant four bean bags and tell him to throw them one by one at any of several predrawn chalk circles on the floor. Award a point for each bag successfully thrown within a circle on the floor. (See Bean Bag Throw on page 238.)

Chopsticks and Marbles

Equipment: Four chopsticks, forty marbles, two cups, and two plates.

Give the contestant two chopsticks and tell him to pick up one marble at a time from a cup and deposit it on a plate. Allow thirty seconds for each try and award a point for each marble successfully placed on the plate.

Leg Toss

Equipment: Two chairs and eight rope rings about 5 inches in diameter.

Have the contestant throw four of the rope rings at the legs of an overturned chair. Award a point for each ring that lands on a chair leg.

Cork Spearing

Equipment: Two dozen small corks in a large pan of water, and six straight pins.

The object is to spear as many floating corks as possible with a pin within a set period of time. One point is scored for every cork speared.

Nail Driving Contest

Equipment: Wooden planks or boards, nails, and two hammers.

See page 196.

Hit the Doll

Equipment: Three or four wood shelves and uprights to hold the shelves, gymnasium mat, six to twelve cloth stuffed dolls, and two softballs.

Hang or set the padded mat behind the shelves. Place the dolls in a standing position on the shelves. Hand a ball to the participant and tell him to throw it at a doll in an attempt to knock it off the shelf. Permit three tries and award a point for each successful throw.

Playing Card Toss

Equipment: Two empty waste baskets and two decks of playing cards.

Prop the basket up slightly so that its opening faces the card thrower. Have the player at a stated distance throw twenty-six playing cards (one-half deck), one at a time, into the basket. Award a point for every card successfully tossed into the basket.

Chicken Feed

Equipment: A paper soda straw for each participant, two plates, and a pile (about three dozen) of hard beans.

Hand a soda straw to each person. Tell him to place it in his mouth and try to attach a bean on the other end by drawing in the breath; then expell and drop bean onto a plate. Establish a time limit of thirty seconds and a point for every bean deposited on the plate.

Card Cutting

Equipment: Two decks of standard playing cards.

Give each person three opportunities to cut a deck of playing cards (by picking up a part of the pile and turning over the top part). Give a point for every face card (Jack, Queen, or King) turned up and two points for every Ace.

Suggestion: Try other booth activities like rubber pointed dart throwing, bingo table, penny pitching, golf putting, and improvised bowling (using paper milk containers and a rubber ball).

Entertainments　　　• A • C • GMS • MR • NP • TB •

Equipment: Stage, room, or auditorium large enough to accommodate the entertainment, microphone, loud speakers, and a chair for each spectator.

Plan in advance a type of entertainment that will be of interest to the group. Make arrangements with the entertainers that are to put on the performance. Pay any nominal fee necessary for their services and check on any other items that will make the entertainment more successful. A check list of some of the preliminaries is as follows:

Fees or compensation
Orientation of performers to
　type of patients

Any necessary medical clearances
Directions to the hospital

Parking arrangements	Stage lighting and equipment
Length of performance	Heat and ventilation
Sound system	Letter of thank you
Dressing rooms	

Advertise and promote the coming entertainment through the newspaper, bulletin boards, posters, and announcements. Tell other appropriate personnel the beginning and terminating hours of the performance so that arrangements may be made in escorting persons to and from the entertainment.

Typical types of entertainment are these:

Band concerts	Lectures with films
Clown and animal acts	Magicians
Comedians	Puppet shows
Dancers	Singers
Drama groups	Sports programs

Be sure to orient performers carefully as to obvious limitations of handicapped spectators. This is especially important when entertaining the neuropsychiatric. Try to secure volunteer performers to lessen expenses. Stress to entertainers that they should avoid overly-sympathetic attitudes toward disabled persons. All program content should be well within the limits of good taste and not likely to cause the audience undue excitement.

Some of the possible sources of entertainment for handicapped persons are:

Musicians' unions
Employee groups from large companies
Community service clubs
University extension services

Pageants   • A • C • GMS • NP •

Consider past school, hospital, or community celebrations in ascertaining the possibility of a pageant. If there is sufficient interest, select a committee of employees to lay plans for the event. Determine a theme for the event and select as many participants as possible to carry out necessary roles. With the selection of an appropriate theme, many plans need to be made regarding scripts, costumes, props, and staging.

As a main part of the pageant, select or write a script, and direct rehearsals of the presentation. Bring in key skills of personnel and handicapped persons in making the pageant a meaningful performance. Gear the pageant around certain holidays (Christmas, May Day, Independence Day, or St. Patrick's Day) or seasonal themes (Harvest Festival or Winter Wonderland).

Seek the assistance of occupational therapists in making costumes that may be needed for the production. Use donated clothing, materials issued by the institution, or crepe paper for costumes and props to save costs.

Consider the advantage of holding the pageant out-of-doors, perhaps on a concrete tennis-court dance-floor that may also be used for concerts and pageants. Make maximum use of physical facilities and natural terrain. Remember the need for alternate dates and locations for any out-of-doors event in case of adverse weather.

Plan on twenty to a hundred active participants in such a large undertaking as a pageant.

Talent Shows   • A • C • GMS • MR • NP • TB •

Equipment: Piano, stage, microphone, loud speakers, and paper for printed programs.

Locate suitable talent for the show through interest finders, the patients' council or by word-of-mouth. Secure a well qualified pianist who, if necessary, may be a staff member. Hold rehearsals sufficient to organize a logical sequence of numbers for the show. Consider a theme or title for the talent show. Include if possible a general sampling of these acts:

Dramatic skits	Magic tricks
Group dances	Readings
Hillbilly band	Record pantomimes
Imitations	Tap dancing
Instrumental selections	Vocal selections

A complete number-by-number rehearsal of all the acts is not necessary in this kind of a variety show. Select someone who has a pleasing personality and skillful voice direction as a master of ceremonies. Look for one who is a skilled speaker rather than a good joke teller. In the event that some pieces are not performed, use the piano for improvising and filling in.

Advertise the talent show and invite patients and staff to view it. On the last day before the performance when the cast is well established, print programs with selections and performers' names.

Tournaments   • GMS • NP •

Equipment: Tournament chart and pencil.

The tournament is a good device to determine individual or team champions from among a group of skilled players or teams. Usually sporting events like table tennis, badminton, chess, and ball games utilize tournaments for determining winners.

Use any of these generally accepted tournament plans in the activity program:

Round Robin

In this type of tournament every team or player must play every other competitor in the tournament.

Whether an odd or even number of teams has been entered, play the same number of rounds. Assign to each team a number and then use these figures in working out the schedule. In a league with seven teams, commence with number one in this way:

7	6	5	4	3	2	1
6-1	5-7	4-6	3-5	2-4	1-3	7-2
5-2	4-1	3-7	2-6	1-5	7-4	6-3
4-3	3-2	2-1	1-7	7-6	6-5	5-4

The figures go in a clockwise motion. The last team (team seven) draws a bye in the first round and those remaining play as directed in the schedule.

Plan for one less number of games than teams with an even number of teams. Revolve the numbers about number one until the beginning combination of team games is reached:

1-2	1-8	1-7	1-6	1-5	1-4	1-3
8-3	7-2	6-8	5-7	4-6	3-5	2-4
7-4	6-3	5-2	4-8	3-7	2-6	8-5
6-5	5-4	4-3	3-2	2-8	8-7	7-6

First, second, and third places are determined by the percentage of the games won by the respective teams. Divide the number of games won by the total games played to get the percentage. For example: when eight games are played and six of them won, six is divided by eight and equals 75 per cent.

Challenge Tournaments

Afford competition for those of near equal ability and keep interest in an activity over an extended period through this type of tournament. Use challenge tournaments for maximum interest in many situations. Rate the players by a committee or draw by lot and then place in position according to draw. The two common methods of arrangement are the ladder and triangle. Inscribe names on cards that can either be placed in a slot or hung on a hook.

In a ladder tournament a player may challenge anyone one or two rungs above him. If successful, he exchanges places with the person whom he has defeated.

In a triangle tournament a player may challenge anyone in the row above him. If successful, he exchanges places with the person whom he has defeated.

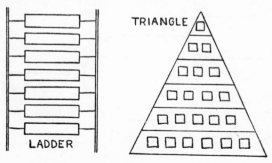

Elimination Tournaments

Consider the question of byes in every tournament where the number of entrants is not an exact power of two (two, four, eight, sixteen, thirty-two, or sixty-four). If the number of entries is an even power of two, then pair the names in a column and note that two of the players will meet in the finals. Follow this example:

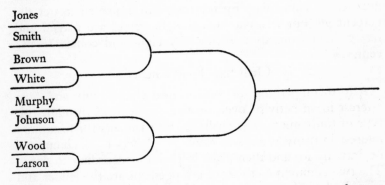

When the number of entrants is not an even power of two, give byes in the first round so as to avoid having three players left to compete in the final round. Move a team up without playing a match when it receives a bye. Give sufficient byes in the first round to assure an even power of two in the second round. Notice the position of byes:

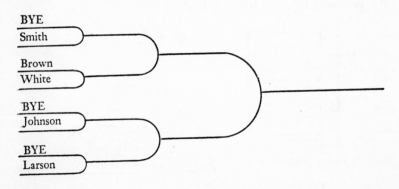

Determine the number of byes by subtracting the total number of entrants from the next higher power of two. For example if there are eleven entrants subtract eleven from the next higher power of two which is sixteen. This leaves five byes, two of which should be placed in the upper half of the bracket and three in the lower. The total number eleven minus the five byes leaves six players in the first round. After these persons have played, three of them will be advanced to the second round in line with five byes. These are now three plus five or eight players in the second round and as eight is a power of two, only two players can meet in the final round. In this example there are eleven entrants and five byes:

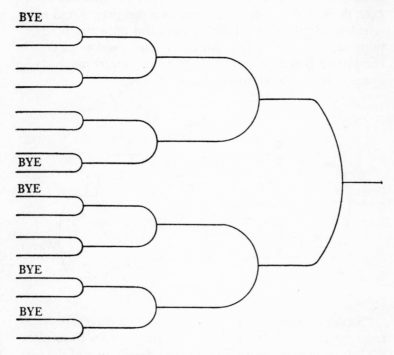

Consolation Tournament

This is a single elimination tournament held for all the losers of the first round in the main tournament. Apply all the laws of byes and location of teams used in single elimination.

Double Elimination

In this type of tournament every team or player must lose twice before being eliminated from play. This method of determining a champion is one of the fairest methods. However, do not use this method when time permits a round robin schedule. Apply all the rules of byes and drawings for positions discussed previously. An example of eight team double elimination is as follows (if number two defeats number one in the finals, a second match must be played):

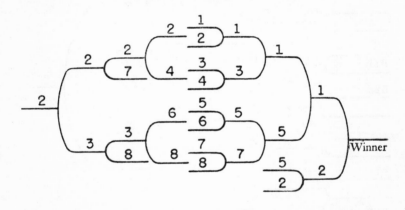

"Seeding" of entrants prevents the two best players or teams from meeting in the first round. "Seeding" means to so place the best competitors as to have an even distribution of the best players. Place the seeded teams or players as far from each other as possible in each bracket. This plan minimizes the chance of an anticlimax in the final round of play.

Trips and Tours   • A • C • GMS • MR • NP •

Remember that life from day to day in the same restricted setting can get dreary and monotonous. Make plans for occasional trips away from the home or ward for those who can go. Discuss the plan with physicians and if they concur, make arrangements for a journey with selected persons. Use a wise, fair manner of deciding who is to go. Study over the possibilities of where to go and how to get there before the actual departure.

Follow these steps in setting up a trip or tour:

1. Determine where to go
   a. consider the time available
   b. think of beaches, zoos, industries, farms, camping, fishing, or sports events
   c. check permissions, reservations, tickets, refreshments, and any needed equipment
2. Transportation
   a. hospital cars and buses
   b. chartered bus
   c. insurance coverage of vehicles
3. Supervision
   a. recreation staff members
   b. physicians, nurses, and/or teachers
   c. parents and volunteers
4. Invitations
   a. check with those who desire to go and have approval
   b. promote and publicize the type of things that can be seen during a trip

Plan to spend the time within the vehicle watching points of interest about the selected area. Allow the tourists to get off the vehicle to look around or purchase refreshments. Consider taking selected groups to county or state fairs. Wherever there are milling crowds, be sure the group has ample supervision. Break a large group into subgroups of two or three persons with a leader in a fair or other crowded event.

HOLIDAY CELEBRATIONS

Christmas Activities   • *A* • *C* • *GMS* • *MR* • *NP* • *TB* •

Equipment: A Christmas tree (pine or spruce) and tree decorations for each ward.

Give considerable thought and planning to the Christmas season from about December 18th through January 1st. Synchronize and coordinate schedules so there is a minimum of conflict between regularly scheduled activities and special Christmas programs. Carefully lay out work assignments so that the many details of this period can be smoothly handled. Work closely with a minister, priest, or chaplain in carrying out the spiritual aspects of Christmas programs through proper emphasis in activities.

Decorate the rooms or halls in appropriate Christmas materials. Contact grades or wards about Christmas trees and decorations. Let the handicapped decorate their own trees.

Provide some or all of these activities for a well-rounded Christmas program:

1. A gift wrapping and personal service for the handicapped. Let volunteers assist with this. Have them collect contributions of wrapping paper, seals, ribbons, and cards.
2. Gift shopping service. Let volunteers assist in purchasing articles or even provide free of charge items that handicapped persons can use as gifts.
3. Have as many as possible make decorations. Put on a decorating party.
4. Make available a calendar of Christmas events in separate printed form or as a part of the newspaper.
5. Sponsor hall decorating contests. Have employees serve as judges in determining the most appropriately decorated halls and rooms.
6. Invite volunteer groups from nearby communities to sing Christmas carols.
7. Lead Christmas carols as a part of group singing.

8. Make Christmas favors for use on bed trays on Christmas day.
9. Put on Christmas parties in rooms or in the recreation hall.
10. Select a Santa Claus to distribute gifts on Christmas eve.
11. Cooperate in observance of special Christmas religious services.
12. Distribute sheets (or in newspaper) of information on the location and time of specially recommended Christmas television programs for groups to watch.

Include a Christmas Scavenger Hunt in the activity at this time of the year. Let the ambulatory and nonambulatory both aid in locating the named articles. Divide the group into small teams and have them secure articles as described on written lists:

1. Star
2. Picture of Santa Claus
3. Ribbon
4. Mistletoe
5. Christmas sock
6. Candles
7. Silver bell
8. Ornament
9. Poinsettia
10. Christmas greeting postmarked in New York
11. Tinsel

One variation of the Christmas Scavenger Hunt for those confined to beds is to provide them with scissors and magazines. Tell them to find pictures of all the articles and cut them out of magazines.

See *Better Homes and Gardens, Good Housekeeping, McCalls*, and similar magazines for suggestions on Christmas decorating, stories, and ideas.

Let the handicapped person make Christmas greetings. Secure a variety of materials, including colored construction paper, aluminum foil, paste, black drawing ink, gummed dots and stars, assorted colors of gummed crepe paper, sequins, airplane cement, glitter specks, pencil, eraser, and scissors.

Start greeting card making by December first or before so that the finished product is available for mailing by December eighteenth.

A good source of additional ideas for Christmas events is *Let's Celebrate Christmas* by Horace J. Gardner.

Field Day   • MR • NP •

Schedule this outdoor "track and sports" activity on a day when there are sufficient numbers who can physically participate in and enjoy such activities. Always plan an alternate activity of indoor gymnasium events in case of inclement weather. Plan on several hundred spectators and participants. Secure medical sanction of the event and a representative committee of key personnel to plan the afternoon festivities. Center field day around a traditional once-a-year celebration or holiday such as Independence Day.

Study the activities described under Carnivals (see page 218), and decide which ones to include in the program. Secure a number of helpers and judges to assist with the field day events. Plan some of the following field activities for participation:

> 100 yard dash
> Backward race
> 220 yard race
> Team relay race
> Left foot hopping race
> Right foot hopping race
> Walking race

Serve refreshments of cake and ice-cream bars or possibly weiners in buns.

Conclude the afternoon with a softball game between teams of handicapped persons. Plan on spectators to watch the game.

Holiday Activities   • A • C • GMS • MR • NP • TB •

Plan holiday festivities around major holidays of the year. Consider the holiday's meaning to the handicapped persons in question. For instance, Valentine's Day means much more to a child than an adult. St. Patrick's Day is more meaningful to certain adults of Irish descent. Plan these activities for appropriate age and interest levels.

Form a committee and develop plans for the type of celebration that will be most meaningful for the participants. When there is religious content in the holiday, call in the chaplain, priest, minister, or rabbi for their advice. Do this for Easter, Thanksgiving, and Christmas. Always include other personnel, along with medical approval, for an event that will require cooperation from all.

See Valentine Party (page 204), St. Patrick's Day Party (page 203), Field Day (page 232), and Christmas Activities (page 230).

Suggestions: See Chapter 17 of E. O. Harbin's *The Fun Encyclopedia*, Chapter 9 of Helen and Larry Eisenberg's *The Omnibus of Fun* and *Social Games for Recreation* by Evelyne Borst and Elmer D. Mitchell for additional program ideas on holiday activities.

See Chapters 6, 7, and 8 of Evelyne Borst's *The Book of Games for Boys and Girls* for many children's games of interest during holiday seasons.

Thanksgiving Festival   • A • GMS • NP •

Equipment: Several packages of assorted colors (mostly brown, orange, and yellow) flameproof crepe paper, paper and cardboard cut-outs of turkeys, about 100 small paper cut-outs of turkeys, two small prizes, rock one foot or more in diameter.

Consider the afternoon of, or even anytime prior to, the Thanksgiving Day dinner for this activity. Lead the festival like a party, but remember the more serious aspects of and reason for Thanksgiving Day.

Secure the assistance of several in advance for the purpose of decorating the room with a Thanksgiving theme. Make the crepe paper decorations simple, but symbolic of the day.

Have the staff conceal in advance of the party the 100 small paper cut-outs of turkeys in out-of-the-way places and hidden corners of the room. Hide them well.

When the festival begins, tell the group to look about the room for small paper turkeys. Allow five minutes and award a small prize to the one who finds the most turkeys.

Invite selected individuals prepared to recite poetry or prose that is appropriate for Thanksgiving. Also have a brief musical selection in keeping with the season.

Direct attention of the group to the rock on a table which has been weighed prior to the beginning of the party. The label on the rock says *Plymouth Rock*. Let persons make guesses aloud as to what it weighs. Record the guess of each one and award a small gift to whoever guessed its correct weight, or nearest to it.

Divide the participants into two teams and have one staff member or volunteer serve as quiz master for The Thanksgiving Dinner Quiz. Ask questions to the teams with a turn for each team member. Specify someone to tally the correct answers and serve as judge for the teams. The object is to guess the Thanksgiving food item that is suggested by the hint:

1. Some people ride in this train (Gravy)
2. From Iowa (Corn)
3. Frozen water and milk (Ice cream)
4. For the Irish (Potatoes)
5. A kind of cloth (Duck)
6. A country in Asia (Turkey)
7. Some musicians like this kind of session (Jam)
8. A measure in music (Beat [Beet])
9. Necessary for the salad (Dressing)
10. Three and one seventh (Pie [π])
11. When you're on the spot you're in a (Pickle)
12. Mulligan's (Stew)

Chapter 13

Sports and Games

THE HEART OF many recreation programs for the handicapped is athletic interest and participation. It cannot be doubted that sports command more current enthusiasm from the masses than any other leisure time activity. Those pursuits that involve the observation of or participation in activities of a physical, competitive nature constitute athletics. The vital interest of American people in athletics requires either the inclusion of regulation sports in programs for the handicapped or some acceptable modification of them. Low organization games, small group sports, team sports, and exercises of a physical nature are contained in this skill area. Low organization games are as necessary to the child or regressed person as are the more competitive team sports to the physically healthy adult. Regulation rules of sports and games should be followed when possible. In any case for the benefit of treatment or rehabilitation, a partial or complete modification of established rules of a game or sport is legitimate and preferable.

There are certain sports and physical activities which are too rigorous and therefore detrimental to handicapped persons. However, substitutes, alterations, and modifications of the sports are quite valuable as a part of the progressive program. Watching sports events on television, listening to sports events on radio or other major adaptations of these activities are within the reach and consideration of the resourceful leader.

Athletics may open the way for competition to turn into conflict. With the sick and injured person, cooperation is an objective often desired as a result of partaking in activities. Yet, the very nature of sports involves a sense of competition. This aspect needs to be controlled and restrained, but not eliminated. Unmitigated competition can easily turn into conflict and lose all value as a therapeutic or beneficial recreation program. Friendly competition, mature judgment, self-confidence, and a temporary forgetfulness of one's handicap can typify the well-directed sporting event.

Stopping activities at the high point of participants' interest is of unusual importance with sports and games. A physical exercise can easily become tedious repetition if it is overworked and repeated to an extreme. Variety, balance, and limited pursuance of an activity at one time characterize good program planning.

The sports and games in this chapter are divided into three sections: low organization games, small group sports, team sports and exercises (lists of references).

Low organization games are those physical activities that involve a minimum of organization and team cooperation. These can be easily engaged in by children and adults with little preparation or experience in the activity. Small or large groups of contestants may participate in these games in indoor or outdoor settings. Thirteen games with variations and three relays are described here. These are representative of the kinds of activities to include in the program.

Small group sports usually feature one to four or slightly more persons in the activity. The action and procedure are more complex than in low organization games and entail more involved rules. A certain amount of skill is often necessary for the mastery of the sport. Since handicapped groups of general equal physical ability are usually few in number at any time and location, the small group sports activities contain definite programming possibilities.

Team sports include those physical activities that require the coordination and cooperation of a team in order to achieve satisfying participation. Team sports require cooperative sharing by a number of players. The rules and directions are advanced and require some study and practice. Therefore, the five team sports listed (basketball, softball, swimming, touch football, and volleyball) are not described. Instead, special books are recommended that discuss directions and plays needed to master such team sports. Each of the five team sports in this section highlights adaptations of value in working with the handicapped.

Exercises are those physical pursuits that characterize activities requiring repetitious movement and occasional strain. Make certain that any handicapped person engaging in these routine activities has medical approval. These physical stress outlets can be useful for wholesome release of pent-up energies and tensions.

For additional games, contests, and sports refer to *Active Games and Contests* by Richard J. Donnelly, William G. Helms, and Elmer D. Mitchell, and *Sports for Recreation* by E. D. Mitchell (editor).

LOW ORGANIZATION GAMES

Balloon Push Ball   • GMS • NP •

Equipment: One inflated toy balloon, piece of chalk, and room cleared of all furnishings.

Divide a room in half with a line. Evenly divide the players into two teams. Direct the teams to stand on opposite sides of the line and face the center. Throw the balloon into the air at the center line. Each team attempts to bat the balloon ball to the opposite wall. Players travel around the entire floor in trying to get the balloon toward the opponent's wall. When any team causes the ball to touch the opposite wall, a point is scored for that team's side. Any number of points determined in advance by the teams constitutes the game.

Variations: Have a member of each side standing on a bench in his opponent's court. That player is holding a common pin and attempts to puncture the balloon when it is tipped his way by fellow team mates. Each balloon punctured constitutes a score for the side that tipped the balloon to its goalie on the bench.

Use a large beach ball instead of a balloon in a large room or gymnasium with a more physically active group. Adapt this with care in a smaller room for those in wheel chairs.

Ball Roll   • A • C • GMS • MR • NP • TB •

Equipment: Softball and marker (flag, pennant, or stone).

Place the marker in the ground or on the floor about thirty feet away from a designated line. Each player takes a turn in rolling the ball toward the marker and attempts to have the ball come to rest nearest to it. The player whose ball comes nearest the marker is the winner and receives a point. Play a game of ten points with the person who scores ten points first the champion.

Variations: Place the marker about fifty to seventy-five feet or more away and tell the contestants to throw the ball at the marker. Score as described in Ball Roll.

For easier handling, use a large colored beachball or regular basketball.

Try a ball throw for distance with a softball or basketball. Whoever throws the ball farthest is the winner.

Bean Bag Throw   • A • C • GMS • MR • NP • TB •

Equipment: Several bean bags, bean bag board, and chalk.

Set up the bean bag board about ten feet away from a chalk-drawn throwing line. Draw a face on the bean bag board, cutting holes for the mouth, nose, and eyes. The player attempts to toss the bags through the mouth, nose, or eyes which are about four to six inches in diameter each. (The "face" target is desirable because some participants can utilize it properly to release their aggressions against an imagined person represented by the face on the board.) Award points for throwing bean bags through the holes. Let the bed or wheel chair patient also toss bean bags at the board.

Draw a target on the floor if no bean bag board is available. The player stands behind the throwing line and tosses bean bags onto the center of the target. Award points according to which ring the bean bag lands in.

Variations: Throw bean bags into tin cans or other receptacles in addition to the board or floor target. See Bean Bag Toss on page 219.

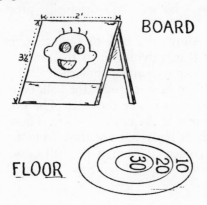

BOARD

FLOOR

Beater Goes 'Round   • NP •

Equipment: Sack stuffed with cloth or rags.

Tell the players to stand in a circle, facing the center, with hands behind their backs. One person designated as "it" stands on the outside of the circle. Give the stuffed sack to "it" and have him walk around the outside of the circle of players. As he moves around, he places the sack in one of the player's hands. This person starts "beating" the person on his right with the sack, breaks from the circle and runs around the players, the beater chasing him. When the chased player reaches his own place in the circle, the chase is over and the person with the sack becomes "it." Try this activity with those patients who may need to release hostilities.

Call Ball   • C •

Equipment: Volleyball or basketball.

Direct the players to stand in a circle, facing center. Select one as "it," and have him stand in the center with the ball. "It" throws the ball into the air and instantly calls the name of a player in the circle who must catch the ball before it hits the floor or ground. If he catches the ball he becomes "it" and has the opportunity of next throwing the ball. If he misses the ball, he returns to his place in the circle formation and the person who was "it" originally proceeds with the game.

Variations: Allow the ball to bounce once before it is caught, rather than catching it in the air.

Tell the children to scatter while the called player is catching the ball. When he has caught the ball, he calls "stop" and all players must stop where they are. The one with the ball attempts to hit one of the others with it. Those being thrown at may move their body but not their feet. If one is hit with the ball, he becomes "it," but if the ball misses a player, the person who threw the ball remains "it" for the next game.

Cat and Rat · C · MR ·

Select one player to serve as the rat and one to be the cat. Arrange the players in a circle with each member holding hands.

The cat takes his place at any spot outside of the circle while the rat goes to the opposite outside of the circle. The cat exclaims, "I am a cat" while the rat says, "I am the rat." The cat replies, "I'll catch you," and the rat's comment is, "Try and do it." Change the dialogue, or omit it when the players are older children. The cat then attempts to tag the rat. Players in the circle help out the rat by letting him pass under their arms in and out of the circle, but obstructing where possibile the cat's tries to catch him. When the cat catches the rat, they go into the circle formation and choose their runner replacements.

Variations: Select two cats who simultaneously try to catch the rat.

Croquet · A · C · GMS · MR · NP ·

Equipment: Ten croquet arches, two stakes, six wooden croquet mallets, six wooden croquet balls, and an area of level grass ground about 30 by 60 feet.

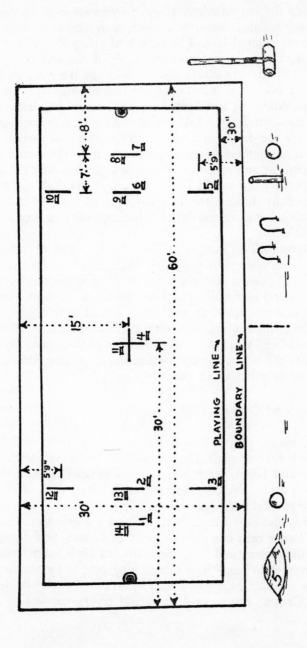

Place the ten wire arches and two stakes in the ground in a croquet court formation. Give each player a mallet and different colored ball. The object of the game is to hit the ball with a mallet through the series of ten arches.

The first player places his ball between the stake and arch number one. Tell him to hit the ball through the first two arches. Allow an additional turn for every arch that the ball goes through. Players take turns and compete in hitting balls through the fourteen arches (arches one and two are repeated as numbers thirteen and fourteen on the course as are numbers six and seven for numbers eight and nine) with his ball is the winner. Hit both stakes with the ball along with successfully hitting the ball through the arches. Award a two-shot bonus to the hitter whenever his ball hits another person's ball.

Variation: Play croquet indoors. Instead of wire arches, use raised cup containers that allow the ball to go up the metal incline and down through the circular opening onto the floor. Make metal cup inclines and put numbers on them. Arrange them in a croquet pattern or other desired layout.

Write to the General Sportcraft Company, Ltd. in regard to the official rules of croquet and the purchase and procurement of them. Local sports dealers also have rules and descriptive information about croquet.

Crows and Cranes   • C • NP •

Divide the players into two teams. Draw two parallel lines about three feet apart. Draw two base lines about twenty feet away and behind each of the two parallel lines. Line the players up by sides, facing each other, along each of the two inside parallel lines, one side on a line.

Designate one side as "Crows" and the other as "Cranes." The leader calls out either Crows or Cranes, and the called side then turns and runs back toward their own base line, attempting to reach it without being caught by members of the other side. If the word "Cranes" is called out by the leader, the "Crows" run toward them and try to tag one or more of the Cranes who have turned and are running in the direction of the Cranes' base line. Whichever team ends up with the largest number of players (or all of the players) is the winner.

Variations: Use the words, "Blink" and "Blank" instead of Crows and Cranes.

Instead of the leader calling out Crows and Cranes, name the sides "Heads" and "Tails." Toss a coin in the air and call out the name of which side is to turn and run towards their respective base line, according to the way the coin falls.

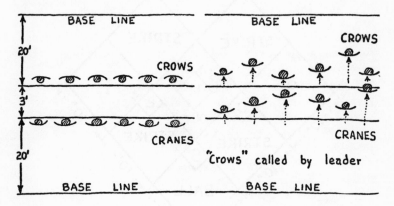

Dartball   • A • C • GMS • NP •

Equipment: Three darts or short arrows with rubber suction cups on ends for each player, and dart board.

Place the dartboard against a wall with the middle of it (home plate) about five feet above the floor. Divide the players into two sides as in a regular game of baseball.

Players stand at a line fifteen feet away from the board. Whichever side is "up to bat" in turn throws darts at the board. Each player is allowed three strikes or four balls as in regular baseball. When the player at bat makes a hit, he leaves his dart in the square. When a succeeding batter hits, he advances his dart an equal number of bases. If a batter hits "E" (error) or "D" (dead ball) he takes his base. If a dart does not hit the board when thrown, it counts as an out. Play dartball as a regular game of baseball. Use metal-pointed darts when the players are not neuropsychiatric. Count any dart that does not stick on the board as an out. For variety use a small bow with arrows, or a toy dart gun and darts that have suction cups on the ends, and play dartball.

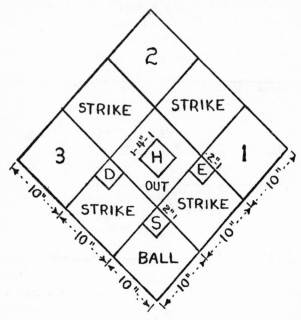

Be sure that the dartball board surface is appropriate from the standpoint of the darts sticking to it. Use concrete or smooth brick wall type of surface that will hold darts with suction cups. Use wallboard or wood boards for metal-pointed darts.

Dodgeball   • C • GMS • MR • NP •

Equipment: Volleyball, basketball, or beach ball.

Have a group hold hands and form a circle around an equal or smaller number of persons scattered within its center. Ask any person in the outer circle to throw a ball at the legs of anyone in the center in an attempt to hit them as they scatter about. Tell those who are hit to join the circle formation. The last remaining one in the center is the winner. Be sure that the players throw the ball at a spot on the body lower than the shoulders, preferably at the legs.

Variations: Allow two balls to be used with an advanced and physically fit group; use a colored beach ball with the mentally retarded as it is easier to see, more attractive to play with, and lighter to handle.

Play as a competitive activity with two teams. Do not let those hit with the ball join the circle, but have them stand aside until all of their encircled team members have been hit. When all have been hit, have those from the other side in the circle formation go into the center. The other group has now formed a new circle around the previous throwers. Keep track of the time that each side is in the center. The team that stays longer in the center is the winner.

Drop the Handkerchief   • C • MR •

Equipment: Handkerchief or cloth.

The players stand in a circle facing center. One player designated as "it" stands outside the circle with handkerchief in hand. "It" walks or runs around the outside of the circle and quietly drops the handkerchief behind any person. When this person discovers that the handkerchief has been dropped behind him, he picks it up and runs around the circle in the same direction that "it" is going. He tries to catch "it" before he reaches home (the place left vacant in the circle). If the player who found the handkerchief cannot catch "it," he becomes the new "it" for the next game.

Variations: Lead the group in the singing of "A-Tisket A-Tasket" as "it" goes around the circle. Stop singing at the moment "it" drops the handkerchief.

Play "Drop the Handkerchief" to recorded music. The person chosen as "it" goes around the circle slowly or fast in time with the music. When the music stops, "it" and the person pursuing him must stop.

Follow the Leader   • C • GMS •

Select a child who is alert and well liked by the others. Tell the group that they are to follow and imitate each action made by the leader. Have the leader start out marching with his hands in a certain position. All others follow in line and duplicate the leader's movements. The leader changes actions and the others follow the leader's example.

Change leaders often and encourage hopping, skipping, and other movements of an exercise type.

Variations: Play "Follow the Leader" with general, medical, and surgical patients who are physically limited and allow only small movements in accord with the medical restrictions upon the patient.

Tell the children to sit down in a circle formation. Select one person to be "it" and designate one player unknown to him to serve as the leader. "It" stands in the middle. The leader starts arm-hand movements that the other children follow. "It" turns around and attempts to guess who the person is who serves as the leader. When "it" correctly guesses who the leader is, he takes the leader's place in the circle formation and the leader now becomes "it" for the next time.

Hot Potato   • A • C • GMS • NP •

Equipment: Any soft type of ball, large or small, and a whistle.

Arrange the participants in a circle formation. Hand the ball to anyone. Ask the seated players to pass the ball from one another and about the circle in any direction to the left or right as rapidly as possible. The object is quickly to get rid of the ball as it is supposedly "sizzling hot" and undesirable to have in one's possession. Every ten seconds or so blow a whistle, and whoever is holding the ball when the whistle is blown has one "hot potato" against him. The person who has been caught holding the "hot potato" for a total of three times is the loser and is either eliminated from the game or given something to do, such as blowing the whistle (instead of the leader blowing the whistle). He may also stand in the circle center and cheer the others.

Kickball
• C • GMS • MR • NP •

Equipment: Volleyball, soccerball, or basketball, and a softball diamond in a gymnasium or outdoors.

Divide the group into two teams. Toss a coin to determine who is at "bat" first. Have both teams determine positions they will assume (catcher, pitcher, first baseman, second baseman, third baseman, shortstop, right fielder, center fielder, and left fielder). The catcher who is a member of the batting team is the first one to stand near home plate and face the pitcher. He holds his foot in readiness to kick the ball as it is rolled by the pitcher across home plate. The object is to kick the ball when it rolls across the home plate. The pitcher rolls the ball across the home plate and the "batter" kicks the

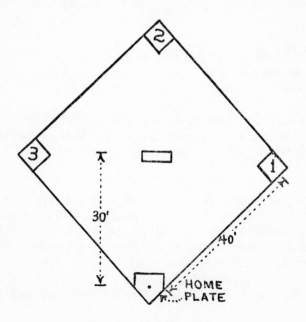

ball into the field as far as he can so that he can round as many bases as possible. He runs the bases as in softball.

The runner may be put "out" by an opposing team member hitting him with a thrown ball or throwing the ball to the baseman the runner is advancing toward before he reaches the base. A ball caught in the air by a fielder constitutes an out. Each team is allowed three outs during any inning.

Award a point to the team for each person who is able to run around the three bases and successfully reach home plate without being put out. Before starting a game of kick-ball, determine the number of innings that will be played. Agree on as few as two innings or as many as nine innings (times each side is at "bat") for a game.

Variations: Shorten the pitching distance and base lines and allow the batter to hit the ball with his fist rather than kicking it.

Permit the batter to tip a beach ball that is pitched under-hand. Let him walk (instead of run) or move in some uniform manner from base to base.

Relays   • C • MR • NP •

Divide the group into two or more relay teams with the same number on each team. If there is one less on any side, have one team member from that side run or go twice to the goal.

To start, direct the teams to line up in parallel lines behind a specified mark, the starting line, on the floor or ground. On the signal of "go" have the teams start the relay.

Over and Under Relay

Equipment: A volleyball or basketball for each team.

The first person on the team passes the ball over his head to the person behind him. This person then takes the ball and passes it between his legs to the person behind him. They alternate over and under and continue from player to player until the ball reaches the last person in line. The last player then runs to the front of the line with the ball and passes the ball over his head to the person behind him. This passing of the ball and running to the head of the line continues until the first person on the team is back to his original place in line. The first team to finish wins.

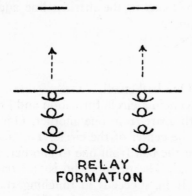

RELAY
FORMATION

Junk Relay

Equipment: A basketball, croquet mallet, book, shuttlecock (or similar miscellaneous items) for each team.

Indicate a junk spot about twenty feet in front of each team. Give each team several of the selected items. The object of the relay is for the first person on each team to pick up all the items and carry them to the designated spot and put them down. He then runs back and touches the next player who runs to the spot, picks up all the items, and carries them back to the starting line. This picking up and carrying continues until each player of a team participates. The first team to finish wins.

Balloon Relay

Equipment: A balloon for each participant.

Hand out balloons to the team members and have them blow up the balloons. Tie the ends by twisting them in slip knots.

Mark off a line about twenty feet in front of each team. The first person on each team tips the balloon in the air and

runs to the marked line at the same time. He then similarly
tips it back to the starting line and his own team. When the
first person returns to his team starting line, the second individual tips his balloon to the designated line twenty feet away
and returns. The first team to successfully have all of its members tip their balloons to the marked line and return is declared the winner.

Ring Ball   • C • MR • NP •

Equipment: One basketball.

Place the players in a circle formation and have them about
one arm's length apart from one another. One person is "it"
and remains in the center of the circle. The players begin the
game by tossing the ball from one to another, trying to keep
it away from "it." The person who is "it" tries to touch or
catch the ball. If he succeeds in touching the ball, the last
person who threw it is the new "it." They trade places and
the game resumes with the new "it." In case of a wild throw
by a player, make him the new "it."

Variations: Use a medicine ball for young male neuropsychiatric patients instead of the lighter basketball, or use
a football (during the fall of the year) or any other type of
ball such as a beach ball during summer months.

Bounce the ball once between players instead of throwing
it.

Ring Toss   • A • C • GMS • MR • NP •

Equipment: Three rope rings for each player, and two ring
toss stands.

Each player holds three rope rings and stands near one ring
toss stand. The object is for each player, in turn, to throw
the rings at the distant stand (about fifteen or twenty feet
away) and attempt to have the rings land on the stand pole.
Each successful throw counts one point.

The rings are thrown one at a time, with players keeping
their own scores. After the throws are made at one ring toss

stand, go to that stand, retrieve the rings, and continue the game by throwing toward the other stand.

Set a maximum number of points such as fifteen. Whoever reaches that number first is the winner.

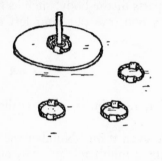

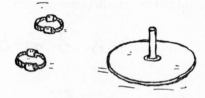

Simon Says   • C • GMS • NP •

A leader, or some person designated as "it," faces a group and calls out a series of action commands, some of which members of the group must perform, depending upon the command. For example, if the command is preceded by the words, "Simon says" (Simon says hand on head; Simon says hands on hips) the action must be performed; those failing to follow the command have a point scored against them. As "it" gives the commands, he may either perform the action commanded or a different action, in an attempt to confuse the players. If the players follow "its" incorrect action instead of performing the commanded action, a point is scored against them. To confuse players further, "it" may say "Hands on hips" or "Clap hands." Any player carrying out this kind of command has a point scored against him, since the command was not preceded by the key words "Simon says." At the end of a designated time, the player with the fewest points wins the game and changes places with "it."

Variation: With those confined to beds or wheelchairs, play Simon Says by using limited parts of the body, such as fingers and hands. An example is, "Simon says put your left thumb on your right ear."

Steal the Bacon   • C • MR • NP •

Equipment: A handkerchief, ten pin, or stick (called the bacon).

Divide the players into two even teams. Number the members of the teams with two sets of numbers, each starting with number one. Urge the players to remember their numbers as they line up in two parallel lines about fifteen feet apart. Place

the bacon in the center between the lines. Have someone designated as a leader call out one of the numbers assigned to the two teams. The player from each team with that number runs out to the bacon and tries to steal it and return to his own line without being tagged by the opponent. Award a point for each time the bacon is returned to a side without the bacon retriever being tagged by the opponent. If he is tagged, the opponent receives a point. The team which accumulates a predetermined number of points first wins the game. Call out all numbers so that each person has an opportunity to participate.

Variation: Call out two numbers at once so that four players will be competing in an effort to return the bacon to their respective lines.

Tetherball   • A • C • GMS • MR • NP •

Equipment: A wooden paddle for each player, tetherball (tennis ball enclosed in a net casing) attached to cord, and pole.

The object of the game is to hit the tetherball in an effort to wind the cord around the pole above the six foot mark on the pole. The opponent attempts to wind the cord in the opposite direction.

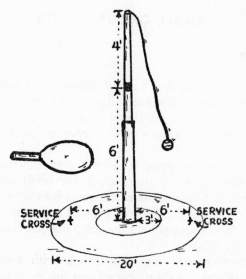

Start the game with the server standing on a spot a few feet from the pole where the tetherball will swing around. Have the server hit the ball with a side-arm swing of the paddle. The opponent stands opposite to the server with the pole between them and tries to strike the ball with the paddle so the ball swings in the other direction from which it was served. Each player moves around, stretches, and swings the paddle in an effort to hit the fast-moving ball. Whoever hits the ball around the pole with the tetherball winding and stopping above the six foot mark wins the game.

Variation: For a slower, but more vigorous game, attach a volleyball to a cord for the tetherball. Strike it with the fist. Purchase a volleyball with a hook and cord on it for this purpose from sporting goods concerns.

Some concerns manufacture tetherballs about the size and shape of volleyballs that have a sturdy cord attached to them. Write to the Voit Rubber Corporation for prices and information on tetherballs, rules, court layouts, and installation instructions.

SMALL GROUP SPORTS

Badminton   • C • NP •

Equipment: Badminton net and standards, badminton court, a badminton racquet for each player, and one shuttlecock.

To begin the game, ask the opponents to toss a coin in the air to determine the choice of first serve or for choosing ends on the court.

The object of the game is to hit a cork and feathered (or plastic) object called a shuttlecock (or bird) over the net with a racquet. The purpose of the game is to keep the shuttlecock from striking the floor or ground and at the same time to hit it back to the opponent in such a manner that he cannot return it.

The server serves (hits shuttlecock with forehand grip below the waist) the shuttlecock from the right hand service court into the receiver's right hand service court. The receiver attempts to return the shuttlecock over the net in such a way that the server cannot return it. If the server commits a "fault" (failure to serve to proper service court), the opponent becomes server. A point is scored for the server if the receiver cannot successfully return the bird that has just been served over the net. A game consists of either fifteen or twenty-one points (as determined in advance by players) and only the server or serving team can score.

Variation: Play an indoor variation of badminton on the ward or elsewhere. Bend an iron rod into a two foot or larger circle that is about three or four feet above the ground (distance to bottom of circle), and attach a stand. Let two persons use ping pong paddles to hit a shuttlecock back and forth through the circular loop. Mark a ten foot by four foot court

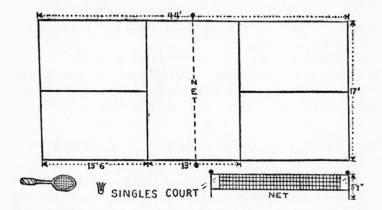

SINGLES COURT   NET

on the floor or ground with chalk, and place the standard in the center. Make up simple rules that fit local needs. Keep a score of twenty-one points as in table tennis.

If badminton racquets are not available, use table tennis racquets; you may also substitute a sponge rubber ball for a shuttlecock.

Suggestions: Purchase shuttlecocks that are made of plastic. These are sometimes more expensive than cork and feathered ones, but are far more durable and better for repeated use.

Play the regulation badminton game either indoors or outdoors. If outdoors, select any relatively flat grass area for a court. Mark off exact feet and area for advanced players.

Write to the American Badminton Association for a copy of official badminton rules and to the American Association for Health, Physical Education, and Recreation for an official guide on badminton for women.

Bowling on the Green   • A • C • GMS • NP •

Equipment: A smooth lawn area about 120 feet square surrounded by a 6-inch trough, two nearly round bowls (balls) made of wood for each player and one jack (small white ball).

One of the four players rolls the jack onto the lawn where it remains as the target for others. Each player in turn attempts to roll his bowl near the jack. Award a point for the bowl nearest the jack. Indicate all bowls rolled into the trough as being out of play.

Variation: Use croquet balls for bowls if regular balls for lawn bowling cannot be secured. If there is no trough, mark this boundary off in some other manner. Write to the American Lawn Bowlers Association for rules of lawn bowling.

Deck Tennis   • GMS • NP •

Equipment: A deck tennis rubber ring and deck tennis net.

Two or four may play. The object is to throw the ring across the net in such a way that the receiver cannot catch and return it. The server stands behind the rear line and throws the ring slightly upward with an underhand motion into the opponent's court. There is only one attempt available for the server in making a good serve. In the event the ring hits the net top and falls into the "dead" area, the served ring counts as a bad serve, and it goes to the opponents for their attempt at service. If a served ring, after hitting the net top, falls into the opposite court, it is called a "let" and is served again unless the receiver chooses to play it. After being served, the ring is tossed back and forth over the net. One hand only is used by the players, with the ring being caught in this hand and immediately thrown back over the net. The ring must also be tossed back from the spot where it was caught. When the receiver catches it and returns it to the server with the server failing to catch and properly return it, the serve then goes to the opponent.

Only the server makes a score and he continues to serve as long as he is winning. One point is made by the server when the opponent fails to catch and return the ring within the server's court. In the event the ring falls into the "dead" area, the point is lost. If a ring falls on a line, it is considered to be in. If the server does not serve the ring properly, or fails to return the ring in accordance with the rules, he loses his service. Fifteen points constitute a game.

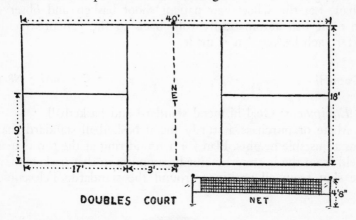

DOUBLES COURT — NET

Variation: Adapt and modify the rules so that the game can be played by wheelchair patients.

Suggestions: Make a ring out of manila rope with ends spliced together. If a net is not obtainable, string a rope across the court and 4 feet 8 inches above the ground or floor.

Write to General Sportcraft Co., Limited, for information and printed rules on Deck Tennis.

Free Throw Shooting • C • GMS • NP •

Equipment: Basketball and basketball backboard with hoop.

Have persons stand on the free throw line of a basketball court and throw the ball in turn at the basketball hoop in an effort to get the ball through the hoop. The object is to successfully throw the ball in an underhand manner through the hoop. Keep track of the successful throws made by the several players, or suggest that each one remember his own score. Limit the game to ten points, with one point being awarded for each basket made.

Variations: Place a basketball hoop on a plywood backing and take to the wards for use with general medical and surgical patients.

Try placing a volleyball net or similar net under the basketball ring and netting on the backboard to the base of a wheelchair. Let the wheelchair patient shoot baskets and observe that the ball automatically rolls back to the patient's hands after each basket that is made.

Goal-Hi   • C • GMS • NP •

Equipment: Goal-hi metal standard and basketball.

Make or purchase a sturdy metal basketball standard that has adjustable heights. Plan for a round ring at the top that is held from the bottom by sturdy supports so that baskets may be shot from all positions around the standard. Telescopic

pipes with heavy catches provide the needed variation in height of the basket ring.

Have participants shoot baskets with any point system desired and agreed upon in advance. Place the standard in various locations since it is portable and can be used indoors or outdoors.

Golf   • A • C • GMS • MR • NP •

Equipment: Golf clubs, golf balls, and a golf course.
Try these modified forms of golf:

Miniature Golf

Secure a quantity of surplus material (troughs, pipes, rings, boards, grates, wires, sand, and poles) from around any school or hospital. Use an accessible area for the course and construct it so that it is usable during clement months of the year. Utilize a minimum of specially purchased material. Make various inclines, drops, holes, tunnels, and runways that make an entertaining course. Sink tin cans into the ground for holes. Make flags to indicate the numbers of the holes on the course. Be sure that hole number two begins near where hole number one ends. Secure a number of used golf balls and putter clubs for use on the miniature course.

Have players start at hole number one and putt the ball around the course. Follow the flag numbers and attempt to hit the ball into the appropriately numbered cup in the ground with the fewest number of strokes. Keep a written score of the strokes required to hit the ball in any one of the numbered holes. The player with the lowest score after playing the course is the winner.

Putting Green

Select a flat lawn surface and sink several tin cans into the ground for holes. Place a small flag by each hole. Number the flags beginning with number one for the first hole and so on numerically for each successive hole. Plan a definite sequence of holes so that a game can be played among the eight or nine putting holes.

The game is started by first putting for hole number one. Try to hit the ball into the number one hole using the fewest number of strokes. Keep an account of the score and proceed putting the ball toward each successive hole on the lawn.

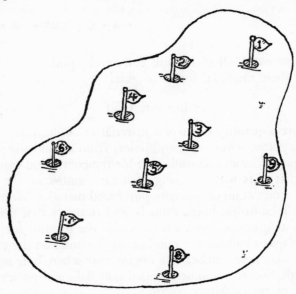

Suggestion: Secure an area for a "driving range" of about one hundred yards by three hundred yards that is generally free of obstruction and somewhat close to the people who will be using the range. Make teeing off stands on one end and large wooden upright markers at certain distances (150, 175, and 250 yards and so on) to indicate yardage that a ball can be hit. After balls have been hit out on the range, let selected persons pick up balls and return them to the driving tees.

Self Approach

Place a cup or can in the ground and a peg just behind it. Draw two concentric circles with lime in a target manner around the sunken cup.

Give a number of balls to the players, and have them hit the golf balls with clubs toward the peg. Any balls that are hit into the hole receive three points. Those that are hit within the closest ring drawn around the cup receive two points. Those balls that are hit within the next ring receive only one point each.

Suggestions: Since new golf clubs are expensive, ask volunteers to search for used clubs and golf equipment that they might procure through voluntary sources. Write to the United States Golf Association for rules of golf and to the American Association for Health, Physical Education, and Recreation for an official guide on women's golf.

Horseshoes   • A • GMS • MR • NP •

Equipment: Two horseshoes per contestant and two stakes in the ground.

Give each contestant two horseshoes and have one start out by throwing his horseshoes, one at a time from near one stake to the opposite stake located forty feet away. The object is to get the horseshoe to encircle the stake (called a ringer). The shoe closest (within a maximum of six inches) to the stake scores one point unless it is a ringer and in that case it scores three points. Fifty points constitute a game.

The order of pitching (throwing) is player A throwing his horseshoes, then player B following suit. On the next turn, player B throws first, followed by player A.

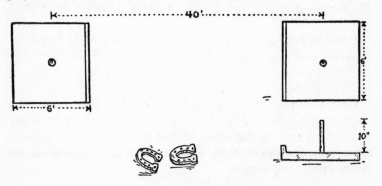

Suggestions: Try this activity with older men. Its success with many older handicapped men is nearly certain.

Write to the National Horseshoe Pitchers Association for rules on the game of horseshoes. If there is a marked interest in horseshoes, consider the organization of a Horseshoe Club. Some clubs sponsor exhibitions, tournaments, contests, and social activities. Clubs also assist in the setting up of horseshoe team leagues.

Purchase official horseshoes, steel horseshoe stakes, pitching boxes, and score sheets for any group that is actively interested in the sport. Write to the Diamond Calk Horseshoe Company for additional information and prices on horseshoe equipment. Also try local sporting goods dealers for horseshoe supplies.

Medicine Ball   • NP •

Equipment: One four pound, six pound, or heavier medicine ball.

This very heavy stuffed ball is slightly larger than a basketball and is used in a number of ways. Throw it into the air and have a player catch it. Toss it back and forth between two or more persons.

Variations: Have a circle pass game wherein players pass the ball between their legs, over their heads, one-handed, and so on. Use several balls and have relays.

Shuffleboard   • A • C • GMS • MR • NP •

Equipment: Eight circular wood discs—each six inches in diameter and one inch thick, four that are red and four that are black; a cue (stick) with a five-foot handle for each player; and a shuffleboard court.

Give each player or team of two a total of four discs and a cue for each person. The object is to push the disc with a cue to a scored area on the other end of the court, or to prevent the opponent from scoring. The two men at either end of the court will be opponents.

Shoot the discs in alternate turns until each player or team has shot four discs. Determine the score by counting all discs that are on a scoring marker with those touching any lines not counting. Keep the score as the game is played until a pre-determined number of points (25, 50, 75, 100) is reached. Limit the game to 25 points for beginning players. In case of a tie, the eighth disc is shot from each end and the side with the highest score then is the winner. In playing, the discs that stop nearer to the player's end than the farthest dead line are "dead" and therefore removed at once.

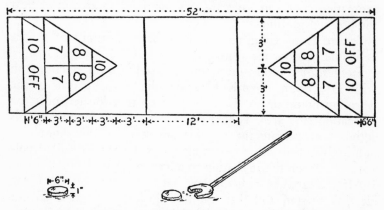

Suggestions: Paint a shuffleboard court on the floor in several key places where handicapped persons are apt to congregate. Have the cues and discs available for ready use at these spots. In case a new play area is being planned, consider laying asphalt tile which has shuffleboard scoring areas. Consult Armstrong Cork Company for information about asphalt tile shuffleboard sets.

Write to the National Shuffleboard Association for deck (floor) shuffleboard rules and to the American Shuffleboard Leagues, Inc. for table shuffleboard information and rules.

Skating   • A • C • NP •

Equipment: A pair of ice skates or roller skates for each person and an ice or roller rink.

Select those who are physically able to engage in skating. Participants must have the ability to use legs freely and have some degree of coordination. Try either of these two types of skating, depending upon interests of skaters, season of year, and appropriate facilities.

Ice Skating

Locate a suitable flat area for an outdoor rink that it accessible and has an adjacent warming house facility. A safe and hard skating surface is necessary. Use a rink in a municipal recreation center in a nearby city, or flood an area in or near the hospital grounds.

Secure from volunteers or elsewhere a supply of skates. Schedule outdoor ice skating.

Suggestions: Hook up a sound system and a phonograph with 33⅓ r.p.m. records. Play melodic waltz records in the warming house or elsewhere with a speaker located near the recreation rink area. Where there is a marked interest in this activity, investigate the possible advantage of spotlights for lighting the rink during evening hours. Recruit a skilled volunteer to teach figure skating to advanced skaters.

After clearance with the hospital administration, open the ice rink to staff and their families during hours that do not conflict with patient's scheduled hours.

Roller Skating

Secure opinions on use of the gymnasium floor for roller skating. If it is sturdy and practical for this purpose, plan roller skating indoors to recorded music. Purchase or secure roller skates with rubber or composition wheels. Check on types of wheels which will do minimum or no damage to the floor.

Play recorded music and schedule periodic roller skating sessions.

Suggestions: Roller skating, under proper conditions and with adequate floor maintenance does not injure wood gymnasium floors. Write to the Hillyard Chemical Company for information on the maintenance of gymnasium floors.

Write to the Chicago Roller Skate Company for roller skate prices and additional information on roller skating as an activity.

Stall Bar Activity   • NP •

Equipment: One set of stall bars and gymnasium mat.

This set of bars affixed to the wall provides an anchor for body exercise. Have the participant assume any of the following positions for exercising various parts of his body:

1. With feet close to bar nearest floor, stand with back to the apparatus, grasp the bar with hands, lean forward, and then move back and forth. This provides exercise for the chest, shoulders, and arm muscles.
2. Follow procedure in number one, but reverse position with participant facing the apparatus. In addition to exercising the shoulders and arms, this provides exercise for the back.
3. With one foot under bar nearest floor and arm on same side holding a higher bar, move toward and away from

the apparatus. This strengthens the arm and leg in use, in addition to the shoulder and hips.

4. Lie down with feet linked under lowest bar and hands clasped behind head; rise to a sitting position (facing apparatus). These are known as "sit ups" and involve alternate sitting up and reclining with back on floor. This strengthens stomach and back muscles. Use this exercise, along with an appropriate dietary program, in reducing stomach of excess tissue. Use in moderation and with judgment whenever middle-aged or older persons are involved.

Try these gymnasium or ward activities:

Heavy Bag

Equipment: Heavy canvas (like a sailor's sea bag) filled with sand, sawdust, rags, and stuffing; strong metal swivel mechanism; and strong board or standard to hold bag.

Use the heavy bag for disturbed or distressed neuropsychiatric patients when they are working off excess energy and steam. Encourage them to lunge at the bag and strike at it in releasing tensions and aggressions.

Wall Pulley

Equipment: A weight attached to cords that move around small wheels with a handle on end of cord or cords.

Have patient stand, sit, or lie down while lifting or pulling these weights. These provide benefits similar to those of stall bar activities but involve an even type of stress to arms.

Striking Bag

Equipment: Striking bag (punching bag), swivel mechanism, and a sturdy standard to hold the bag.

Place a striking bag on selected wards and in recreation hall for patients to hit. This is of major benefit to neuropsychiatric patients who need a physical release. Hitting the punching bag is an acceptable outlet for the active mentally ill male.

Table Tennis   • C • GMS • NP •

Equipment: Table tennis paddle for each player, table tennis celluloid ball, net, net brackets, and table designed for the game.

Tell players to take their places with paddle in hand at opposite ends of the table. The object is to hit the ball over the net to the opponent in such a way that he cannot return it. A game consists of twenty-one points unless the score is twenty to twenty. In the latter case, the next person to score two consecutive points wins the game. One point is always scored for the opponent when an individual fails to return the ball.

Commence the service by striking the ball with the paddle so that it bounces on the server's side of the net and then passes over the net and bounces on any portion of the table on the opponent's side. Player A serves five times. Player B then serves five times. Continue this alternation throughout the game. The player winning two out of three games wins the match. If player A makes eleven points before player B can make one, player A wins the game through a "shut-out."

Suggestions: If there are a number interested in table tennis, plan a tournament within the school or hospital. Study official rules for the correct method of playing doubles with four players. Write to the United States Table Tennis Association for information and rules.

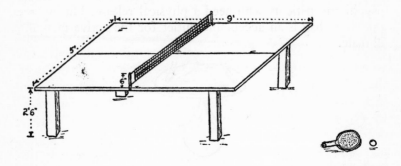

Twenty-One   • C • GMS • NP •

Equipment: Basketball and basketball backboard with hoop.

Give each player two shots at the basket, one called a "long," taken from beyond the free throw line on the floor, the second shot called a "short" and taken close to the basket. Award one point for every short made and two points for every long that is made. Opponents take turns with two shots each until one person accumulates a total of twenty-one points.

Variations: Try playing twenty-one with the rule that exactly twenty-one points must be scored. If a player scores twenty-two points, have him start over with zero points.

When only limited space is available, try this variation. Set up a basketball ring and backboard. The game is played like twenty-one, but with a tennis ball instead of a basketball. Set a time limit on the game (five or ten minutes) and whoever scores the most points in that period is the winner.

Suggestion: Play twenty-one in any area inside or outside where there is a basketball hoop and backboard. Improvise a free throw line if necessary. If there is no basketball hoop and backboard available, use a wastebasket for the "basket."

Volleyball   • GMS • NP •

Equipment: Volleyball (or balloon or beach ball), volleyball net (or rope for net), and flat area for court.

Divide the players into two teams of the same number and have each team take positions as indicated on the diagram. Player A of Team I has the ball. Player A serves the ball with an underhand swing, hitting it with the palm of his hand over the net to the opposing team. If the opponents fail to return it, a point is scored for the serving side. Scores are made only by the serving side. In attempting to return the ball, three different players may touch it if necessary, but the same player may not touch it twice consecutively in one service. If the server fails to hit the ball over the net, or the serving side fails to return it when it is tipped over to them, the service then goes to the other team. At any change in service, all players on the serving team rotate clockwise (in diagram, the last server A moves to B's spot, B to C, and so on, as well as F to A's serving position).

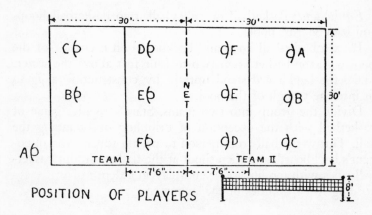

POSITION OF PLAYERS

Fifteen or twenty-one points constitute a game. Agree before starting the game which of these totals to play for. A tie at fourteen or twenty requires that two points be scored in succession to end the game.

"Fouls" occur when the ball is caught, hit with the fist, hit more than once in succession by the same player, or when a player gets into the opponent's territory or touches the net with his body. When a foul occurs, the service changes or a point is given to the serving side. The latter takes place when the offender is on the side that is not serving the ball.

Variations: Use a balloon instead of a volleyball for bed or wheelchair patients. This allows for playing inside without the hard impact of a regulation ball and still provides fun and exercise. Use a rope in place of the regulation net at net height. See Balloon Push Ball on page 237.

For a change, use a large light beach ball instead of the regulation leather volleyball. Change the rules to allow for a "help-over" or "assist" on the serve when unskilled persons are playing.

Secure the complete rules for mens' volleyball from the United States Volleyball Association Printer. Secure the rules for womens' volleyball from the American Association for Health, Physical Education, and Recreation.

Water Basketball   • C • GMS • NP •

Equipment: Basketball or volleyball, two basketball hoops and backboards, pool.

Place a basketball hoop and backboard on each side of the pool with the basket from two to four feet above the water. Make the backboard stand upright by constructing a jig to fit into the trough of the pool.

Divide the group into two teams. Start a regular game of basketball with the exception of dribbling or bouncing the ball. Throw the ball from person to person toward the opponent's backboard, and then shoot at the basket. Adopt basketball rules with modifications and play in a depth of water according to capabilities of the swimmers.

TEAM SPORTS AND EXERCISES

The team sports and calisthenics in which the handicapped can engage are only listed by title in this section. Extensive practice, direction, rules, and care are necessary in teaching team sports to the handicapped. These activities tend to have a complex organization, require a good degree of cooperation and practice, and take time in the development of real skill. The reader is encouraged to secure recommended books in pursuing study of selected team sports and calisthenics. Several team sports of special popularity with handicapped persons are:

Basketball   Swimming
Bowling   Tennis
Exercises   Touch football
Soccer   Water polo
Softball

Basketball   • C • GMS • NP •

AAU Basketball Rules and Guide. Amateur Athletic Union, New York, New York.
ANDERSON, FORREST AND TYLER MICOLEAU. *Basketball Techniques Illustrated.* New York: The Ronald Press Co., 1952.

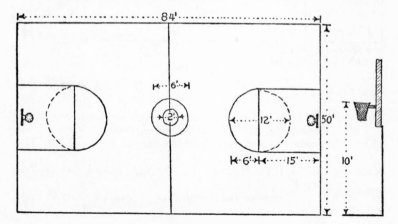

BEE, CLAIR AND KEN NORTON. *The Bee-Norton Basketball Series.* New York: The Ronald Press Co., 1959. 5 vols.: Basketball Fundamentals and Techniques; Man-to-man Defense and Attack; The Science of Coaching; Zone Defense and Attack; Individual and Team Basketball Drills.

DEAN, EVERETT S. *Progressive Basketball: Methods and Philosophy.* Englewood Cliffs, N.J.: Prentice-Hall, Inc., 1950.

MEISSNER, WILHELMINE E. AND ELIZABETH Y. MEYERS. *Basketball for Girls.* New York: The Ronald Press Co., Rev. Ed., 1950.

Official Basketball Guide. American Association for Health, Physical Education, and Recreation, Division of Girls' and Women's Sports, Washington, D.C.

Bowling · A · C · GMS · NP ·

FALCARO, JOE AND MURRAY GOODMAN. *Bowling for All.* New York: The Ronald Press Co., 3rd ed., 1957.

GOODMAN, MURRAY AND JUNIE MCMAHON. *Modern Bowling Techniques.* New York: The Ronald Press Co., 1958.

NISENSON, SAM. *A Handy Illustrated Guide to Bowling and Duck Pins.* New York: Garden City Books, 1949.

Official American Bowling Congress Bowling Guide. American Bowling Congress, Milwaukee, Wis.

Official Bowling, Fencing, Golf Guide. American Association for Health, Physical Education, and Recreation, Division of Girls' and Women's Sports, Washington, D.C.

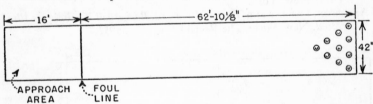

APPROACH AREA FOUL LINE

Exercises · C · GMS · MR · NP ·

COTTERAL, BONNIE AND DONNIE. *The Teaching of Stunts and Tumbling.* New York: The Ronald Press Co., 1936.

HORNE, VIRGINIA L. *Stunts and Tumbling for Girls.* New York: The Ronald Press Co., 1943.

KIPHUTH, ROBERT J. H. *How To Be Fit.* New Haven, Conn.: Yale University Press, 1942.

MCCLOW, L. L. *Tumbling Illustrated.* New York: The Ronald Press Co., 1931.

PRUDDEN, BONNIE. *Is Your Child Really Fit?* New York: Harper & Bros., 1956.

——. *The Bonnie Prudden Fitness Book.* New York: The Ronald Press Co., 1959.

RYSER, OTTO. *A Teacher's Manual for Tumbling and Apparatus Stunts.* Dubuque, Iowa: W. C. Brown Co., 1948.

Soccer   • NP •

DICLEMENTE, F. F. *Soccer Illustrated.* New York: The Ronald Press Co., 1955.

Official NCAA Soccer Guide. National Collegiate Athletic Association, Chicago, Illinois.

Official Soccer-Speedball Guides. American Association for Health, Physical Education and Recreation, Division of Girls' and Women's Sports, Washington, D.C.

WATERS, EARLE C., JOHN R. EILER, AND A. E. FLORIO. *Soccer.* Annapolis: U.S. Naval Institute, Rev. Ed., 1950.

Softball   • C • MR • NP •

MITCHELL, A. V. *Softball for Girls.* New York: The Ronald Press Co., 3rd ed., 1952.

NOREN, A. T. *Softball.* New York: The Ronald Press Co., 3rd ed., 1959.

Official ASA Softball Guide. Amateur Softball Association, Newark, New Jersey.

Official Softball–Track and Field Guide. American Association for Health, Physical Education, and Recreation, Division of Girls' and Women's Sports, Washington, D.C.

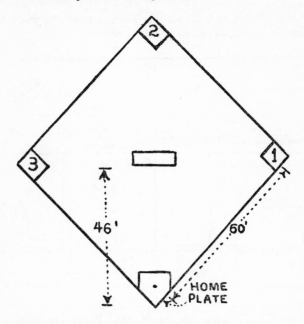

Swimming   • C • GMS • MR • NP •

AMERICAN RED CROSS. *Life Saving and Water Safety.* New York: Doubleday & Co., Inc., 1956.

——. *Swimming and Diving.* New York: Doubleday & Co., Inc., 1939.

LUKENS, PAUL. *Teaching Swimming.* Minneapolis: Burgess Publishing Co., 1948.

Official AAU Swimming, Water Polo and Diving Rules. Amateur Athletic Union, New York, New York.

Official Aquatics Guide. American Association for Health, Physical Education, and Recreation, Washington, D.C.

SPEARS, BETTY. *Beginning Synchronized Swimming.* Minneapolis: Burgess Publishing Co., 1957.

HORNEY, J. A. *Swimming.* New York: McGraw-Hill Book Co., Inc., 1950.

YATES, FERN AND THERESA ANDERSON. *Synchronized Swimming.* New York: The Ronald Press Co., Rev. Ed., 1958.

Tennis   • C • NP •

BUDGE, J. D. *On Tennis*. Englewood Cliffs, N.J.: Prentice-Hall, Inc., 1949.

BUDGE, L. *Tennis Made Easy*. New York: The Ronald Press Co., 1945.

DEWHURST, E. *Lawn Tennis Simplified*. New York: Pitman Pub. Corp., 1950.

MACE, W. AND TYLER MICOLEAU. *Tennis Techniques Illustrated*. New York: The Ronald Press Co., 1952.

MURPHY, BILL AND CHET MURPHY. *Tennis for Beginners*. New York: The Ronald Press Co., 1958.

Official Tennis–Badminton Guide. American Association for Health, Physical Education and Recreation, Division of Girls' and Women's Sports, Washington, D.C.

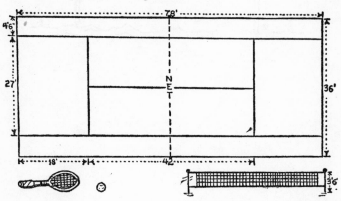

Touch Football   • C • MR • NP •

CRISLER, H. O. *Modern Football*. New York: McGraw-Hill Book Co., Inc., 1949.

GROMBACH, J. V. *Touch Football*. New York: The Ronald Press Co., 1958.

MOORE, JIM AND TYLER MICOLEAU. *Football Techniques Illustrated*. New York: The Ronald Press Co., 1951.

Official NCAA Football Guide. Latest Ed., National Collegiate Athletic Association, Chicago, Illinois.

Water Polo   • C • MR • NP •

BARR, ALFRED R., BEN F. GRADY, AND JOHN H. HIGGINS. *Swimming and Diving*. Annapolis: U.S. Naval Institute, Rev. Ed., 1950.

Official AAU Rules for Swimming, Diving, Water Polo. Amateur Athletic Union, New York, New York.

Official NCAA Swimming Guide. National Collegiate Athletic Association, Chicago, Illinois.

SMITH, J. R. *Playing and Coaching Water Polo.* Los Angeles: Warren F. Lewis, 1948.

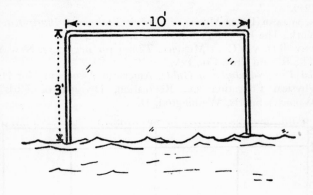

APPENDIX 1

Try interest finders as a key to program planning. Use this leadership aid in determining the activities in which persons want to take part. Make up interest finder sheets and distribute one to each person along with a pencil.

To prepare the interest finder, list a variety of activities on a piece of paper. Be sure there are sufficient facilities and equipment available for each activity listed on the sheet. After the title of each activity leave a blank in which the person may check his possible interest. If there are a number of people in the program, mimeograph the interest finders so there is one for each person to check.

```
┌─────────────────────────────┐
│    INTEREST   FINDER         │
│  Check activities that       │
│      you enjoy:              │
│                              │
│   Bird Watching  —           │
│   Charm School   —           │
│   Fingerpainting —           │
│   Papier Mâché   —           │
│   Photography    —           │
│   Record Listening —         │
│   Stamp Collecting —         │
└─────────────────────────────┘
```

Give the interest finder to the participant and tell him to check only activities in which he is interested in participating at a future time. Have him write his name on the questionnaire and, upon completion, give it to the leader or therapist.

Make an analysis of the interest finder results and plan a program of activities to fit the needs and desires of participants.

277

Suggestions: Mentally handicapped persons do not always accurately and honestly check just those activities they are interested in. The questionnaire therefore has a limited value with such a handicapped individual. Interest finders also have only limited value with children under about ten years of age since they have not necessarily been exposed to the whole gamut of activities that could possibly interest them.

Secure adequate clerical help for tabulating results if there is a large group of persons who check the interest finders.

State the directions clearly on the sheet so there will be few if any questions as to procedure on completing it. When a number of persons are involved, advertise the fact that interest finders will be passed out. Allow time for participants to think over planned responses.

What the handicapped individual wants to do is not necessarily that which is medically desirable for his rehabilitation.

APPENDIX 2

The Recreation Calendar

Look up additional activity ideas on the suggested pages.

JANUARY

1 *New Year's Day.* Watch a football game on television (p. 87)

FEBRUARY

2 *Ground Hog Day.* Play some nature scrambles (pp. 174–75)

7 *Charles Dickens' Birthday.* Show a Dickens' movie (pp. 80–82)

11 *Daniel Boone's Birthday.* Have a square dance (pp. 106–12)

12 *Abraham Lincoln's Birthday.* Put on a quiz program (pp. 196–99)

14 *St. Valentine's Day.* Plan a Valentine's party (pp. 204–6)

22 *George Washington's Birthday.* Do a paint-by-number patriotic scene (pp. 38–39)

MARCH

11 John Chapman ("Johnny Appleseed") died 1847. Tell his life story with flannelgraphs (pp. 79–80)

17 *St. Patrick's Day.* Plan a St. Patrick's Day party (pp. 203–4)

21 First day of spring. Start a Nature Notebook (p. 181)
Easter Sunday falls between March 22nd and April 25th. Do various Easter and springtime activities (pp. 184–85)

APRIL

1 *April Fool's Day.* Put on a "Springtime" dance (p. 90)

26 *John J. Audubon's Birthday.* Make a bird feeder (p. 169)

MAY

1 *May Day.* Make a May Basket (pp. 44–45)

12 *Florence Nightingale's Birthday.* Start a correspondence course today (p. 137)

30 *Memorial Day.* Have a picnic (pp. 188–90)
Mother's Day falls on the second Sunday in May

JUNE

14 *Flag Day.* Plan a badminton game (pp. 254–55)

21 First day of summer. Feature a "Stardust" dance (p. 90)
Father's Day falls on the third Sunday in June

JULY

4 *Independence Day.* Plan a field day (p. 232)

AUGUST

   9 *Izaak Walton's Birthday*. Go on an orienteering trip (pp. 186–88)

SEPTEMBER

   23 First day of fall. Have a county fair (pp. 218–21)
     Labor Day falls on the first Monday in September

OCTOBER

   12 *Columbus Day*. Plan for a harvest festival complete with country music (pp. 222–23)
   31 *Halloween Day*. Make a paper bag mask (pp. 41–42)

NOVEMBER

   11 *Veteran's Day*. Challenge someone to play "Battleship" (pp. 206–8)
     Thanksgiving Day falls on the fourth Thursday in November. Take part in a Thanksgiving Festival (pp. 233–34)

DECEMBER

   21 First day of winter. Make some crepe-paper flowers (pp. 40–41)
   25 *Christmas*. Plan for holiday season activities (pp. 230–32)

APPENDIX 3

Selected References

A B C's of Hand Tools, Detroit: General Motors Corporation, 1945. A cleverly illustrated booklet with many practical ideas on the use of hand tools.

AMERICAN RED CROSS, *Life Saving and Water Safety,* New York: Doubleday & Company, Inc., 1956. An up-to-date handbook on procedures and principles of water safety techniques. Among the topics included are rescue forms, personal safety, drowning, and resuscitation. Photographs illustrate the methods used in rescue of drowning victims.

——, *Swimming and Diving,* New York: Doubleday & Company, Inc., 1939. A handbook illustrating the various strokes in swimming, along with pointers on diving. Considerable information on learning how to swim and methods of improving strokes.

BORST, EVELYNE, *The Book of Games for Boys and Girls,* New York: The Ronald Press Company, 1953. Complete step-by-step directions on indoor and outdoor games for boys and girls. Good organization makes the book easy to follow. Well illustrated in the how-to-do-it aspect of game leadership. A special feature on holiday games for all seasons of the year.

BORST, EVELYNE AND ELMER D. MITCHELL, *Social Games for Recreation,* New York: The Ronald Press Company (2nd edition), 1959. A complete guide to games of use in social settings. Step-by-step directions on the procedures of leading many group games.

BRICKER, WILLIAM PAUL, *The Complete Book of Collecting Hobbies,* New York: Sheridan House, 1951. Hints on how to start a hobby. Collecting hobbies featured are art, furniture, ceramics, clocks, jewelry, glass, books, firearms, playing cards, shells, stamps, coins, minerals, buttons, and dolls.

BURGER, ISABEL B., *Creative Play Acting,* New York: The Ronald Press Company, 1950. Illustrates step-by-step progress from simple pantomime to the completed play. Innumerable suggestions, by age group, of situations for the child to enact. Stories for dramatization, two complete plays of moderate length, and a full-length drama appear in the appendices.

CARROLL, ALICE (ed.), *The Good Housekeeping Needlecraft Encyclopedia,* New York: Rinehart & Company, Inc., 1947. A complete and profusely illustrated book containing all techniques and steps in sewing and needlework.

Coit, Lottie Ellsworth and Ruth Bampton, Follow the Music, Evanston, Ill.: C. C. Birchard & Company, 1948. A collection of twenty-five musical games of a finger, hand, rhythm, and party type. Complete with words, music, and directions for the games.

Dennison Paper Arts and Crafts for Teachers and Group Leaders, Framingham, Massachusetts: Dennison Manufacturing Company, 1957. Directions for various paper crafts with special emphasis on decoration, posters, bulletin boards, and dramatics.

Donnelly, Richard J., William G. Helms, and Elmer D. Mitchell, Active Games and Contests, New York: The Ronald Press Company (2nd edition), 1958. Contains about 2000 games and contests, each described in detail and categorized for ready reference.

Educational Film Guide, New York: H. W. Wilson Company (11th edition), 1953. A subject and title catalog of current 16 mm. motion picture films. Some 11,000 films are described and graded according to the age group for which they are intended.

Eisenberg, Helen and Larry, The Omnibus of Fun, New York: Association Press, 1956. An idea book on many recreational activities that can be done in varied settings. Directions and suggestions for the successful leadership of program events. There is included a separate section on leading recreation for the handicapped.

Fitzgerald, Gerald B., Leadership in Recreation, New York: The Ronald Press Company, 1951. The theory and methodology of working with groups in recreation. Special features on supervision and leadership techniques applied to the recreation setting.

Fun with Crafts, Framingham, Massachusetts: Dennison Manufacturing Company, 1956. A colorfully illustrated booklet on beginning crafts. Some craft projects described are puppets, costumes, animals, games, and paper pottery. Patterns and diagrams are an aid to the leader.

Gallinger, Osma and Oscar Benson, Hand Weaving with Reeds and Fibers, New York: Pitman Publishing Corporation, 1948. Illustrations and thorough descriptions on basketry for the advanced person in this craft.

Gardner, Horace J., Let's Celebrate Christmas, New York: The Ronald Press Company, 1951. Contains parties, plays, legends, carols, poetry, and stories. Recipes, customs, and directions for a variety of Christmas activities.

George, R. F., Speedball Textbook, Camden, New Jersey: Hunt Pen Company (17th edition), 1956. This booklet contains many pen and ink drawings and lavish diagrams on the uses that are possible with the speedball type of pen. Various lettering styles and decorative flourishes are shown for one who wants to do drawing and printing with pen and ink.

GRIMM, GRETCHEN AND CATHERINE SKEELS, *Craft Adventures for Children*, Milwaukee: The Bruce Publishing Company, 1952. A wide variety of interesting crafts are illustrated and described in this handbook for the leader of craftwork for children. The materials and directions necessary for each activity are clearly presented in this loose-leaf bound book.

Handbook for Boys, New York: Boy Scouts of America, 1950. A comprehensive handbook that outlines the boy scouting program and the various merit badge requirements. Numerous line drawings and illustrations make the book valuable for those interested in nature and the out-of-doors.

Handy, Delaware, Ohio: Cooperative Recreation Service, 1937-1941. A loose leaf collection of booklets in kit form. Many practical helps for the group leader on party planning, mental games, leadership, outdoor games, mixers, stunts, musical games, and active outdoor games.

HARBIN, E. O., *The Fun Encyclopedia*, Nashville, Tennessee: Abingdon Press, 1940. Contains a wealth of material for the program leader. A wide range of ideas dealing with banquets, hobbies, games, sports, dramatics, puppetry, holiday parties, magic, and countless others.

HARMER, G. R. AND E. N. COSTALES (eds.), *Scott's Standard Postage Stamp Catalogue*, Vols. I and II, New York: Scott Publications, Inc., 1958. The most universally accepted catalog that illustrates and describes all postage stamps used throughout the world. Values of stamps are included. Many other facts of interest to the postage stamp collector are brought out in this encyclopedia of philately.

HAWLEY, ESTHER M. (ed.), *Recreation Is Fun, A Handbook on Hospital Recreation and Entertainment*, New York: American Theater Wing, 1949. A collection of program ideas that have worked well under volunteer leadership in hospitals. Many party plans, quizzes, and social games are described.

HILLCOURT, WILLIAM, *Handbook for Patrol Leaders*, New York: Boy Scouts of America, 1947. Activities that take place in the out-of-door camp or nature setting are contained in this useful book for the leader. Dramatic stunts, nature ideas, and helps on working with boys are some of the subject matters covered.

Hobby Dyeing Book, Indianapolis: Rit Service Bureau, n.d. The use of dye and its program possibilities in recreation are presented throughout this booklet. Ideas are featured on sponge dyeing, batik dyeing, raffia, sewing, and dye color recipes.

HOROWITZ, I. A. AND FRED REINFELD, *First Book of Chess*, New York: Sterling Publishing Company, Inc., 1952. Moves in chess are discussed and many diagrams help the beginner better understand chess technique. The descriptions are very complete and useful for the novice in this activity.

How to Make Flowers, Framingham, Massachusetts: Dennison Manufacturing Company, 1955. Over thirty different varieties of flowers and how they are made out of crepe paper are discussed in this booklet. Diagrams show how the flowers are put together and instructions are furnished on the preservation of them.

ICKIS, MARGUERITE (ed.), *Handicrafts and Hobbies for Pleasure and Profit*, New York: Hawthorne Books, Inc., 1948. There are numerous drawings and photographs in this combined approach to hobbies and handicrafts. The book is divided into detailed and informative subject sections. Some of the topics covered are plastics, whittling, boats, cars, railroading, planes, stamp collecting, soap sculpture, book binding, finger painting, miniature furniture, block printing, metal craft, lettering, and card tricks.

KIPHUTH, ROBERT J. H., *How To Be Fit*, New Haven: Yale University Press (Rev. ed.), 1956. All of the major exercises that benefit the human body are described in detailed sequence along with accompanying photographs. Hints and steps to good physical health and exercise for men and women are in the book.

Learn How Book, New York: Spool Cotton Company, n.d. A guide book for those interested in needlework and the first steps in this activity.

LEEMING, JOSEPH, *Papercraft*, Philadelphia: J. B. Lippincott Company, 1949. A wealth of paper projects that a child would enjoy. Paper folding, cutting, and tearing are used as methods of making toys and games. Papier mâché, stunts, and other unusual items made from paper are described.

LEONHARD, CHARLES, *Recreation Through Music*, New York: The Ronald Press Company, 1952. Many practical helps and specific suggestions are contained in the 160 pages along with particular aids to the leader in directing a music participation and appreciation program. Instrumental and vocal aspects of music are thoroughly covered for the music recreation leader.

MAYALL, R. NEWTON AND MARGARET L. MAYALL, *Skyshooting: Hunting the Stars with Your Camera*, New York: The Ronald Press Company, 1949. Explicit and understandable information as to how the "outer neighbors" can be photographed and what equipment is necessary and desirable.

MENKE, FRANK G., *The Encyclopedia of Sports*, New York: A. S. Barnes Company, Inc. (Rev. ed.), 1953. A historical and informational approach to all sports. Rules, records, and interesting facts are presented about sports known to the western world.

MITCHELL, ELMER D. (ed.), *Sports for Recreation and How to Play Them*, New York: The Ronald Press Company (2nd edition),

1952. Describes and illustrates the skills and techniques for learning to play fifty different sports. Includes basic rules.

Photographic Production of Slides and Filmstrips, Rochester, New York: Kodak Company (Kodak Publication S-8), 1955. Methods of making slides and filmstrips by amateurs is discussed. A help to the advanced amateur who seeks additional information on how to produce slides and filmstrips.

Postage Stamps of the United States, 1847-1957, Washington, D.C.: U.S. Government Printing Office, 1957. This book contains considerable information and illustrations of interest to the stamp collector who specializes in United States postage stamps. An excellent publication for the price and one worthwhile for any philatelist.

RCA Victor Educational Record Catalog, Camden, New Jersey: Radio Corporation of America, 1957. This catalog not only lists record titles, but contains additional descriptive information on care of phonograph records, types of music that are recorded, and general music appreciation information.

Recreation Program, Chicago: The Athletic Institute, 1955. A description of the over-all recreation program with many types of activities described in general.

ROGERS, MATHILDA, *Flower Arrangement, A Hobby for All*, New York: William Morrow & Company, Inc., 1948. A small, illustrated book that introduces the satisfaction of flower arranging as a hobby. Holders, equipment, centerpieces, and other needed items are described.

SANDS, LESTER B., *Audio-Visual Procedures in Teaching*, New York: The Ronald Press Company, 1956. A textbook on how to effectively use audio-visual aids in a teaching program. All major audio-visual methods are discussed and illustrated in black and white.

STEVENSON, ISABELLA (ed.). *The Big Book of Knitting*, New York: Hawthorn Books, Inc., 1948. An illustrated book containing ideas on the skill of knitting. Finished products are shown with helpful suggestions.

"This Projector Cart Is Practical," *The Modern Hospital*, November, 1951, Vol. 77, No. 5, p. 74. Details on a practical cart for motion picture equipment or other things that are heavy and need to be transported about a hospital. Directions for how to make one at a nominal cost.

TRIEB, MARTIN H., *Handbook of Couple Dances*, Los Angeles: Martin H. Trieb, Author, 1954. A handy book with specific directions on a variety of couple dances.

VAUGHN, CY, *101 Uses for Craftstrip*, West Acton, Massachusetts: The Rex Corporation, 1953. A complete booklet that gives all the directions that are necessary to do various craftstrip projects. Some of the topics that are covered are flat weaving, winding with twists, overbraiding, square knot braiding, kerchief slides, tie clasps, barrettes, belts, lanyards, and several other subjects. Many illustrations and drawings facilitate an understanding of this craft.

WARD, WINIFRED, *Playmaking with Children*, New York: Appleton-Century-Crofts, Inc., 1947. Types of stories, references, story lists, and other helps to the leader of creative dramatics groups. Suggestions by ages are offered along with a useful bibliography.

ZIM, HERBERT S. AND IRA N. GABRIELSON, *Birds*, New York: Simon & Schuster, Inc., 1949. A guide to 267 species of the most familiar birds in the United States; of interest to the beginning bird watcher. The 118 full-color paintings are accurate.

ZIM, HERBERT S. AND ROBERT H. BAKER, *Stars*, New York: Simon & Schuster, Inc., 1951. A guide to constellations, sun, moon, planets, and other features of the heavens. The 150 color illustrations make study fascinating.

APPENDIX 4

Firms and Organizations

A. B. Dick Company, Chicago, Illinois.
Amateur Roller Skating Association of America, New York, New York.
Amateur Softball Association, Newark, New Jersey.
American Art Clay Company, Indianapolis, Indiana.
American Association for Health, Physical Education, and Recreation, Washington, D.C.
American Badminton Association, Wellesley Hills, Massachusetts.
American Baseball Congress, Battle Creek, Michigan.
American Bowling Congress, Milwaukee, Wisconsin.
American Camping Association, Martinsville, Indiana.
American Checker Association, Benton Harbor, Michigan.
American Congress of Physical Medicine and Rehabilitation, Chicago, Illinois.
American Crayon Company, Sandusky, Ohio.
American Lawn Bowlers Association, Buffalo, New York.
American Library Association, Chicago, Illinois.
American Music Conference, Chicago, Illinois.
American National Red Cross, National Headquarters, Washington, D.C.
American Nature Association, Washington, D.C.
American Nurses Association, New York, New York.
American Occupational Therapy Association, New York, New York.
American Optical Company, Chelsea, Massachusetts.
American Orienteering Service, New York, New York.
American Philatelic Society, State College, Pennsylvania.
American Physical Therapy Association, New York, New York.
American Psychological Association, Washington, D.C.
American Recreation Society, Inc., Washington, D.C.
American Shuffleboard Leagues, Inc., Union City, New Jersey.
Ampro Corporation, Chicago, Illinois.
Ansco Company, Binghamton, New York.
Armstrong Cork Company, Lancaster, Pennsylvania.
Association Films, New York, New York.
B and I Manufacturing Company, Burlington, Wisconsin.
Ball Jar Company, Muncie, Indiana.

287

Bausch and Lomb Optical Company, Rochester, New York.
Bell and Howell Company, Chicago, Illinois.
Bicycle Institute of America, New York, New York.
Billiard Association of America, Chicago, Illinois.
Bingo King Company, Littleton, Colorado.
Boy Scouts of America, New York, New York.
Camp Fire Girls, Inc., New York, New York.
Charles Beseler Company, Newark, New Jersey.
Chicago Roller Skate Company, Chicago, Illinois.
Cleveland Crafts Company, Cleveland, Ohio.
Childrens Book Council, New York, New York.
Cooperative Recreation Service, Delaware, Ohio.
Coronet Films, Chicago, Illinois.
Cosom Industries, Inc., Minneapolis, Minnesota.
Dennison Manufacturing Company, Framingham, Massachusetts.
Diamond Calk Horseshoe Company, Duluth, Minnesota.
Ditto Company, Chicago, Illinois.
Dramatic Publishing Company, Chicago, Illinois.
Dudley Sports Company, New York, New York.
Eastman Kodak Company, Rochester, New York.
Encyclopaedia Britannica Films, Wilmette, Illinois.
Eye-Gate House, Inc., Long Island City, New York.
Famous Artists Course, Westport, Connecticut.
General Sportcraft, Limited, New York, New York.
Girl Scouts of America, New York, New York.
Handicrafters, The, Waupun, Wisconsin.
Hillyard Chemical Company, Saint Joseph, Missouri.
Hobby Institute of America, New York, New York.
Indiana University, Audio-Visual Service, Bloomington, Indiana.
International Film Bureau, Inc., Chicago, Illinois.
J. C. Larson Company, Chicago, Illinois.
Keuffel and Esser Company, St. Louis, Missouri.
Life Magazine Filmstrips, New York, New York.
Lightner Publishing Corporation, Chicago, Illinois.
McGraw-Hill Book Company, Text-Film Department, New York, New York.
Mekeel's Weekly Stamp News, Severn-Wylie-Jewett Co., Portland, Maine.
National Amateur Athletic Union, New York, New York.
National Association for Music Therapy, New York, New York.
National Audubon Society, New York, New York.
National Federation of Music Clubs, Chicago, Ilinois.
National Federation of State High School Athletic Associations, Chicago, Illinois.
National Gallery of Art, Washington, D.C.

National Geographic Magazine, National Geographic Society, Washington, D.C.

National Golf Foundation, Chicago, Illinois.

National Horseshoe Pitchers Association, Crestline, California.

National Recreation Association, New York, New York.

National Shuffleboard Association, Saint Petersburg, Florida.

National Wildlife Federation, Washington, D.C.

Nature Magazine, American Nature Association, Washington, D.C.

Needlework Guild of America, Philadelphia, Pennsylvania.

Palmer-Pann Corporation, Toledo, Ohio.

Popular Science Publishing Company, Audio-Visual Division, New York, New York.

Portland Cement Association, Chicago, Illinois.

RCA Victor Division, Radio Corporation of America, Camden, New Jersey.

Rit Products Division, Indianapolis, Indiana.

Samuel French Company, New York, New York.

Slide Supply Service, Canton, Ohio.

Society for Visual Education, Inc., Chicago, Illinois.

Square Dance Associates, Freeport, New York.

Swank Motion Pictures, Inc., St. Louis, Missouri.

Tandy Leather Company, Fort Worth, Texas.

Toastmasters International (Clubs), Santa Ana, California.

Together, Chicago, Illinois.

United States Golf Association, New York, New York.

United States Lawn Tennis Association, New York, New York.

United States Playing Card Company, Cincinnati, Ohio.

United States Table Tennis Association, Chicago, Illinois.

United States Volleyball Association Printer, Berne, Indiana.

Voit Rubber Corporation, Los Angeles, California.

Western Stamp Collector, Van Dahl Publications, Albany, Oregon.

Index by Diagnostic Groups

General Index

301